WILLA CATHER IN CONTEXT

Willa Cather in Context

Progress, Race, Empire

Guy Reynolds
Lecturer in English and American Literature
University of Kent, Canterbury

St. Martin's Press
New York

WILLA CATHER IN CONTEXT
Copyright © 1996 by Guy Reynolds
All rights reserved. No part of this book may be used or reproduced
in any manner whatsoever without written permission except in the
case of brief quotations embodied in critical articles or reviews.
For information, address:

St. Martin's Press, Scholarly and Reference Division,
175 Fifth Avenue, New York, N.Y. 10010

First published in the United States of America in 1996

Printed in Great Britain

ISBN 0–312–16070–4 cloth
ISBN 0–312–16071–2 paperback

Library of Congress Cataloging-in-Publication Data
Reynolds, Guy.
Willa Cather in context: progress, race, empire / Guy Reynolds.
p.   cm.
Includes bibliographical references and index.
ISBN 0–312–16070–4 (cloth).— ISBN 0–312–16071–2 (paper)
1. Cather, Willa, 1873–1947—Political and social views.
2. Literature and society—United States—History—20th century.
3. Imperialism in literature.   4. Progress in literature.   5. Race
in literature.   I. Title.
PS3505.A87Z813   1996
813'.52—dc20   95–53265
                                                            CIP

Contents

Preface

This book examines the major novels written by the Nebraskan writer, Willa Cather, during and after the First World War. The aim of the study is to read her novels contextually, by providing a series of frameworks within which their ideological complexity can be understood. This enables us to read Cather as an *engagée* author whose works were bound up within the intellectual, political and social debates of her age, rather than the secessionist writer suggested by some of her readers (an image partly encouraged by Cather herself). I believe that Cather's work was enmeshed within many of the key cultural and intellectual discourses of early twentieth-century America: intensely contested discussions concerning, for instance, 'progress', 'Americanisation', and what we would now term the developing multiculturalism of the United States. Bringing this material to Cather's fiction enriches her work; it 'problematises' our sense of Cather's relationship to her culture (to use one of modern criticism's many ungainly terms). Cather cannot be thought of simply as an author reacting to her culture's failings, although she came to portray herself as an escapist disgusted with many facets of modern culture. Indeed, some of her fiction might now strike us as liberally progressive in its magnanimous openness to a range of peoples and cultures, from the settlers of French Canada to the Pueblo Indians of the South-west. The complexity of Cather's work, I hope to show, lies in its often volatile mixture of elements as the writer seems to shift from one pole to another, from reaction to progress, in the space of a single fiction.

My methodology was suggested by this contextual approach. Cather's letters (from archives in Nebraska and Vermont) are used to discover her unpublicised views on her art's relationship to its context. The works of her friends and fellow-novelists provide a web of analogies and parallels, an intellectual milieu. Beyond this sense of an immediate context, I have suggested numerous writers, contemporaries in other fields, whose work can provide surprising and suggestive analogies to Cather's writing. These authors range from the social scientist, Thorstein Veblen, through to the sociologists who researched the 'Americanisation' of immigrants and on to President Wilson (whose commentary on the First World War provides an intriguing key to Cather's novel about the conflict, *One of Ours*).

The structure of the book is as follows: Chapter 1 examines the theoretical questions raised in reading Cather; discusses 'progress' as a key term; introduces the letters; asks whether there is an 'American ideology' and if such a concept would help us to read Cather. The second chapter explains why Cather was misread in the 1920s and 1930s and why those early misunderstandings have led critics to appreciate Cather, but not primarily as a novelist responsive to her culture. A survey of critical writings from a range of important pundits (for example, Van Wyck Brooks, H. L. Mencken) demonstrates the codes of this criticism. Literary criticism demonised women's writing and writing about the frontier, thereby damning Willa Cather.

The remaining five chapters discuss five major novels, from *O Pioneers!* through to *Death Comes for the Archbishop*, relating them individually to the specific areas of American culture mentioned above. Inevitably, a project that draws on contextual material necessitates a focus on a limited number of texts; I hope extend my approach to Cather's later fiction (*Shadows on the Rock* and *Sapphira and the Slave Girl*) in forthcoming articles.

All page references within the text are to the Virago paperback editions of Cather's novels, published in London in the following years: *O Pioneers!* (1983); *My Ántonia* (1980); *One of Ours* (1987); *The Professor's House* (1981); *Death Comes for the Archbishop* (1981).

Acknowledgements

I am indebted to the staff of the Cambridge University library and the Love library at the University of Nebraska at Lincoln. Further help was given by the staff at the Willa Cather Pioneer Memorial and Educational Foundation in Red Cloud, Nebraska, especially by Pat Phillips. Jeffrey Marshall at the University of Vermont helped me to sift the Canfield Fisher papers and introduced me to the wonders of 'Ben and Jerry's' ice cream. Professor Susan Rosowski has, over the years, helped me with many, many enquiries about Cather, and has been unflaggingly attentive, even given the vagaries of the fax machine connections between South-eastern England and the American Midwest.

Several chapters of this work were read (in various forms) at seminar groups in Cambridge. Many thanks are due to the members of the American Graduate seminar and the Women and Literature seminar for their questions and disagreements. J. H. Prynne kindly lent me his collection of books by Haniel Long.

The Master and Fellows of Selwyn College, Cambridge provided a congenial environment in which to write much of the early draft of this text. Charmian Hearne, at Macmillan, was equally supportive at the other end of the compositional process. And Richard Gray has been encouraging throughout.

Thanks are due to the University of Nebraska Press for allowing me to reprint 'Death Comes for the Archbishop: The Ideology of Cather's Catholic Progressivism', an earlier version of which appeared in Cather Studies 3 (1995).

My greatest debts are due to Dr Jean Chothia, who read my work with fiendish attention while encouraging me to further my research in the United States, and to my wife, Cal Anton-Smith, who displayed a welcome, robust indifference to the whinges of an impecunious graduate student.

Extracts from The Professor's House, O Pioneers!, My Ántonia, One of Ours and Death Comes for the Archbishop, by Willa Cather are reprinted by kind permission of the publishers, Virago Press.

Thanks are also due to Random House; extracts are reprinted as follows:

From DEATH COMES FOR THE ARCHBISHOP by
Willa Cather
Copyright 1929 by Willa Cather and
renewed 1955 by The Executors of the
Estate of Willa Cather   Reprinted by
permission of Alfred A Knopf Inc.

From ONE OF OURS by Willa Cather
Copyright 1922 by Willa Cather and
renewed 1950 by Edith Lewis, Executrix
and City Bank Farmers Trust Co.
Reprinted by permission of Alfred A
Knopf Inc.

From THE PROFESSOR'S HOUSE by Willa
Cather
Copyright 1925 by Willa Cather and
renewed 1953 by Edith Lewis and the City
Bank Farmers Trust Co   Reprinted by
permission of Alfred A Knopf Inc.

GUY REYNOLDS

1

Introduction

Willa Cather thought of herself as an American writer. Although the point might seem an obvious one, discussions of Cather's work have failed to address a creativity that was deeply rooted in her native soil. We have been given instead a Cather who is at odds with America, if not wholly marginalised. Cather herself helped to create the image of a disenfranchised writer, an author on the edge of modern American life. Her published statements suggested minimal contact with her culture; she claimed that her novels had one thing in common – the theme of escape. Her collection of critical essays, *Not Under Forty* (1936), was given this title because she felt alienated from contemporary America; she wrote that her work would have 'little interest for people under forty years of age'. She increasingly attacked the spirit of modern America, its commercialism and materialism; her work turned to a golden age that now appeared to have passed. Thus the epigraph to *My Ántonia* was a nostalgic tag from Virgil: 'Optima dies prima fugit' – the best of days are the first to fly. Cather's historical account of her home state, 'Nebraska: The End of the First Cycle' (1923), was similarly overshadowed by the recognition that a phase of American civilisation had come to a close; its title encapsulates her keen sense of an ending.[1]

Cather the escapist, the nostalgist, the elegist – these are the various guises she adopts in her public comments. Despite the caprices of critical fashion, Cather's readers have followed this lead; many regard Cather as a novelist who was fundamentally out of touch with the contemporary scene. In the 1930s, to a left-wing critic such as Granville Hicks, Cather seemed to be damagingly uninterested in social movements and 'the masses' ('The Case against Willa Cather'). In 1937, Lionel Trilling accused Cather of being closeted within a domesticated, bourgeois world, implying

1

that she was unaware of wider social currents. Others, though, have admired Cather's nostalgic or elegiac mode. In 1985 Harold Bloom wrote that, '*A Lost Lady* elegises a lost radiance or harmony, a defeat of a peculiarly American dream of innocence, grace, hope'. He praised this novel, together with *My Ántonia* and *The Professor's House*, as 'three profound studies of American nostalgias'. Across 50 years, the terms and opinions coalesce to unite the critics with the author: whether for good or bad, these critics effectively say, Cather was a secessionist or retrospective author with little interest in contemporary life.[2]

But Cather's correspondence offers a rather different picture. The letters, which are chatty, inquisitive and sympathetic, reveal a writer in touch with the immediate realities of American life. They demonstrate that her writing life had been predicated on very different assumptions about the author's relationship to the national culture. She wrote early in her career that her work would be the fictionalisation of the American life around her, and she posited a reciprocity between the writer and the nation. The voice of the letters is unlike the tight-lipped and disillusioned tone sometimes heard in her public statements, but unfortunately, because of the stipulations in Cather's will, her letters cannot be quoted verbatim. They can, however, be paraphrased.

A 1905 letter to Kate Cleary stated Cather's desire to render an America that had not yet been portrayed in fiction – the small-town, Midwestern world of Nebraska. Writing to Carrie Sherwood in 1922, Cather affirms her love of Nebraska and its people and voices doubts about being true to the experience of the Nebraskans. She told Sherwood in 1934 that her imagination was transformed by the immigrants in Nebraska; after an upbringing amongst them she was destined to write *My Ántonia*. Other letters detail the technical problems she encountered in writing about immigrant culture. According to a letter of 1916, for example, she tried to write the German sections of *The Song of the Lark* using single and double quotation marks to indicate the translated nature of the language, but abandoned this because it was unwieldy and turned instead to indirect discourse. A letter of 1943 testifies to Cather's success in representing the varieties of American culture. *Death Comes for the Archbishop*, she tells Carrie Sherwood, has found its own devoted Catholic audience.[3]

The letters provide a unique perspective on the question of Cather's relationship to American culture. They reveal a gap between the author of the letters and the 'public' Cather. On the one hand is a writer who claims to have found a new subject-matter, namely, the immigrant experience in the Midwest. On the other is a Cather who stresses her remoteness from contemporary American life. The first is an *engagée* novelist aware of cultural change in America and eager to comment upon it; the second is a fugitive from her age. The letters provide, at the very least, a commentary on her work that runs parallel to the 'secessionist' account of her work. Following the lead given by the letters, we see how Cather can be placed in context; the letters show that Cather *had* a context and they map out intersections between the writer and her culture, notably in their concern with Nebraska, immigrants and Catholicism.

This book is inspired by Cather's commentary on American culture and society. Before we examine how the novels can be contextualised, however, it is necessary to understand why Cather was positioned on the margins of 'America'. Why did one Cather become prominent, displacing the other? As we have just seen, critical argument has taken its cue from Cather's public self-portrayal as marginalised, as an elegist or nostalgist. In other words, the institutionalised view of Cather has the author's (partial) blessing. The letters help us to see why that institutionalisation took place. They show that she had specific ideas about the social and cultural terrain of modern America; in her novels she created a fictional America based on these observations. Nebraska, pioneers, immigrants, Catholicism: these are the subjects of the letters and the themes of her major novels. And here is the reason why her fictional world (Cather's America) has been seen as an evasion or retreat from contemporaneity: it was the wrong America that she chose to portray, at least as far as the dominant critical voices in American letters were concerned.

As I demonstrate in the next chapter, literary criticism (in newspapers, journals and academic studies) became increasingly dogmatic about what was or was not quintessentially 'American'. During the early twentieth century, while Cather was establishing her career, a consensus developed about the American writer and what he – for the writer is definitely male – ought to write about. In the course of this debate certain areas of the national life, for instance the pioneer inheritance and the 'feminisation' of culture, were subject to intense criticism. Cather's work was coded with the wrong signals in this ideological controversy. She wrote about pioneers and women when such subjects were under attack. To be concerned with these topics was to signal one's disenfranchisement from modernity or one's complicity with outmoded and destructive cultural forces. Thus, the fugitive Cather was easily appropriated by the pundits and became the author to whom we are still accustomed.

The reduction of Cather's work to a set of cultural signals is epitomised by two dismissive comments on her fiction. Ernest Hemingway attacked her novel about the First World War, *One of Ours* (1922), in a letter to Edmund Wilson:

> Then look at *One of Ours*. Prize, big sale, people taking it seriously. You were in the war weren't you? Wasn't that last scene in the lines wonderful? Do you know where it came from? The battle scene in *Birth of a Nation*. I identified episode after episode, Catherized. Poor woman she had to get her war experience somewhere. (*sic*)[4]

Resenting Cather's success (*One of Ours* won the Pulitzer Prize) and unable to accept that a woman could write about conflict, Hemingway asserts his soldierly fraternalism with Wilson (even though both served with hospital and not front-line units). Catherized: the uncomfortable surgical pun implies a bodily unease with this invasion. Hemingway's prickly jokiness stems from a position of not fully vindicated bravery and chafing literary apprenticeship (Hemingway had to wait until 1925 to make his reputation with *In Our Time*).

Yet when Cather confined herself to the feminine world – for example, the domestic sphere of hearthside and kitchen – she remained indictable. Thus Lionel Trilling:

> Miss Cather's later books are pervaded by the air of a brooding ancient wisdom, but if we examine her mystical concern with pots and pans, it does not seem much more than an oblique defense of gentility or very far from the gaudy domesticity of bourgeois accumulation glorified in the *Woman's Home Companion*.[5]

Just as Hemingway summed up Cather's fictional world in one word, so Trilling deploys a nexus of value-laden terms: 'mystical', 'gentility', 'domesticity'. Fictional complexity is reduced to a series of cultural signals which Trilling imperiously decodes. For both men much can be assumed and shared with their readers. The word 'mystical', for instance, is used by Trilling in 1937, but echoes the infamous 'Case against Willa Cather' written by Granville Hicks in 1933. That piece referred to the 'mystical conception of the frontier' in *O Pioneers!*, adding that *The Song of the Lark* and *My Ántonia* were 'merely mystical'. We see here the creation of a coded critical language which can be used to dismiss Cather, even though a full account of its terminology is never given (what does 'mystical' really *mean*?). Indeed, there is an intellectual clubbishness here – the kind of club founded on a shared rhetoric. The critic's language sets down clear demarcations of who is and who is not acceptable, at the same time obscuring the reasons for drawing the critical perimeter at that particular point: without an explanation of *why* Cather is mystical, it is difficult to refute these accusations. But the meaning of a work of art must exceed, in complexity and scope, this simplistic reduction to themes alone. In a novel, form, structure, and the very texture of the prose itself are part of the work's significance. Readings of fiction must be close readings in order to explicate these layered meanings. Even on a thematic level, as I will demonstrate in this book, Cather's novels are 'about' much more than Trilling admits. They encompass a spectrum of themes: the rise and fall of empires, racial diversity, conflict between pastoralism and technology, the Americanisation of European immigrants.

THE AMERICAN IDEOLOGY

The early reception of Cather's work by readers such as Trilling and Hemingway would today be regarded as intensely 'ideological'. Recent work in American studies deploys 'ideology' as a key term, adopting a concept whose origins lie in the work of the Frankfurt school to a new American context. Sacvan Bercovitch identified a specific 'American ideology' in his essay, 'The Problem of Ideology in American Literary History'. He argued that the need to define, consolidate or subvert what 'America' means is the manifest or covert activity of the American writer; the literary critic – attuned to the codes and signals of the culture – deciphers these ideological configurations. But the American ideology possesses a double-faced and paradoxical quality. It is at once fixed and hegemonic, but also discontinuous or shifting. Having described

America as 'a rhetorical battleground, a symbol that has been made
to stand for diverse and sometimes mutually antagonistic out-
looks', Bercovitch continues: 'I would urge that, in spite of all that
diversity and conflict, the American ideology has achieved a
hegemony unequalled elsewhere in the modern world'. Bercovitch's
case is deployed in critical terminology, but the point is fundamentally a simple one. On the one hand, 'America' seems to cover a
volatile and mutating range of meanings; it can mean almost whatever the writer wants it to. As Allen Tate wrote in 'Religion and the
Old South' (1930), 'the very idea "America"must give us pause, for
it is almost anything that a determined apologist may wish to make
it'. On the other hand, certain concepts or values do appear to
constitute 'American-ness': individualism, the democratic ideal,
self-reliance, free enterprise. Such ideals, recurring in literary, cultural or political discourses, achieve a mythic status or what
Marxists would term a 'reified' permanence.[6]

Perhaps Bercovitch manages to have his cake and eat it too in this
essay. He has either alighted upon a complex truth about the
American ideology – its contradictory doubleness – or he has
tacked his way between dichotomous positions. Difficulties with
Bercovitch's position are apparent when, in discussing the
American literary canon, he cannot decide whether canonical texts
subscribe to the dominant ideology or form a dissenting tradition.
He suggests that the American ideology defuses oppositional texts
by incorporating them into the canon; oppositionality, at the very
moment it proclaims itself, becomes a feature of the status quo:

> In this view, our classic texts re-present the strategies of a
> triumphant middle-class hegemony. Far from subverting the
> status quo, their diagnostic and prophetic modes attest to the
> capacities of the dominant culture to co-opt alternative forms to
> the point of making basic change seem virtually unthinkable,
> except as apocalypse. This is not at all to minimize their protest.[7]

The turns in Bercovitch's prose illustrate the paradoxes in his
position; he claims that the American canon represents both 'status
quo' and 'protest', conservatism and subversion. His is a troubling
mixture of the two propositions that underpin many discussions of
literature and ideology: the text is an artistic transcendence of ideology (here, the subversive text escapes from the constrictions of the

'American ideology' in its fixed, dominant guise); but the text is also a manifestation of the prevailing ideology, serving to 'represent the strategies of a triumphant middle-class hegemony'.

One reason for Bercovitch's confusion is the static nature of the model he proposes. For all his talk of subversion and protest, his cultural model is undynamic: Bercovitch's America is a curiously static culture where literature is permanently locked in a frozen dichotomy. There is no dialectic between the poles; the production of ideology is absent from Bercovitch's discussion. What his essay needs is a local, detailed example of American ideology in action, forming itself in a work of literature. Cather's fiction and the reactions of her early readers provide an ideal example of the American ideology at work. Bercovitch's essay impinges upon our discussion of Cather because a debate about ideology featured in the critical evaluation of her novels. In 1933 Granville Hicks published 'The Case against Willa Cather', claiming that the novelist had fallen into 'supine romanticism' and had recoiled 'from our industrial civilization': 'She tried, it is true, to study the life that had developed out of the life of the frontier, but she took essentially marginal examples of modern life, symbolic of her own distaste rather than representative of significant tendencies'.[8]

The key phrase is 'significant tendencies'. For Hicks the tendencies of modern America are to be found in the urban world, in technology and mass production – the world of Dreiser, Norris and Dos Passos. In contrast, Cather remains a novelist of the frontier, and since American civilisation has shifted from the small-town and agrarian to the urban, industrialised environment, she is inevitably outmoded.[9]

Cather replied to Hicks in her essay, 'Escapism' (1936), by attacking *la littérature engagée*:

Why does the man who wants to reform industrial conditions so seldom follow the method of the pamphleteers? Only by that method can these subjects be seriously and fairly discussed.

In the great age of Gothic architecture sculptors and stone-cutters told the same stories (with infinite variety and fresh invention) over and over, on the faces of all the cathedrals and churches of Europe. How many clumsy experiments in government, futile revolutions and reforms, those building have looked down upon without losing a shadow of their dignity and power

– of their importance! Religion and art spring from the same root and are close kin. Economics and art are strangers.[10]

Art and social issues (or politics, or economics) are divorced; art is akin to religion; art endures, remote and inviolate above the petty contortions of political change. References to Gothic architecture shift the geographical and temporal locale away from Hicks's industrial America to a Europe that is spiritual and artistic. The thrust of Cather's polemic is that art should not be coupled to ideology, but in the wake of Marxist critiques of literature's encoded ideology, its 'political unconsciousness', we can now see that Cather, while denying economics and politics, nonetheless adumbrates an inherently conservative stance in which social change is effaced by the unchanging permanence of art.

Cather was indeed a conservative rather than a radical or liberal – at least in terms of attested political conviction. She was, as far as we know, a Republican throughout her life, and kept her distance from radical political movements. The latter is surprising because due to accidents of geography and occupation Cather's career intersected with some of the crucial political issues and movements of the period 1890–1930. As a young woman in the Midwest Cather was at the centre of the Populist upsurge in the 1890s. Populism advocated measures to increase the political and economic power of the agricultural Midwest, primarily through the circulation of a currency based on silver, a metal that the mining states had in abundance. The West wanted to limit the East's economic power (based on the gold supply). Populism affected national politics: the 1896 Presidential election became the 'Battle of the Standards' (silver vs. gold). The Democratic candidate, William Jennings Bryan, was a Nebraskan; he adopted the Populist programme but was nonetheless defeated by the Republican, William McKinley.[11]

Cather was well placed to observe this agitation. Nebraska was one of the Midwestern states affected by Populism's rise. While Cather was at the state university a Populist journal, *Wealth Makers*, was published in Lincoln.[12] Moreover, she reported on the 1896 election in a piece for *Home Monthly* magazine: 'Two Women the World is Watching' profiled the candidates' wives. In 1900 the *Library* published Cather's article on the politician himself, 'The Personal Side of William Jennings Bryan'.[13]

These articles illustrate Cather's bafflingly aslant relationship to American politics. When her journalism turns to these topicalities the writing is anodyne or reticent. On Bryan:

> So I think William Jennings Bryan synthesizes the entire Middle West; all its newness and vigor, its magnitude and monotony, its richness and lack of variety, its inflammability and volubility, its strength and its crudeness, its high seriousness and self-confidence, its egotism and its nobility.[14]

The overflow of characteristics undercuts our sense of what makes Bryan unique. Bryan is, it seems, all things; and so is the Midwest. The bite of words like 'inflammability' and 'volubility' is deadened in the overwritten rush of Cather's sentence. Actual details of Bryan's politics, the agenda that convulsed America, are absent. Cather gives the reader what the genre (the personal profile or character sketch) requires and nothing more, sidestepping political complexities.[15]

Cather's journalism brings us to the question of how we identify the ideology of a writer's work. Her article abjures commentary on the prominent manifestations of ideology (politicians and elections); but ideology permeates a culture in more ways than simply through the confessedly political expression. It is evident, too, in languages that seem at first to be distanced from politics, such as the language of fiction. Here, ideology can manifest itself in a host of ways: choice of theme, point of view, structure, turn of phrase. As the 'Case against Willa Cather' demonstrated, the choice of novelistic theme might constitute in itself an ideological act, a recognition or renunciation of the 'significant tendencies' of American life. That article also showed that readings of an author are themselves part of the creation, maintenance and overturning of ideologies: Hicks uses the term 'case' in a legalistic way, as if to achieve a courtroom objectivity, but his article is predicated on a narrowly partisan set of assumptions about the American writer. If we were to adopt a different set of assumptions, broader and more fluid, then Cather could be read for her encounters *with* American culture.

To demonstrate this, we can take another article written in 1933. Cather's friend, Dorothy Canfield Fisher, a fellow-novelist, wrote 'Willa Cather: Daughter of the Frontier' for the *New York Herald-*

Tribune. Fisher proposed that Cather was a major novelist because she understood the salient characteristics of her society. Cather's letters show that she was worried when Canfield Fisher began the article; she felt that her friend would read the novels more closely than other critics. Canfield Fisher, to Cather's pleasure, realised that her work offered unique insights:

> I offer you a hypothesis about Willa Cather's work: that the only real subject of all her books is the effect a new country – our new country – has on people transplanted to it from the old traditions of a stable, complex civilization. Such a hypothesis, if true, would show her as the only American author who has concentrated on the only unique quality of our national life, on the one element which is present more or less in every American life and unknown and unguessable to Europeans or European colonials... Is there any one of Miss Cather's novels which is not centered around the situation of a human being whose inherited traits come from centuries of European or English forebears, but who is set down in a new country to live a new life which is not European or English, whatever else it may be?[16]

Canfield Fisher's article anticipates precisely the discussion of ideology and culture developed in this introduction. Her argument is a simple and persuasive one: Cather explores unique aspects of American life that are still unaccounted for in the national literature. The word 'only' is used repeatedly in this piece to point to the exceptional qualities of American life and the singularity of Cather's achievement in recording them. We read Cather, Canfield Fisher tells us, for the most fundamental reason: she writes about a realm of experience that has been beyond the purview of fiction. Canfield Fisher demonstrates that her friend *was* aware of the significant tendencies of her age: immigration, cultural transmission and the 'new life'. In the light of this hypothesis, the readings of Hicks and Bloom look less tenable.

But Canfield Fisher's hypothesis never became an established way to read her friend's novels. 'The Case against Willa Cather' has been reprinted, whereas this eulogy has appeared only in its original form. Similarly, the Cather letters remain beyond most discussions of Cather and American culture due to the copyright restrictions. Taken together, the letters, the Canfield Fisher article and the novels themselves suggest an alternative 'Case for Willa

'Cather'. They suggest a 'progressive' Cather, a writer liberally attuned to the broad currents of early twentieth-century American life – race, immigration and multiculturalism.

PROGRESSIVISM

'Progressivism' was a significant term when Cather wrote her major novels. The period when Cather became a novelist (1890–1920) is often described as the 'Progressive Era'; but this provokes the enquiry, 'what exactly *was* progressivism?' Historical opinion has been divided to the extent that recent commentators conclude that progressivism can only be defined *ex negativo* – by what it was not. Progressivism was not, in spite of the fact that Presidential candidates (Theodore Roosevelt, Robert LaFollette) ran for office under the Progressive banner, a single movement or simply a political platform. It was, according to Robert Crunden, 'a climate of creativity', but even this expansive definition is undercut by Peter Filene's wariness: 'The more that historians have analyzed it, the more doubtful that identity. In each of its aspects – goals, values, membership and supporters – the movement displays a puzzling and irreducible incoherence.' [17]

Nonetheless, we can distinguish between the immediately political and economic aims of progressivism and the broader intellectual *Zeitgeist* it created. The former were defined by Benjamin De Witt in 1915 as the exclusion of privileged interests from centres of political or economic control, the expansion of democracy and the use of government to protect the weak and oppressed.[18] The broader sense of progressivism at first resists definition but has been analysed by historians in terms of underlying social and intellectual structures. Three features are particularly worthy of note.

First, that progressivism was the product of a 'status revolution'; the rise of the professional middle classes (lawyers, teachers, scientists) at the turn of the century found its political corollary in calls for reform of the Establishment. Richard Hofstadter has shown that these groups were opposed to the entrenched business and political interests who, it seemed, had monopolised power and money for their own ends and were undermining American democratic ideals.

Second, that progressivism was basically a Protestant movement and bore similarities to earlier American Utopian movements; it was a form of secular 'Great Awakening'. In a well-argued account of 'The Religion of Progress', covering thinkers such as Henry Demarest Lloyd and Herbert Croly, David W. Noble concluded that 'the rapidly rising religious enthusiasm of American intellectuals...suggests the necessity for fundamental qualifications of the thesis that postulates conversion of these intellectuals to Darwinism'.[19] Much religious energy went into the 'Social Gospel' movement, the drive by middle-class Protestant reformers to improve the lives of the poor, especially in the cities. The Social Gospel marked a break with the earlier Protestant attitude to economics, where the system was seen as justifiably beneficial to the morally righteous, by expressing an outright dislike of unregulated capitalism. Now the social role of the church became important.[20] Progressivism was in general a profoundly Utopian politics. Alongside the specific reform programmes (attacks on business trusts, missions to help the urban poor) sat a generalised and mythic language which envisaged the outcome of these measures. Progressives thus formulated a Utopian imagery of a purified nation, a fervent language of renewal. Their secular heaven was squarely in the tradition of American idealism, a redeployment of the classic image of the godly city on the hill. In J. A. Thompson's words, 'Progressivism, at its heart, was an effort to realize familiar and traditional ideals under novel circumstances'.

Examples of this Utopian myth are found throughout progressivism; they occur in fiction, anthropology, economics and politics. Edward Bellamy's novel *Looking Backward* (1887) features a collectivist Utopia. Thorstein Veblen eulogised primitive craft communities in *The Instinct of Workmanship and the State of the Industrial Arts* (1914). And liberal sociologists at Chicago University, surveying the immigration and assimilation of Europeans in their *Americanization Studies*, forecast a Utopian multicultural United States.[21] All of these works project the idealised progressive community, the harmonious and fulfilled good society.

Third, that although the title 'progressive' implies a forward-looking movement, in fact progressivism often looked backwards. In his major study of the broad currents of progressivism, Robert Crunden uses the phrase 'innovative nostalgia' to describe this simultaneous retrospective and proleptic envisaging of America.

How does Cather fit into this scheme? We can, I believe, examine the overall pattern of her career and the local features of her fiction in terms of progressivism. Her life followed an exemplary progressive pattern: journalist, teacher and writer – Cather entered those professions which had emerged at the turn of the century to create an articulate, reforming middle class. Her upbringing in the recently-settled Midwest; the entry into one of the new state universities; work in regional newspapers and magazines; editorship of the major progressive, muckraking journal, *McClure's* – as a life it is an almost archetypal progressive success story. Cather's life bears many similarities to other progressive life stories in actuality and fiction dating from this period. Like her mentor S. S. McClure and like Scott Fitzgerald's fictional Midwesterners, Jay Gatsby and Nick Carraway, Cather moved upwards from provincial obscurity to East Coast fame as part of a rising middle class. Many of her closest friends had lives that were similarly various and professionally chameleon-like. The Cather circle was provincial in origin and social standing, but in classic 'status revolution' manner these friends moved into positions of authority and cultural power. She knew Louise Pound and her brother Roscoe, both of whom had academic careers which spread across a range of disciplines; Louise was a folklorist, philologist and the first female president of the MLA, while her brother was an eminent Harvard lawyer and a key figure in introducing unions into American academe. Another friend, Dorothy Canfield Fisher, was well known as a novelist and journalist. It is worth stressing the mobility of these careers and their professionalism (the Pounds especially were involved in the creation of professional bodies which gave their members a political voice). Cather emerged from a distinctive social group which could be designated the progressive, professional middle class.

The life was progressive; the fiction deploys, sometimes indirectly and sometimes squarely, the themes and motifs of progressivism. Cather alludes to, echoes, modifies and recasts progressivism's main features. Reading Cather in conjunction with progressivism enables us to see how her novels are implicated in a 'war of ideas'. Rather like Jane Austen, this apparently *désengagée* author was caught up in a fictional exploration of many of the leading intellectual, social and political ideas of her time.[22] Throughout this book I use several progressive motifs as touchstones when reading Cather's work: professionalisation, Protestantism and Utopianism, depoliticised reform, 'innovative nostalgia'. All four elements occur in the fiction, providing a series of stencils through which we can read the novels in their ideological context and, in so doing, also reread the context. My major methodological means to demonstrate this is by suggestive juxtaposition. Placing the novels alongside key progressive texts we can see the congruences or disjunctions between Cather and her contemporaries. Figures such as the sociologist Robert Park, the polymathic theorist Thorstein Veblen, the muckraking journalist Lincoln Steffens and the politician William Jennings Bryan provide a route – through their lives and writings – to illustrate the intersections between Cather and progressivism. I quote their work to compare it with Cather's and to demonstrate how Americans in the progressive milieu worked out different approaches to the issues outlined above.

Cather's relationship to these ideas was distinctive, if not idiosyncratic. We can read her *in conjunction* with progressivism but not *as* a straightforward progressive; we must recognise the distinctiveness of Cather's progressivism. There are two major reasons to stress her singularity. First, there are the chronologies of Cather's career and progressivism. The longevity of her writing life was an important factor in enabling her to oversee the rise, establishment and eclipse of progressive ideas. She began working as a journalist in the 1890s, reaching her peak as a novelist in the 1920s – and this span of time coincides with the progressive era. Chronologically, then, Cather's work asks to be read in this way. But her major phase – the stretch of years from 1913 to 1927 dealt with in this book – saw the twilight of progressivism or, if one looks at the period from a slightly different perspective, the blurring of progressivism into the first stirrings of New Deal politics. Writing with hindsight, Cather was ideally placed to survey the aspirations and achievements of the progressive era (1890–1920). And what she saw was the splintering of progressive idealism during the First World War.

Historians frequently remark on the moral absolutism of progressivism, its idealism. There was inevitable disillusion when this idealism foundered against historical contingencies; the War was this turning-point for the progressives. The transformation of the tone of progressive politics is echoed in Cather's fiction, also structured around polarities of idealism and disillusion. As the 1920s advanced, her fiction struck increasingly sour and disillusioned notes (climaxing in the embittered final stages of *The Professor's House* when St Peter seemingly acquiesces in a nearly fatal accident); but buried within the most disgruntled stories are intimations of idealism and glimpses of the great good American places beloved of the progressives. In several of the novels ideal communities are envisaged: cliff-dweller pueblos, Catholic missions in the South-west, bilingual homesteads on the Plains. Her characters find themselves at ease in these places, at one with themselves, with each other and the landscape. For example, in *The Professor's House* St Peter's disillusion is juxtaposed against the exuberant idealism of 'Tom Outland's Story' where the hero finds an earthly heaven on the Blue Mesa. At first, these earthly heavens and Utopias might seem ahistorical – purely and simply mythic ideal communities. However, if we place the novels in the context of progressivism, we change the lens through which Cather's Utopianism is perceived. An apparently mythic discourse is revealed as historically-conditioned; the great, good places of Cather's fiction emerge as part of a larger cultural pattern, namely the Utopian idealism of progressive America and its reforming drive to recreate the nation as an earthly Eden. An important aspect of Cather's revision of progressive Utopianism was that she also imagined the dream's failure. Writing after the progressive heyday, she could see the obverse of Utopianism: dystopia. Her Utopias often contain their own mirror-image, the Utopia gone wrong or failed. Even at the most heightened, enthused or rapturous moments there are disquieting tremors, intimations that the idyll, the vision of the ideal community will soon vanish. The idyllic Blue Mesa, for example, is found to contain barbaric relics such as the mummified remains of a woman punished for sexual impropriety. Later chapters in this book explore ambiguous passages where the upswing towards idealism is checked and then falters as Cather comes up against the disconcerting failures of the progressive ideal.[23]

The second reason to stress Cather's idiosyncrasy is that her views on some issues dealt with by the progressives marked out a distinctive position. In particular, she rejected the insularity of progressivism in favour of a more cosmopolitan and outward-looking vision of the ideal community. For progressivism was often a highly insular, overly *American* movement. As the First World War and its aftermath demonstrated, American idealism did not export easily. Within the US, progressivism was hardly hospitable to the foreign or the alien. Some progressives were probably nativists – that is, strong believers in the Anglo-Saxon, protestant 'native' traditions of America who were suspicious of immigration and racial or religious variety. Progressivism's strength lay in the application of American Protestantism to secular problems; it is thus hardly surprising that the movement was coloured by an almost theological resistance to other ways.[24]

But Cather's imagination could be characterised in the opposite fashion: she was unusually receptive to *difference*, weaving into her novels a broad-minded acceptance of the foreign or the strange. The novels harness many progressive themes – reform, earthly Utopias, moral idealism – to a highly unprogressive awareness of the cultural variety of America. As my chapter on *Death Comes for the Archbishop* demonstrates, Cather even envisaged such progressive ideals as a reforming authority and an earthbound Utopia within the context of the Catholic Church. Against the narrowly Protestant idealism of the progressives, Cather places her own multicultural vision. Geographically and culturally, she envisaged a range of American Utopias, situating them in Indian settlements and in the Catholic South-west. In her multiculturalism Cather was, oddly, more progressive than her reputation or her professed politics suggest.

It would be foolish to overlook the biographical origins of this broad-minded, progressive sympathy. As a girl, Cather loved to talk with the hard-pressed immigrant women from Bohemia and Scandinavia who were forging a life on the Nebraskan plains near the family home:

> The early population of Nebraska was largely transatlantic. The county in which I grew up, in the south-central part of the State, was typical. On Sunday we could drive to a Norwegian church and listen to a sermon in that language, or to a Danish or a Swedish church. We could go to the French Catholic settlement in the next county and hear a sermon in French, or into the Bohemian township and hear one in Czech, or we could go to church with the German Lutherans. There were, of course, American congregations also.[25]

Her girlhood in Nebraska fostered an understanding of the varieties of American experience. Indeed, the 'American congregations' are incidental to this polyglot, religiously varied culture, deserving only an ironic aside. This cataloguing of races or nationalities became, as we shall see, a favourite tactic in Cather's writing. She seemed to take pleasure in simply *listing* the different peoples of America.

But it is also important to place her intellectually. Cather, perhaps more than many of her contemporaries, was attuned to the revolutions in social science, anthropology and archaeology that had occurred at the end of the nineteenth century. She understood that our definitions of 'progress', 'culture' and 'civilisation' must change in response to conceptual shifts. My chapters on *O Pioneers!*, *Death Comes for the Archbishop* and *The Professor's House* set the novels against the changing intellectual climate of the period. Definitions were broadened: geology and archaeology opened up history beyond the short span of modern occidental 'progress'; anthropology introduced other peoples, other cultures into the story of civilisation; the study of mankind began to be relativised. Most of these developments occurred in the late nineteenth century, of course, but their impact on American culture was delayed. This is shown by the reception of Darwin in America. While Darwin's work received immediate acclaim in Britain and exerted enormous influence on novelists, in America the osmosis of his ideas was prolonged.[26] In 1925, as I show in my chapter on *The Professor's House*, controversy still raged over the teaching of evolutionary theory in schools. At the centre of these changes was a new attitude to the 'primitive' and an almost italicised sense of progress: how can civilisation's development really be 'progress' if so many worthwhile cultures were left behind or destroyed? Cather's intellectual peers are other quirky progressives, figures such as the maverick social scientist Thorstein Veblen. He also dealt with the anthropological dimensions of progress, including praise for 'primitive' societies alongside characteristically progressive jeremiads on the ills of contemporary America.

FICTION, MYTH AND HISTORY

The question now arises of *how* the novels interact with their context. How, for instance, can we begin to map progressive motifs onto the fiction, but avoid the simplistic reduction of texts to passive reflections of their context? Is there a transformation of historical actualities when they are inscribed into the texture of fictional prose? How, in other words, are texts *produced* in early-twentieth-century America?

I here want to cite a recent discussion of 'myth' and 'history' in nineteenth-century American fiction. Robert Clark argues that in classic American novels complex social, economic and political actualities ('history') are condensed and displaced into 'myth'. In this process, which Clark discusses using a Freudian terminology, there is often a 'wish-fulfilling' drive; the American writer turns history the 'other way round' to create a myth of what America should be like. Troublesome realities – exploitation of nature and subjugation of Indians or blacks – are transformed into the comforting myths of the innocent in the garden (Natty Bumppo) or the comradely pairing of black and white (Natty and Chingachgook, Ishmael and Queequeg). Myth is the 'inversion of real conditions'. Clark then distinguishes between ideological discourse, 'combining real conditions with varying amounts of the imaginary but always retaining a basis of material address', and myth, which 'would be reserved for areas of acute contradiction between beliefs and practices of the social formation'. 'Mythic signs' are used to preserve order 'at those points where the belief system threatens to reveal its arbitrary and paradoxical nature'. In the early and mid-nineteenth century, Clark writes, 'terms such as "natural right to the land", "freedom", "civilisation", "savagery", "providence", "manifest destiny", appear in political rhetoric at those points where the contradictions of social experience are too acute to allow further ideological elaboration'. The examples adduced are drawn from work by Cooper, and deal with the fates of peoples extinguished by historical progress. Clark frequently discovers in his texts 'contradictions of social experience' which centre on race, progress and civilisation.[27]

Robert Clark's work is part of the so-called 'New Americanist' school of criticism. The New Americanists react against the founding fathers of American Studies, such as Henry Nash Smith, Leo Marx, R. W. B. Lewis and Leslie Fiedler. These earlier critics seemed to be working to enmesh history and literature; but their critical practice, in the eyes of New Americanists, failed to create an adequate analytical methodology. For, even as they called for closer attention to the actualities of their culture, the early Americanists posited a series of mythic or symbolic figures, scenarios and motifs: the American Adam, the machine in the garden, the flight into the wilderness, the buddy duo of white man and Indian. The reader leaves these critical works believing that the cultural patterns described are *archetypal*. They are, in Robert Weimann's words, 'anthropological, symbolic, or mythical concepts, which replace the more strictly sociological and economic tools of analysis'. This led to the 'vogue of a disembodied history of ideas', producing the image and symbol criticism which came to dominate the emerging discipline of American Studies. Surveying the achievements of

American Studies' programmes recently, Gerald Graff concluded that, 'As often as not, the history in question rested on little more than bold assertions, buttressed by the occasional quotation from Tocqueville, Lawrence, or Frederick Jackson Turner'. When Warner Berthoff reviewed Richard Poirier's *A World Elsewhere* (a book whose basic premise is that the writer creates an alternative America, a world outside of society and history) he remarked that 'America' featured as 'an almost completely unanalyzed historical integer'. The value of Clark's work is that it gets a purchase on America as a 'historical integer' while creating a space for the rehabilitation of myth: he combines analysis of the social, political and economic factors conditioning the literary text with readings of the mythic registers of American fiction. Myth, Clark demonstrates, is a *discourse*, and as such it is one in a range of discourses within which the novelist writes 'America'. More often than not, Clark shows, myth is an evasive discourse by which the problems of history and ideology are suppressed or evacuated from the text. Myth is grafted back on to readings of American texts, becoming historicised; it is then understood as a way for the American writer to 'read' his or her historical situation. His emphasis on myth does not lead, as it did in earlier criticism, to the exclusively mythological coding of literature. The critic now asks the questions overlooked by her predecessors: what is myth for and how is it used?[28]

Clark's thesis shows that the slide from history into myth often took place when the author considered the knotted relationships between the white man and the Indian. At these points the very identity of America is focused. Race, the progress of civilisation, the conflicting ideals of ecological pastoralism and technological advance: there is a sudden proliferation of the dilemmas which underlay America's development but usually remained hidden or deliberately overlooked.

Clark's discussion raises questions about race and civilisation which are pertinent to this book. Clark locates the crux of Cooper's historical imagination in his tales of extinguished races; Cather also told stories about the victims of historical 'progress' (for instance, the Navajo and Pueblo Indians in *Death Comes for the Archbishop*). Cather's fictional world – that diverse patchwork of Pueblo Indians and European immigrants, mesa settlements and university buildings – juxtaposes different orders of American civilisation. She was fascinated by the idea of cultural conflict, by the shibboleth of historical progress and by the question of what 'civilisation' really means.

However, we need to stress the differences between Cather and her predecessors: we can locate a thematic continuity linking Cather to her forebears, but in its representation of history her fiction marks a significant break from the nineteenth-century model. Two formal or structural features of the novels are especially significant for their ideological implications. First, in Cather's fiction the mythic discourse is overtly present. She writes myth into her novels, self-consciously foregrounding a symbolic, parable-like form of story-telling. Examples include the stories of Peter and Pavel (*My Ántonia*), the Cliff-City and the Enchanted Mesa (*The Professor's House*), the destruction of the Navajos (*Death Comes for the Archbishop*), and Ántonia's homestead (*My Ántonia*). When these stories begin there is a sundering of the realist text by other voices; a thickened, knotty density enters the prose; the narrative turns towards symbol and parable, taking on a layered complexity. The text is then overloaded, saturated and suffused with concentrated and condensed meanings. These are moments when the writing becomes intricate and difficult to interpret, even as it seems to demand decoding. For this reason, then, my discussion pays a great deal of attention to those moments when Cather's writing shifts into what I call the mythic register.

The second feature of the novels I want to draw attention to is their increasing 'gappiness' during the 1920s. Cather's fiction became increasingly fractured or open in its narrative form. The episodic openness of *My Ántonia* or *O Pioneers!* was succeeded by the radical structural disjunctions of *Death Comes for the Archbishop* and *The Professor's House*, in which Cather showed scant regard for preserving unities of place or time or point of view. She defended the form of *Death Comes for the Archbishop* (a book that seemed formless to many readers) on the grounds that this was a *narrative* not a novel. Her experiments with novelistic form have major implications for the meanings of the texts: structure, the architecture of a novel, help to define its ideological configuration. Narratology has taught us to read for the oddities in the construction of a text; we now search for moments of incoherence or asymmetry rather than formal coherence, organic wholeness or symmetry. At these nodal points the text's engagement with history is found as historical actuality erupts into the text or is silenced and suppressed. To use two geographical metaphors: we can think of the parable-like or symbolic discourse of Cather's fiction as a fold in the terrain of the novel, a sudden thickening of its density; and the gaps in her novels are fissures, rents in that same terrrain. In charting the ideology of Cather's fiction, particularly her negotiations between myth and history, I will often concentrate on these two features of the novels.

CATHER'S PROGRESSIVISM

Having defined 'progress' in its early twentieth-century senses, we now need to understand the ways in which we, as late twentieth-century readers, understand the word.

'Progressivism' is a matter of great concern to contemporary literary critics. The drive of much criticism – deconstructive, feminist, ideological – is to gauge how progressive, that is liberal or radical, the chosen author is. And, not surprisingly, evaluated against the tenets of twentieth-century Western liberalism, most writers of the past emerge as conservative at best, and more often as virulently reactionary. Alvin Kernan, in what is admittedly a caricatured account of contemporary criticism, has gone so far as to claim that the most popular university courses are those 'that demonstrate how meaningless, or paradoxically, how wicked and antiprogressive, the old literature has been'. To take but one example of this critical adjudication, Laura Brown's recent study of Pope, we find openly damning references to the poet's politics; the mission of the critic is to expose these iniquities: 'As a consistent advocate of the beliefs and ambitions of the capitalist landlords and of an imperialist consensus, Pope must be scrutinized, doubted and demystified.' The implication of this commentary is that to read Pope is to encounter an alien and repugnant politics; our responses will always be conditioned by the basic fact of his anti-progressive ideology. Brown's argument is nowadays a familiar one and received its pithiest expression in Alan Sinfield's assertion that 'most literary texts...will be reactionary'. The next move for some critics is to rehabilitate writers who appear to be reactionary but, it is contested, can be read as closet revolutionaries. Kiernan Ryan, countering the arguments of Sinfield, repeatedly uses the words 'progress' and 'progressive' in his account of a radical Shakespeare: 'it ought to be possible to work towards a more productive way of re-reading Shakespeare's plays frankly but plausibly from a progressive modern viewpoint'.[29]

How does Cather fit into these arguments? She cannot be said to stand out for impeccably unbesmirched liberal credentials. There is, for instance, the issue of her alleged anti-Semitism. The evidence against her is partly biographical, though there are flashes of apparently racist caricature in the fiction. First, several stories feature references to Jews, and Cather's characterisation makes them graspingly greedy. In 'The Marriage of Phaedra', a story which appeared in *The Troll Garden* collection (1905), a casual anti-Semitism is part of the hero's character. The fact that the anti-Semitism is mediated through a character means, one might claim, that we have to qualify the attribution of such sentiments directly to the author. But there is no antiphonal voice in this story, no commentary to suggest that the following sentence, for example, is not endorsed by the author: 'Later, however, the man's repulsive personality and innate vulgarity so wore upon him that, the more genuine the Jew's appreciation, the more he resented it and the more base he somehow felt it to be'.[30] Second, in her diagnosis of America's decline into gaudy materialism she partly attributed this decay to figures who are either overtly or covertly Jewish. The 1914 essay, 'Potash and Perlmutter', attacked the growing commercialism of America and seemed to place the blame on Jews. In her fiction she attacked the commercial and intellectual vulgarities of her age, sometimes caricaturing America's Jews, who were made synonymous with acquisitive materialism. *The Professor's House* extensively features a Jewish character, Louie Marsellus, whose job (electrical engineering) and pursuits (building kitsch houses) contrast unfavourably with the disinterested intellectual brilliance of the novel's gentile hero, Tom Outland. It is probable that Louie Marsellus was inspired by the marriage of her old friend Isabelle McClung to the Canadian Jewish violinist, Jan Hambourg. Isabelle had been her closest friend, and it appears that the marriage soured the relationship between the two women. There are intriguing parallels between the scenario of *The Professor's House* – the Professor is devoted to his old house and disturbed by the prospects of moving to a new home and study – and the situation when Cather visited the Hambourgs at their French home: Cather, like the Professor, was offered a new home and a new study, both of which she turned down. Cather's affective life might seem progressive, but closer investigation shows disturbingly reactionary moments.[31]

The critics have not been sure what to make of all this. James Schroeter is trenchant, pointing out that Cather dealt sympathetically with many immigrant groups but 'There was one important group...that played little part in Willa Cather's fiction, the Russian and Polish Jews who were coming to America in such large numbers.' He nicely contrasts the 'assimilative and Whitmanesque hug' she extended towards most immigrant groups with the coldness or even 'hatred' she showed towards Jews. *The Professor's House* thus becomes an anti-Semitic fable, a bleak dissection of the putative take-over of America by the Jewish inheritors (Marsellus marries St Peter's daughter and exploits Outland's scientific discoveries for profit). But the consensus is that Cather's anti-Semitism must be interpreted within its cultural context. James Woodress points out that there are good Jews in the fiction and the life; many of her villains are white and Protestant. 'She had what one might call a typical Midwestern bias against Jews in the aggregate, the result of growing up in a culture almost devoid of Jews; but to call her anti-Semitic is to exaggerate considerably.' Sharon O' Brien, keen to foreground Cather's sexual radicalism, summarily accounts for her racist recidivism as 'the unfortunate anti-Semitism Cather shared with many American writers of her generation'.[32]

Underlying this debate is a basic question of, as it were, literary morality: does an occasional lapse of judgement invalidate or cancel out the 'progressive' impulses evident elsewhere in a writer's life and work? This is the difficult terrain over which Christopher Ricks travelled in his study of T. S. Eliot and prejudice.[33] The problem of Cather's anti-Semitism is analogous, though perhaps not as extreme (there is a wider range of troublesome comments in Eliot's work, and his alleged prejudice fits all too easily into the larger framework of his political conservatism); the questions are, again, how we can account for views that appear to the modern reader distasteful or deserving of censure. If we adopt a 'correspondence-theory' of truth, so that each element in a writer's foundational beliefs has to correspond absolutely with the next, then there has probably never been (and never will be) an author whose works cannot be deconstructed to demonstrate how self-contradicting and self-subverting their ideas were.

Contradictions, however, might simply be what they are. Cather is a major example of a writer whose inconsistencies are just that: messy ambiguities, anomalies, paradoxes, aberrations and blunt contradictions. For we can set alongside the anti-Semitism many instances when Cather was scrupulously attentive to the culture and psychology of the 'Other'. Throughout this book I refer to such moments, noting Cather's sympathy for alien peoples like Navajo or Pueblo Indians. Indeed, these moments establish Cather as a writer whose work, almost in spite of her own occasional lapses, manifested a breadth of sympathy and a genuine progressivism. There is also evidence that she was aware of earlier lapses in her work. For the revised version of *The Song of the Lark* (1937) she cut at least one barbed aside (a character sneers at 'Kosher clothes').[34]

Two assertions need to be made on behalf of Cather's progressivism. First, Cather demonstrates the ability of art to create a 'hinterland' in which the creative intelligence fathoms problems given simplistic answers or avoided in other discourses. In her fiction she countenanced ideas, areas of American life and structures of human feeling overlooked in her journalism. Thus, the political documentation in her newspaper writing hardly prepares us for the political commentary in the novels. Second, in order to understand Cather's progressivism we need to contextualise her writing. One of the problems with our accounts of literature's political complexion is that to compare earlier texts with a modern ideological agenda is almost inevitably to dehistoricise literature. We need to ask how progressive Cather was within her age, otherwise our readings of the fiction will be *of* the past and not of the fiction situated *in* the past. Such a historical reading can be developed in several ways.

We can interpret Cather's major themes in a more favourable light by taking them as an illustration of her engagement with, rather than rejection of American culture. One instance of this is her fascination with memory, retrospection and nostalgia. In Dorothy Canfield Fisher's words the new American, focus of Cather's interest, is 'a human being whose inherited traits come from centuries of European or English forebears'. Inheritance necessitates a search of the past to discover where the traits originally came from. This then means that memory becomes a centre of fictional investigation. Memory and inheritance are akin to the nostalgia and elegy which Hicks and Bloom identified as topics in the novels; but now they become the very heart of American life and key motifs in Cather's depiction of the contemporary scene. For Cather was a novelist of modern America who portrayed a land of immigrants, a country with a twofold consciousness and a people turned simultaneously towards a lost Europe and the New World.

Second, by reading Cather as a novelist of the 'national life' numerous social and political contexts suggest themselves, enabling us to recover the ideological complexity of her novels. Immigration and cultural migration, in particular, were the subject of intense debate during Cather's lifetime. Academics, journalists, lawyers and politicians interpreted immigration in conflicting ways: some welcomed the newcomers, forecasting a dynamically pluralist culture; others were resistant, fearful that America would be lost beneath the migrant waves. Placing Cather's novels in this context (and others), we can analyse in detail her representations of the 'national life'.

2

'American Literature' and the Failure of American Culture

THE ORDEAL OF THE AMERICAN WRITER

American literary criticism during the First World War and the 1920s was a series of jeremiads about the nation's society and culture. The lament of the critics, reviewers and pundits was that America, a nation of philistine businessmen, withstood artistic creation. Culture, such as it was, had been colonised by the women-folk and reduced to a genteel mockery of itself. The critics whom I discuss in this chapter come from a variety of cultural and political positions, but their work shares two preconceptions: that the weakness of American literature results from the apotheosis of business and commerce; and that culture is 'feminised'. The critic (Van Wyck Brooks, for example, or H. L. Mencken or Harold E. Stearns) demonised the businessman and the American woman: here were the culpable parties responsible for the collapse of literary culture and the disabling of American intellectual life.

When these critics attacked the business mentality of modern America, they often did so by telling a fable about the development of the United States. Their tale began with the pioneers who had founded the country; it showed how the pioneer bequeathed a corrupt culture, becoming, as it were, the father of the business-man. Pioneering set the tone for a preoccupied, pragmatic and fundamentally anti-artistic national life. Culture and art, denied to both businessman and pioneer (too busy or tired to pursue their leisure), therefore became the province of women. Culture is feminised; but because women are not competent enough to undertake artistic work the culture which results is genteel. This reading of American culture achieved a widespread currency because, perhaps for the first time in the United States, *criticism* had become

26

established as a major cultural activity in its own right. The professional critic became a familiar figure (Van Wyck Brooks, H. L. Mencken); small magazines were able to forge a new literary consensus; university departments began to teach American literature as an autonomous subject.[1]

What is surprising, given this increased critical activity, is how often the critics were in agreement. My synopsis provides the paradigm around which many critics from about 1890 to 1940 built their individual accounts of the decline of the national life. Furthermore, this paradigm enables us to see why Cather was regarded as a writer unaware of the 'significant tendencies' of her age: a woman who dealt sympathetically with the pioneer, her fiction appeared to collude with the very forces that hindered American letters. The irony, of course, is that Cather herself was contemptuous of business and commerce; her 1923 *Nation* account of Nebraska, for example, described the 'ugly crest of materialism' now ascendant in her home state. But her fiction gave out the wrong signals. Cather seemed to place herself on the wrong side by dealing with aspects of American life which were repeatedly stigmatised by the loudest voices of the 1920s.

These voices were the culmination of a cultural diagnosis which originated many decades earlier. There are, in fact, striking continuities between successive schools of critics from the 1890s to the 1930s, and we even find correspondences between groups of pundits which disagreed with one another. Moreover, these correspondences converge on the figures of the pioneer and the woman; the attack on these icons of cultural failure is the constant that links the various critical formulae. At the start of Cather's career arguments had already emerged about the baleful influence of the pioneers. Henry C. Vedder's *American Writers of To-day* (1894) and Barrett Wendell's *A Literary History of America* (1900) adumbrate the basic themes: the American writer, standard-bearer of culture, strives against the resistant philistinism of the new pioneer nation. Thus Vedder:

A people that have had to subdue the wilderness, to tunnel the mountains, to bridge rivers, to build railways and telegraphs and factories, to dig wealth out of the bowels of the earth, may be pardoned if they have somewhat neglected the worship of the beautiful in eager quest of the useful. Our country has thus far

been too deeply intent on utilitarian aims, its ideals have been
too gross and unspiritual, for the up-bringing of great poets.[2]

The opposition of 'the beautiful' to 'the useful' or 'utilitarian' is
the polarity which critics used to focus their arguments. Vedder
plays on this opposition, claiming that Americans might be good
labourers and builders, but do not work on their art with sufficient
care: 'The fault of American literature in general is hasty, crude
workmanship.'[3] He praises certain writers and rejects some British
attacks on American writing; but his standards are, on the whole,
Anglophile. Vedder searches for fine writing or an American voice
assimilable to European standards. The latent literary nationalism
implicit in Vedder's title remains merely implied; the difficulty for
the student of American writing lies in the identification of enough
great native authors to make up a viable tradition. For Barrett
Wendell, too, the native literature could hardly be considered self-
sufficient; the common language meant that the standard of judgement had to be 'what America has contributed to the literature of
the English language'.[4]

Several critics inaugurated a tougher, more nationalist mode of
literary criticism; but Van Wyck Brooks was largely responsible for
the idiom in which the new literary nationalism was articulated. In
essays for *Seven Arts* magazine and in books written from 1915 to
1921 Brooks attacked America's literary tradition. Indeed, the
burden of his 1918 essay, 'On Creating a Usable Past', was that
there *wasn't* a cultural tradition: the commercialism and acquisitiveness of American society had stymied the growth of the arts, prevented the establishment of a culture and left the writer alienated.
Brooks's work had two aims: a critique of American commercialism
(continuing the genteel suspicion of business); and the forging of a
cultural past in order to ground the present.[5]

Brooks coined the terms 'Highbrow' and 'Lowbrow' in *America's
Coming of Age* (1915) to condemn the commercialism and gentility
of his country. Commercialism produced gentility, Brooks believed,
and writers 'set themselves to the composition of richly rewarded
trash'.[6] This situation developed because pioneering, although it
enabled Americans to settle a continent, led to the atrophy of art:
culture was deflected by the pioneering drive. Brooks subverts the
commonplace paradisiacal metaphor of America being transformed
from wilderness into garden; in his eyes the pioneer became the

businessman, and business led America into the cultural desert. Hence 'Toward a National Culture' (1917):

> We are like explorers who, in the morning of their lives, have deserted the hearthstone of the human tradition and have set out for a distant treasure that has turned to dust in their hands; but having on their way neglected to mark their track they no longer know in which direction their home lies, nor how to reach it, and so they wander in the wilderness, consumed with a double consciousness of waste and impotence.[7]

Brooks's images pessimistically reverse the wilderness myth; the exploration of America has ended in bewilderment, frustration and waste. Five years later Brooks developed this point in *The Ordeal of Mark Twain* (1920), a work which has been described as a typical work of literary criticism from this period.[8] Brooks's Twain was broken by the severity of the developing pioneer nation. A series of quotations outlines this diagnosis of failing artistry and unremitting philistinism:

> As for the majority of the settlers, it is to the honor of mankind that history calls them heroes; and if that is an illusion, justice will never be realistic. The gods of Greece would have gone unwashed and turned gray at forty and lost their digestion and neglected their children if they had been pioneers: Apollo himself would have relapsed into an irritable silence.
>
> We cannot understand this mood, this creed, this morality unless we realize that the business men of the generation after the Civil War were, essentially, still pioneers and that all their habits of thought were the fruits of the exigencies of pioneering. The whole country was, in fact, engaged in a vast crusade that required an absolute homogeneity of feeling: almost every American family had some sort of stake in the West and acquiesced naturally, therefore, in that worship of success, that instinctive belief that there was something sacred in the pursuit of wealth without which the pioneers themselves could hardly have survived.[9]

Brooks takes the idea that the United States is a theocracy and gives it a remarkable twist. Noting the country's religious fervour, its fondness for the 'vast crusade', he discovers a veneration of the pioneer. Casting an eye backwards and forwards across American history, correlating the desires and compulsions of his society, Brooks discovers a latent pattern that relates these disparate elements: the development of the pioneer spirit, the ever-tightening grip of the pioneer upon the nation.

Twain, a child of business America, was inured to its commercial morality, becoming a literary example of capitalism in action:

> He never thought of literature as an art, as the study and occupation of a lifetime: it was merely the line of activity which he followed more consistently than any other. Primarily, he was the business man, exploiting his imagination for commercial profit, his objects being precisely those of any other business man – to provide for his family, to gain prestige, to make money because other people made money and to make more money than other people made.[10]

The ordeal of Mark Twain, then, is produced by the voluntary sacrifice of artistic genius to the national gods of money and business. The sacrifice is presented as a matter in which Twain hardly had a choice; instinctively he turned writing into commerce. But the ordeal did not stop there. Many pages of Brooks's study are devoted to the writer's domestic life, his relationships with his mother and wife. Brooks there focuses on the second part of the American writer's ordeal: the feminisation of his culture. In his society Twain encountered the endless coveting of riches; but at home he was enmeshed by another code of behaviour – the genteel vacuities of womankind. Twain was tyrannised by women, notably his wife:

> The whole tenor of this new life was to feminize Mark Twain, to make him feel that no loyalties are valid which conflict with domestic loyalties, that no activities are admirable which do not immediately conduce to domestic welfare, that private and familiar interests are, rightly and inevitably, the prime interests of man.[11]

The reader is not surprised when Brooks rails against Mrs Clemens; he earlier traced Twain's despair to a fatherless childhood in the pioneer Midwest and an upbringing at the hands of a woman who incarnated the cultural impoverishment of America: 'And his mother stamps there, with awful ceremony, the composite image of her own meager traditions.'[12] Twain's family, in Brooks's paranoid cultural pathology, were the agents of a system that failed to accept either his creative gifts or the possibility that he might use his talents in a satirical and oppositional way.

Twain is presented as a representative man, a writer with an exemplary career. The 1920s were a decade during which critics looked back over the sorry record of literary failure in America, writing biographies of their neglected, underpaid and misunderstood forebears. Melville was another writer marginalised by commercial America but hallowed in the 1920s for his artistic suffering. Barrett Wendell had only fleetingly mentioned Melville: 'Herman Melville, with his books about the South Seas, which Robert Louis Stevenson is said to have declared the best ever written, and with his novels of maritime adventure, began a career of literary promise, which never came to fruition.'[13]

In the 1920s the reasons why this career failed to flourish became important. Raymond Weaver produced the first revisionist biography in 1921, and Lewis Mumford built upon this portrait of the crucified author in his study of 1929. Melville was now 'the greatest imaginative writer that America has with Whitman, produced', although 'when Herman Melville died in 1891, the literary journal of the day, *The Critic*, did not even know who he was'. Mumford places Melville in the domestic hell which Brooks's Twain inhabited:

Both Melville's father and his mother were monsters... Their correctness, their pettiness, their shallowness, were the correctness and shallowness of a venial society whose pretensions to culture and civilization were, on the whole, pretty thin.[14]

Mumford's book helped to consolidate this distinctive biographical sub-genre about mistreated authors. Biographies were a means to identify the key writers of the emerging American canon; these works helped to validate the forgotten novelist, preparing the ground for the eventual establishment of Melville at the heart of the great tradition in F. O. Matthiessen's *American Renaissance* (1941). Canon-formation in America was from the start a kind of martyrology; the biographies which confirmed the status of major writers are books of martyrs delineating the agonies of the literary life in a land of women and business.

The martyrdom of the writer provided an analogy to the critic's own martyrdom; as American intellectuals discovered their professional identity they found that marginalisation and alienation were their shared lot. The paradigmatic account of this disillusion was autobiographical, *The Education of Henry Adams* (1918), but new historical studies established a revisionist debunking of American civilisation which underwrote Adams's testimony: Charles Beard's *An Economic Interpretation of the Constitution of the United States* (1913) presented the Constitution as a conspiracy of the wealthy against ordinary farmers and workers – his thesis was quickly accepted as a demonstration of the citizen's radical alienation from government and the national life.[15] These texts lie behind 'The Literary Life', an essay which Van Wyck Brooks contributed to an important symposium edited by Harold E. Stearns, *Civilization in the United States: An Enquiry By Thirty Americans* (1922). This book, containing critical, satirical and diagnostic pieces by a group of youngish intellectuals, is sometimes seen as one of the contributing factors in the migration of creative writers to Paris in the 1920s, such were the contributors' doubts about the viability of an intellectual career in the United States. Brooks's essay reiterated the attack on the pioneer, but added that pioneering caused neurosis in the modern psyche. Adopting a Freudian vocabulary of psychological disturbance, Brooks identified a form of pioneer neurasthenia: 'If our writers wither early, if they are too generally pliant, passive, acquiescent, anaemic, how much is this not due to the heritage of pioneering, with its burden of isolation, nervous strain, excessive work and all the racial habits that these have engendered?'[16] Brooks deploys the languages of psychiatry and social Darwinism to picture a neurosis, a collapse of personal confidence, that the pioneer first experienced and that has now become inbred. The writer is the victim of a genetic psychological illness whose aetiology can be traced back to pioneering. The Darwinist and psychiatric diction in this passage demonstrates how the critique of pioneers and business could be endlessly revitalised by the infusion of new terminologies into the basic thesis. In the following passage the word 'utilitarian', used by Henry Vedder in 1894, again occurs. Brooks weaves the genteel fear of utilitarianism into his analysis of an encoded, quasi-genetic pioneer spirit:

That old hostility of the pioneers to the special career still operates to prevent in the American mind the powerful, concentrated pursuit of any non-utilitarian way of life: meanwhile everything else in our society tends to check the growth of the spirit and to shatter the confidence of the individual in himself. Considered with reference to its higher manifestations, life itself has been thus far, in modern America, a failure. Of this the failure of our literature is merely emblematic.[17]

We can now see how these discussions of American literature helped to foster an unsympathetic critical climate for Cather's novels. These jeremiads established a way of thinking, a critical diction which enabled Lionel Trilling and Ernest Hemingway to dismiss her fiction in an elliptical, coded language. Van Wyck Brooks and Harold E. Stearns were on the fringe of literary culture at the start of their careers but quickly moved towards the centre. Their opinions, originally those of the young turk, were absorbed into the literary establishment. Brooks's judgements gained rhetorical power from being part of a larger analysis; his statements were supported by a vision of America's history and identity which gave them cogency and persuasive force. Developments in America's literary culture reinforced Brooks's argument. For the years after 1910 witnessed the growth of a vociferous critics' lobby, the evolution of what Warner Berthoff has called a '*critical* context' and a 'professional milieu'. 'For the first time,' he writes, 'a class of writers emerges in the United States whom we may call, who call themselves, "intellectuals".' Their function was 'to guide literate opinion, to formulate goals and channel energies, above all to stand guard moment by moment over the nation's faltering communion with its own creative destiny'.[18] Thus, for instance, Brooks was not a solitary heckler; he was part of a larger circle, associated with *Seven Arts* magazine, which included Randolph Bourne. The group seems to have been exclusively male. Brooks, working within a fraternal coterie of fellow-critics, almost inevitably concluded that one of the problems with American writing in the past was the lack of fraternal groups, salons and circles. A way towards the 'usable past' was, he thought, to create a sense of literary brotherhood.[19]

This desire to create a 'usable past' was placed in an institutional context when American universities began to teach their national literature. When Brooks published 'On Creating a Usable Past' (April, 1918) American literature was hardly known as an academic discipline. Within a few years the subject had established itself; during the World War and the 1920s, an institutionalised literary consensus developed. Exhaustive details about this institutional-isation (from syllabuses to appointments and publications) can be found in Kermit Vanderbilt's study of American literature and the universities, but the basic process was as follows: articles and books written by the critical clerisy influenced the development of university departments of American literature by defining past ills and positing future remedies. And the message of a critic such as Brooks himself was that pioneering had led to the enervation of writing and writers. The renewal of literature was therefore dependent on resistance to the forces originally responsible for the decline in literary fortunes: pioneers, businessmen and womankind.[20]

At this time Cather too wrote about pioneering, but in an enquir-ing and sometimes celebratory manner. As she began to fictionalise the pioneer past of her home state, Nebraska, critics were incul-pating that very same pioneer past as the cause of cultural failure. Cather might have been regarded as the major novelist who most fully answered Brooks's call for the 'usable past', entwining as she did America's immigrant history and its current multiculturalism (her fiction attempts to see modern America through the lens of the country's history and by so doing make the past quite literally 'usable'); but the Brooks thesis drove a wedge between the pioneer past and serious art. Thus the 'past' became an easy word with which to attack Cather. Not only did Cather appear to overlook the 'significant tendencies' of the age; the tendencies she identified in a *previous* age were the cultural features lambasted by her literary colleagues. Cather was then attacked by a critical 'catch-22': she failed to address the contemporary scene; and her fictions of the past colluded with historical forces that created a hell for modern writers. Articles attacking her, which I discussed in the last chapter, invoked the word 'past' for these negative connotations, just as Brooks, in a diametrically opposite manner, sought an affirmative meaning of the word.

The literary establishment offered two ways in which Cather's achievement could be understood and appreciated. The first channel was the simple weight of sympathetic reviewing. There is no doubt that Cather was often well received by reviewers, but their favourable readings lacked the institutional weight conferred by the cultural pundits discussed in this chapter. James Woodress's recent biography attempts to quantify the positive reviews by counting up the number of critics who liked each novel. He demonstrates convincingly that 'The critics usually have treated Cather very well, though she often thought otherwise'.[21] But this is to misunderstand the equation between literary status and critical approbation: dozens of reviews in minor provincial newspapers carried little weight against Trilling, Hemingway, Hicks and those such as Brooks who, while not dealing with Cather in particular, made it difficult to read the word 'pioneer' without a shudder of distaste. Moreover, it was the pundits whose opinions fed into academic accounts of American literature, not the provincial reviewers. The reviewers sanctioned Cather for her immediate American readership, and Cather's impressive sales figures suggest that journalism probably helped to boost her standing with the public. Yet the reviewers provided little foundation for readings of Cather that would last. Specifically, they could not supply a counter-weight to the corrosive critiques of Cather's failure to deal with her own culture. What was needed, as literary nationalism reached its apogee in the creation of university courses in American literature, was a means to bind Cather to her country.

The second channel would have been an alternative, Cather-oriented school of pundits to extol her work. The Canfield Fisher article quoted earlier demonstrates what this criticism would look like, but the first reader who provided a critical framework for Cather was H. L. Mencken. He was one of her earliest fans, and his views on literary nationalism had suggestive parallels with Cather's notions about immigration, race and multiculturalism. Mencken's study of The American Language (1919) gave the US a means to distinguish itself from the mother-country and the mother-tongue, but his work was equally dedicated to broadening definitions of 'America' and 'American'. He believed that American culture would be invigorated by contact with foreign influences. His essay, 'The National Letters' (1920), reiterated a familiar complaint: the promise of American literature has not been fulfilled; the prophetic hopes of Emerson and Whitman have given issue only to mediocrity; gentility and puritanism reign supreme. The virtues of American writing are 'merely those of an emasculated and often very trashy dilettantism'. He even downplays the significance of the New England literary renaissance, rejecting the equation of one area with the entirety of the US. How, he asks, can we understand from one area 'the whole, gross, glittering, excessively dynamic, infinitely grotesque, incredibly stupendous drama of American life?' Mencken felt that America's Anglo-Saxon tradition was bloodless and dying; the country needed an infusion of foreign stock and alien influences. Mencken was excessively proud of his own German blood, claiming that the 'foreign' was necessary for successful American writing. Good American literature 'takes on a subtle but unmistakable air of foreignness'; 'Intellectual experimentation' was now left to immigrants or Anglo-Saxons enriched by their foreign blood.[22]

Mencken's championing of foreign culture heralds a feeling amongst the avant-garde that American literature would be improved if cultural contacts were forged beyond Anglo-American provincialism. From Mencken one can trace the desire for experience in France and Southern Europe, and also the developing literary interest in 'primitive' or Indian culture. Mencken sanctioned foreignness as a means to discover a new American tradition; his credo underwrites the expatriate American writers of the decade – Hemingway, Stein et al.[23]

Here we come to a central paradox in the relationship between Willa Cather and her age. Cather's work during the period dealt with varieties of foreign experience: French culture (*One of Ours*, *Shadows on the Rock*); Spanish and Indian life (*Death Comes for the Archbishop*), the experience of German and Scandinavian immigrants (*O Pioneers!*, *My Ántonia*). She was fascinated by the Spanish South-west, French life, German opera, and classical literature – all of these interests accord with Mencken's cult of the foreign. Why, then, was Cather not read as a novelist whose work possessed a laudable 'unmistakable air of foreignness'? One reason is that she often chose to depict foreign experience as a form of pioneering – whether literally so in *O Pioneers!* or, more indirectly, as a form of missionary pioneering in *Death Comes for the Archbishop*. Cather's fiction contained two elements that were at the period's literary heart. One of these was regarded sympathetically by her contemporaries (the foreign) and one was not (pioneering). Cather's depiction of foreign experience failed to outweigh her commitment to the pioneer heritage. This trend has continued to the present day, so that while many critics describe Cather as the pioneer-novelist (and a group of revisionists praise her for this), no major study accounts for the range of cultures in her fiction or seeks to understand her sympathy for the 'Other'.

Moreover, no matter how far Cather seemed to anticipate the literary scene's interest in foreignness, her own judgements and works were invalidated in another way: her sex told against her.

Several signs of conformity or revolt were important when decoding the status of the writer: an interest in Europe probably indicated a healthy distance from decayed American culture; the pioneer was an emblem of commercial corruption. But even more important was the sexual division in American literary politics. Gender was the basis of literary conformism and revolt in the 1920s: the mediocre conformity of the literary establishment was frequently attributed to the 'feminisation' of society, while masculinity became an index of revolt.

'THE MEN HAVE BEEN FEMINIZED': SEXUAL POLITICS AND LITERARY CRITICISM

H. L. Mencken gestured towards a cultural map of America which Cather would have recognised, but he also deployed one of the central indictments of America's literary culture. As we saw earlier, in 'The National Letters' he notes that American literature's virtues are 'merely those of an emasculated and often very trashy dilettantism'. 'Emasculated': the culture's mediocre conformity was attributed to the 'feminisation' of America and the undermining of masculinity.

This paranoid, gendered reading of cultural history surfaces repeatedly in the 1920s, and is epitomised in Harold E. Stearns's essay, 'The Intellectual Life' (1922). Stearns was the editor of the *Civilization in the United States* symposium. The collection included contributions on a variety of issues: Lewis Mumford on urban life, Mencken on 'Politics', Brooks on 'The Literary Life'. It was the central document produced by the youngish intellectuals who rebelled against what they saw as an atrophied culture. Stearns, a harsher and sterner proponent of ideas introduced by Van Wyck Brooks, subjected his complex subject to a caustic accusation: the American intellect has been ruined by pioneering and feminisation. The essay begins with a Mencken-like invocation of foreign opinion: 'Hardly any intelligent foreigner has failed to observe and comment upon the extraordinary feminization of American social life, and oftenest he has coupled this observation with a few biting remarks concerning the intellectual anaemia or torpor that seems to accompany it.'[24] And again we come to the obligatory denigration of the pioneer: 'The pioneer must almost of necessity hate the thinker, even when he does not despise thought in itself, because the thinker is a liability to a community that can afford only assets; he is non-productive in himself and a dangerously subversive example to others.'[25]

By now this is familiar stuff: the diagnosis of a cultural disease ('anaemia', 'torpor'); the aetiology of the illness; the attack on the pioneer. For Stearns, however, there is then another stage in the decline and fall of American intellectual life. The nineteenth-century's period of settlement, he writes, gave way to an era of wealth and leisure (Stearns here refers to the late-Victorian 'Gilded Age') when culture was taken over by women:

> That surplus was expended not towards the enrichment of our life – if one omit the perfunctory bequests for education – but towards the most obvious of unnecessary luxuries, the grandiose maintenance of our women.[26]

Here we have another fable of America which combines the key elements – pioneers, women, writers – to castigate the country's philistinism and materialism. Stearns outlined how the immigrant uprooted himself from his homeland and entered the void of America. Eventually the pioneer created wealth through unstinting enterprise, but the result was the bifurcation of society. The men live in their world of business and commerce; the women in a sphere of debased, commercialised, genteel culture. Stearns resentfully adds that American men who are involved in the arts have their masculinity mocked.

Earlier American writers were similarly disturbed by female dominance of the literary marketplace, if not of the general culture. From Hawthorne's bitter comment about the 'scribbling women' of America onwards there is a recurrent nervous flinch which haunts the writer, caught as he is in a profession that seems unsuited for a man. In the early twentieth century this masculine complaint becomes increasingly splenetic. Henry James, for one, trenchantly delineated the sexual division of his society in *The American Scene* (1907): the business man who can never 'hope to be anything but a business man'; the women who 'are all the embroidery while the men supply, as it were, all the canvas'.[27] When American critics now attempted to define their national literature they found a culture completely feminised. For Stearns the placidity of American social life belied the conflict which boiled beneath – a Manichaean struggle between the intellect and a debased literary life, between men and women. He despairingly realised that the men had been defeated:

> Where men and women in America to-day share their intellec-
> tual life on terms of equality and perfect understanding, closer
> examination reveals that the phenomenon is not a sharing but a
> capitulation. The men have been feminized.[28]

As he wrote in his collection of essays, *America and the Young Intellectual* (1921), the word 'Intellectual' carries with it a 'faint aura of effeminate gentility': 'With us it was a natural pioneer tradition that to be interested in the life of reason was in itself rather feminine and sissified.'[29] To stress the point again: this is not a new complaint, but it is the first time that these jeremiads are consistently linked to putatively historical accounts of pioneering and feminisation. It is this convergence of feminisation, pioneering and troubled masculinity which underpins the specific attacks on Cather quoted in my introduction. We can now understand how these comments emerged from a *gendered* rhetoric of cultural disaffection. Stearns's writing exemplifies the flexibility of this rhetoric. He even indicts the feminised world of that utilitarianism previously associated with the male pioneer. He contrasts true intellectual endeavour, described as 'disinterested', with the intellectual work of women. Because women direct themselves towards 'moral reform', Stearns convolutedly explains, their efforts are at root pragmatic, not disinterested, and are therefore another instance of pernicious utilitarianism:

> Hence it is hardly surprising that the intellectual life, as I have
> defined it, of women in America turns out on examination not to
> be an intellectual life at all, but sociological activity. The best of
> modern women thinkers in the United States – and there are
> many – are oftenest technical experts, keen to apply knowledge
> and skill to the formulation of a technique for the better solution
> of problems *the answers to which are already assumed....*what
> women usually understand by the intellectual life is the applica-
> tion of modern scientific methods to a sort of enlarged and
> subtler course in domestic science.[30]

Stearns closes the circle in this sentence. Whereas the feminised sphere seemed to be in opposition to the masculine worlds of the pioneer and the businessman, now it transpires that the pioneers and the 'scribbling women' were different manifestations of the same phenomenon. This conflation is achieved by a contrast between true intellectual endeavour, which Stearns calls 'disinterested', and the intellect of women. Their intellectual effort is directed towards 'moral reform'. By means of this distinction he can link the idea of a feminine intellect to the issue of utilitarianism: women's intellectual achievement is invalidated because it is directed towards practical ends. Stearns's ingenious sophistry enables him to show that the apparent inutility of female culture is deceptive; the women's sphere is, in fact, profoundly utilitarian. Stearns therefore brands the female mind as another manifestation of the pioneer mentality. The underlying opposition, the fundamental struggle in America, is one between intellectuals or writers on one side and pioneers or women on the other.

Stearns's 'domestic science', the ultimate condemnation of women's culture, anticipates Trilling's dismissive comments on Cather and domesticity; Trilling spoke with a vocabulary created by earlier critics. That vocabulary fixed feminine culture within a pathology of American life whose underlying diagnosis was that the male intellectual's predicament was caused by the historical ascendancy of the women's sphere. This argument meant that the simple thematic stuff of Cather's fiction was absorbed within an established discourse about American culture. For a self-conscious inheritor of the American literary mantle like Trilling, aware as he must have been of the laments of Hawthorne and James, Stearns and Brooks, Cather's fiction suggested one thing: the dangerous ubiquity of the 'domestic' and 'feminised' in America.

The attacks on pioneers, utilitarianism and women, read alongside the laments about the woeful position of the writer, add up to a jeremiad. The cultural sway of the jeremiad resulted from these arguments being the complaints of a specific coterie (the emerging voices of 'young America') and of the general literary culture. Attacking the feminisation of America was both the old, old story and a new sport – around the First World War period there was a conflation of these traditional and novel critiques.

To illustrate this we can compare two pieces published during the period. John Dos Passos, then just 16 years old, published 'Against American Literature' in the *New Republic* in 1916. Dos Passos imagined representative women in order to symbolise the inadequacies of American literature. He asserted that:

If any mood predominates in American writing it is that of gentle satire. This tendency to satire, usually vague and kindly, some-times bitter with the unconvinced bitterness of a middle-aged lady who thinks herself wordly-wise, is the one feature pervad-ing all that can be called American among the mass of foreign-inspired writing in this country.

Dos Passos had already realised, in anticipation of Mencken, that American literature was becoming 'foreign-inspired'. Otherwise the literary scene was dominated by the domesticity of women writers:

It is significant that, quite unconsciously, I chose the works of two women to typify American novels. The tone of the higher sort of writing in this country is undoubtedly that of a well brought up and intelligent woman, tolerant, versed in the things of this world, quietly humorous, but bound tightly in the fetters of 'niceness' of the middle-class outlook.[31]

As a young man with something to prove, Dos Passos affirms his integrity by tilting at a familiar target: a caricature of feminised culture. What is surprising about the early twentieth-century literati is the consensus that stretches across the old and the new waves, the establishment and the avant-garde. The fledgeling author proves himself by the verbal ingenuity with which he re-fashions old complaints, displaying his writerly credentials in showy wordplay: Hemingway's pun on 'Catherized'; Trilling's identification of Cather's 'pots and pans'; Dos Passos's sarcastic vignettes.

Another example demonstrates the pervasion of these argu-ments. It also shows how, through a process of cultural osmosis, these ideas permeated the critical avant-garde *and* the middlebrow literary scene.[32] Joseph Hergesheimer, a now forgotten novelist, was at the height of his considerable popularity after the war. In July 1921 he published in the *Yale Review* an article called 'The Feminine Nuisance in American Literature'. Its gist can be imag-ined. There is the usual attack on the 'cowardly mediocrity' of liter-ary life, pithily figured in Hergesheimer's statement 'that literature in the United States is being strangled with a petticoat'.[33] He complains about the neglect or mistreatment of masculine themes such as war or, bizarrely, university athletics. Again we note the dichotomies: men and women, business and a debased art. Hergesheimer presents a vignette which dramatises these oppositions:

> The women had – in the intervals of feeding the children and preparing for dinner – nothing better to do than strum at Chopin; but the men were importantly engaged in – what? – the shredding of codfish, the floating of Texan oil on the troubled waters of private financial dreams, or holding in the clouds the price of wheat and the price of coal.[34]

Which just about sums it all up. But Hergesheimer goes even further than Stearns, Mencken or Brooks in revealing the deep anxiety of America's male writer. He turns the usual argument around – swerves or twists of logic dominate writing on this subject – and claims that it is the women who are really interested in practicalities, while the men are the true artistic sex. 'Again and again', he writes, 'I find in these men of affairs whimsical fancies and echoes of harmonies, poetic memories, and cherished ideals.' He wants to appropriate the utterly stereotyped ideals of the feminised world of culture: fancy, poetry, idealism, whimsy. For this appropriation to take place it was necessary to break the covenant that bound women and art together. Hergesheimer therefore claimed that this cultural sphere, mistakenly placed in female hands, was cynically transmuted into a world of business: 'Feeling, beauty, romance, are delivered to a feminine supervision which promptly syndicates them into the corporation of dressmakers, candy manufacturers, and jewellers.' The language of business ('corporation', 'syndicates') is effortlessly transposed onto women's culture; now the male writer can regain 'Feeling, beauty, romance'. Hergesheimer concludes that what is needed is a literature for men because 'in that way a new and eventually inviolate body of American literature will be established'. Note his use of the word 'inviolate'. The cultural desire here is similar to Hemingway's imagining of masculine experience and literature as a sacrosanct body that needed to be kept 'inviolate', untouched and un-'Catherized' by the intrusions of feminised America. Canonisation, literary nationalism, the antagonisms between men and women or business and art: all these topics merge in Hergesheimer's solution to the dilemma of male authors in America.[35]

THE NEW AMERICAN WRITER

If we group together the numerous pieces written by Brooks, Mencken, Stearns, Hergesheimer, Trilling and Hemingway a pattern emerges. Underpinning their essays are a series of oppositions which can best be represented in a table:

Pioneers	Male writers
The 'feminine'	The 'masculine'
Neurosis	Health
Uprootedness	The 'Usable Past'
Utilitarian	Disinterested
'Low' art	'High' art
Corruption of culture	Renewal of culture
Gentility	A new 'earthy' writing

This table is based on the terms used by American critics during the approximate period 1915–22. What is striking about these antinomies is that they anticipate a writer such as Hemingway. *In Our Time* had yet to be published (Paris edition, 1924, and New York edition in 1925), but a definition and approval of his prose already resided in the criticism of the period. Hemingway's fiction – declaratively masculine, 'disinterested' in its portrayal of codes of stylised behaviour, earthy, permeated by the foreign – embodied that reaction against a feminised gentility promulgated by Stearns, Mencken and Brooks. Hemingway was the antidote to watery, womanly, genteel commercialism. The ease with which he fits into the literary scene and into our conceptions of American writing has much to do with the creation of a critical language before *In Our Time* appeared. Hemingway himself was aware of his position; his comments about the War being 'Catherized' in *One of Ours* indicate a canny understanding of the emerging debate about gender and American culture.

Hemingway's fiction is at once in opposition to the feminine and the *appropriation* of the feminine. His early stories revise the domesticated values of the women's sphere, portraying a spartan and austerely defeminised home-making. In the story 'Big Two-Hearted River' his protagonist, Nick Adams, wanders off into the wilderness and sets up camp. Nothing of significance occurs apart from the simple activities of pitching a tent and going fishing. Isolated as he is from society and family, Nick enables Hemingway to purify pioneering (there is no taint of business or commerce – this is the original untarnished pioneer spirit). Nick enters the tent:

> It smelled pleasantly of canvas. Already there was something mysterious and home-like. Nick was happy as he crawled inside the tent.[36]

Trilling, we remember, attacked Cather for her 'mystical concern with pots and pans'. Hemingway's phrase 'mysterious and home-like' suggests a shared terrain with Cather, a common ground of domestic mysticism, and this suggestion is borne out in Nick's Zen acts of simple household artfulness. The very reverence of Hemingway's writing is important, since it grants a mystique to quotidian trivialities. His prose continually exerts pressure on these routines and chores, bestowing on them a weighty status and elevating them above their origins in the woman's world of homemaking. Note the 'pots and pans' in the following passage:

> Nick laid the bottle full of jumping grasshoppers against a pine trunk. Rapidly he mixed some buckwheat flour with water and stirred it smooth, one cup of flour, one cup of water. He put a handful of coffee in the pot and dipped a lump of grease out of a can and slid it sputtering across the hot skillet. On the smoking skillet he poured smoothly the buckwheat butter. It spread like lava, the grease spitting sharply. Around the edges the buckwheat cake began to firm, then brown, then crisp. The surface was bubbling slowly to porousness. Nick pushed under the brown undersurface with a fresh pine chip. He shook the skillet sideways and the cake was loose on the surface. I won' t try and flop it, he thought. He slid the chip of clean wood all the way under the cake, and flopped it over onto its face. It sputtered in the pan.[37]

Hemingway's exhaustive, pedantic detail attempts to cut away, if not eradicate,the mystical complexities of cooking. The prose demystifies activities linked, in the rigidly coded discussions of Hemingway's peers, with women. Hence the stubbornly ungenteel emphasis in Nick's cuisine on *cans* of food, and hence also the absence of feminine culinary skills such as baking, decorating and serving. The irony, though, is that the exhaustiveness of the passage only serves to remystify food. A mysterious and almost sacred appreciation of the domestic arts is implied by Hemingway's excessive precision. In this two-way movement, the prose denying that which it can only reinscribe, we witness a fictional equivalent to the discursive contortions of a Hergesheimer or Stearns: the simultaneous dismissal and coveting of feminised ideals.

How different were Cather's own writings on food! Trilling attacked her 'mystical concern with pots and pans', but her concern was in fact eminently practical (the pages of her fiction have supplied enough recipes for a Willa Cather cookery-book, a compendium of dishes drawn from the cultures she wrote about). For Cather food had a historical and sociological importance. In *Death Comes for the Archbishop* the priests' ability to bridge Europe and America is demonstrated in their adaptation of French dishes to the exigencies of native provisions. At one point Father Latour says that the history of a country is contained in its soup:

'a soup like this is not the work of one man. It is the result of a constantly refined tradition. There are nearly a thousand years of history in this soup.' (39)

Latour's axiom would have seemed laughable to Trilling or Hemingway, but in her own wry manner Cather was making a great claim for the decried arts of the feminised sphere. She thought that through an examination of cookery a nation's history, its manners and customs, could be shadowed forth. This is Cather's characteristically oblique response to the call of Van Wyck Brooks for a 'usable past'. For Cather that past could be apprehended in the present in the food one ate. And what, after all, could be more 'usable' than a bowl of French onion soup?

3

Imperial History:
O Pioneers! and the
Settlement of the Plains

IMPERIAL TIME

Willa Cather's novels are about empire. They fictionalise the transfer of European empires to America, and the subsequent growth of an American empire. Her novels deal with different empires: French (*Shadows on the Rock*), Spanish (*Death Comes for the Archbishop*), plantation confederacy (*Sapphira and the Slave Girl*). Even the central European immigrants of *My Ántonia* and *O Pioneers!* continue the theme, since they are refugees from the disintegrating Hapsburg empire. Cather understood empire in terms of diversity and variety. As Howard Erskine-Hill has shown, the example of Augustan Rome stood behind Renaissance and Enlightenment literature, uniting genres and authors. But by the nineteenth century the 'Augustan idea' had lost its cohering force. Empires proliferated; examples of empire mutiplied.[1] Cather responded to this multiplicity. This chapter looks at the response of Cather – in her fiction and other writings – to imperial history, and specifically to the ways in which she configured the history of her own country.

Cather drew on several imperial models, of which three have particular importance. First, the Spanish empire served as an example of a power in decline; America's first major steps as an expansive imperial nation were, of course, taken against the remnants of the Spanish empire in Mexico and the Philippines (1846–8 and 1898). In *My Ántonia*, in references to Coronado's explorations of the western United States (243–4), Cather looked back to the founding of Spanish America. In *Death Comes for the Archbishop*, which I discuss in Chapter 7, she examined the waning of Spanish power and the shift from imperial to ecclesiastical authority.

Second, she was fascinated by the growth of France into a unified nation and an empire. Jules Michelet's *Histoire de France* (1833–67) was a major influence on her thought. In *One Of Ours* (1922), after writing a dissertation on Joan of Arc, Claude Wheeler is told by his Professor to 'read what Michelet has to say about her'. The Professor is probably referring to the *History*. In an interview in 1925 with the *New York World* Cather quoted Michelet's maxim, 'The end is nothing; the road is all'. The enthusiasm she felt for his work suggests that in reading Michelet, Cather found confirmation of her own notions about the development of civilisations. Cather pointed out to Dorothy Canfield Fisher that Michelet saw history as a cyclical process.[2] Reading Michelet, she would have found many points where American and French history overlapped, thus confirming the cyclical view of history. Michelet, for instance, described a racial fusion in medieval France which might have reminded Cather of the amalgamation of the races in America's pioneer Midwest.

> In the first, the races deposited themselves one upon the other, so as to fertilise the Gallic soil with their alluvions... In the second age begins the fusion of these races: society seeks to settle down.[3]

Like Michelet, Cather was a historian of immigration and racial fusion who charted the emergence of a nation out of different peoples. Michelet provided her with historical evidence that racial diversity spurred national growth, buttressing the cultural pluralism she favoured. He also emphasised the formative impact of a nation's geography upon its social and political life, an idea expressed in his aphorism, 'mere geography becomes a history' and his image of peoples settling down like layers of soil. Cather, too, as the inhabitant of a state with a powerfully distinctive terrain and climate, understood that the land itself might seem to steer a society's development. Nonetheless, as Cather's novels show, there was a steady societal evolution from homesteads to villages and then towns as America was knitted into a nation. Michelet also concluded that centralisation was the key to imperial growth: 'The nation whose centralization is the most perfect, is likewise that which, by its example, and by the energy of its action, has done most to forward the centralization of the world'.[4] Michelet, then, provided Cather with a parallel history, the history of France, to set

alongside the history of America (where racial interlarding and de-
termining environmental forces were also of paramount importance), and in so doing confirmed that history was recursively
patterned.

The third imperial model provided further evidence of recursion
or cycles in history. She was interested in classical writers who
alluded to empire. Virgil echoes throughout the fiction, often in
specific references such as the epigraph to *My Ántonia*, taken from
the *Aeneid* ('Optima dies...prima fugit'), or Tom Outland's memo-
rising of the same poem in *The Professor's House* or Jim Burden's
devotion to the *Georgics* in *My Ántonia*.[5] Cather found thematic parallels between Virgil's classical world and modern America.
Aeneas, a pioneer, travelled across seas to found a new civilisation
in a foreign land. The duality of his life – migration and homeliness
– was suggestively precursive to the dynamic of immigrant
experience in Nebraska.

The Roman example posed an ambivalent precedent for
American writers. If Rome was a symbol of imperial power, wealth
and artistic achievement, then it also represented the nemesis of
these attributes: Rome had fallen to the barbarians. By exemplifying
the achievements of empire, Rome also served as a warning against
empire's potential decline. America, too, was ominously faced with
its own 'barbarian' incursions as waves of immigrants from the
poorer fringes of Europe poured into Ellis Island. For *ante-bellum*
Americans the analogy with Rome also proved troublesome
because the earlier empire, like their own, was founded on slavery
(the explosive equation between imperial ascendancy and slavery
explored in corruscating detail by Melville in 'Benito Cereno').

But for Cather the Roman parallel had other, more oblique
purposes. The *Aeneid* is a poem which meditates upon the intercon-
nections between imperial destiny and the quotidian detail of lived
experience. Encouraging a broad perspective, the imperial theme
places melodramatic episodes within a larger pattern. Leave-
takings, exile, wandering, return home: Aeneas's intense dramas
are flattened out when placed against the sweep of an empire's rise
and fall. Virgil counterpoints the episodes that make up a lifetime
against the elongated narrative of empire. Paradoxically, then, the
massiveness of the imperial theme returns us to the stuff of everyday life. Cather learnt from this structural principle. Her fiction
places moments of lurid action and intense emotion within

sweeping narratives. By dwelling on the transience of life (*sic transit* – a major Virgilian theme) the writer ponders the status of quotidian experience, appreciating it for its intensity in the lived moment, but then placing it within a longer timescale where it inevitably fades.

In *O Pioneers!* the operatic tone of the doomed love affair of Emil and Maria is never capitalised upon; one can imagine a restructured version of the novel in which this story would have a central, emphatic position. John Bergson's death also illustrates this effect, being casually and unemphatically mentioned: 'For the first three years after John Bergson's death, the affairs of his family prospered' (47). It is only a glancing aside, but the death becomes a touchstone in the developing narrative and is recalled in a later allusive touch: 'It is sixteen years since John Bergson died' (75). While the apparently momentous event is relegated to the margins, the unimportant or trivial is shifted to the centre. Alexandra Bergson lives her life as if it were a string of epiphanies, or inverted epiphanies – moments of supersaturated ordinariness:

> There were certain days in her life, outwardly uneventful, which Alexandra remembered as peculiarly happy; days when she was close to the flat, fallow world about her, and felt, as it were, in her own body the joyous germination in the soil. (203–4)

This sentence tangentially refers to Alexandra's mission to make the land bloom; but the tone is notably unemphatic and quietened – the settlement of the West becomes a meditative reciprocity between pioneer and earth. Cather's pioneer woman feels 'in her own body' the land's awakening. Here is an understated reversal of the archetypal pioneer effort, whereby the land is imposed upon and, as it were, penetrated by the settlers. Instead, Alexandra, a female not a male pioneer, is herself figured as sharing the regenerative, fertile power of the soil.

A single idea underpinned Cather's understanding of the past: history is cyclical. Cather saw civilisations analogously, as if they were linked by a series of cycles (rise, decline and fall throughout the ages). Her major article, 'Nebraska: The End of the First Cycle', began with the empty terrain which greeted the first pioneers. She then described the early settlers, railroads and the arrival of European immigrants. Major change occurred within the span of a generation:

Nebraska is a newer State than Kansas. It was a State before there
were people in it. Its social history falls easily within a period of
sixty years, and the first stable settlements of white men were
made within the memory of old folk now living.

In her telescoped account of society's growth the turn of one
cycle takes just 60 years, from the original pioneers to a commercialised society 'stamped with the ugly crest of materialism'. In
'Nebraska: The End of the First Cycle' Cather regarded the past
ambivalently, at once mourning a lost age and hoping that the
revolution of the historical wheel would return Nebraska to its
earlier condition. The pioneers are now buried, Cather writes, but
then goes on to say, 'I have always the hope that something went
into the ground with those pioneers that will one day come out
again'.[6]

In Nebraska the period for a culture to rise, decline and fall was
compressed. The waxing and waning of empire was foreshortened
into the sixty years it took for civilisation to establish itself and
reach its materialist nemesis. However, Cather's Midwest is also a
place where the steady track of imperial time is crossed and confused with other chronologies. In the Midwest the chronologies of
migration and settlement run up against other timescales. The land
has a geological agedness; traces of prehistoric man remain;
machinery, specifically the train, foreshadows the accelerating
timescales of modernity. On the Plains a kaleidoscopic variety of
timescales ran together.

O Pioneers! is alert to the strangeness of Midwestern time. Early
in the story Carl Linstrum and Alexandra Bergson are sitting together, 'the eyes of the girl who seemed to be looking with such
anguished perplexity into the future' and 'the sombre eyes of the
boy, who seemed already to be looking into the past' (14). Past and
future: the polarities bear down heavily on the present. Cather's
westerners are devoted to the quotidian toil of settlement, but the
pioneering effort also requires an imaginative leap into the future
to the time when untilled earth is ploughed and fertile. *O Pioneers!*
dramatises this conflict in the dispute that Alexandra Bergson has
with her brothers, an argument which sets short-term activity
against long-term aim. The brothers evaluate the homestead
economy on a daily basis, whereas she wants to buy and plan over
a decade. Alexandra hopes that the family will '"sit down here ten
years from now independent landowners, not struggling farmers

any longer"' (67). As she says, '"We ought to do more than they do, and see further ahead"' (68–9).

This responsiveness to different timescales underpins the novel's narrative construction. *O Pioneers!* is organised to follow the expansions and contractions of Midwestern time. Now the narrative follows events methodically, cleaving to the moments as they pass by day and month; and now it cuts across a swathe of time. After the rhythm of Book 1 is established we suddenly jump across time when Book 2 opens: 'It is sixteen years since John Bergson died' (75). A typical Cather technique, this disjunction fissures the evolving, sinuous story. Gradually enlarging her tale *and* cutting from one story to another, or from one time to another, Cather constructs narratives that combine the leisured amplitude of traditional genres (the epic or pastoral) with a mobile adaptability that sometimes reminds the reader of film narrative.[7] In later novels, as we shall see, Cather would be more daring in exploiting this tactic.

The apparent arbitrariness of the form of *O Pioneers!*, its loose construction, pulls against the rigid patterning that is imposed by a cyclical historiography. A cycle implies determinism, an ineluctable revolution from rise to fall, and in novels this inexorable movement can diminish the efficacy of human action in two ways: by dwarfing the characters' actions within a pre-ordained history; and by minimising the novelist's authority within a pre-established narrative pattern. I believe there was a tension in Cather's thinking about these problems which created asymmetries in the novels. Briefly stated, she saw history cyclically but rejected the determinism implied by a recursive historiography. Her method of composition, for example, privileged contingency and open form – the reverse of a determined pattern. The genesis of *O Pioneers!* lay in two stories, 'Alexandra' and 'The White Mulberry Tree', which Cather conflated to provide the novel's basic material.[8] Cather's reliance on the chance processes of writing, as with this fortuitous juxtaposition, distinguishes her work from that of her contemporaries. In a writer such as Dreiser we find a more determined narrative drive, the result of Marxist and Freudian theories of society and psychology. Whilst she could not have failed to come across these theories in Greenwich Village, to which she moved in 1913, Cather's intellectual disposition was to mistrust determinist philosophies – except for cyclical history.[9]

At the beginning of *O Pioneers!* Carl Linstrum and Alexandra Bergson looked simultaneously into the past and the future. This

scene becomes a controlling metaphor for the text, encapsulating
Cather's sense of time's multifacetedness. Cather's elongation of
historical narrative also reaches back before the lives of its central
characters and the foundation of modern America: the novel is
shaped by a post-Darwinian awareness of time's magnitude, deploying a language drawn from the new sciences of geology and
archaeology. One striking sentence places Alexandra against an
enormous chronological backdrop: 'For the first time, perhaps,
since that land emerged from the waters of geologic ages, a human
face was set toward it with love and yearning' (65). Given this ex-
panded historical vision, settlement in the American wilderness
might appear to be the absolute beginning of society, such is the
bleakness and indomitable emptiness of the landscape. The land is
presented at first as blankly uncongenial, harshly resistant to the
progressive human endeavour which settles and colonises empty
space. The title of Part 1 is 'The Wild Land'. Cather figures the
pioneer effort as the inauguration of civilisation: 'But the great fact
was the land itself, which seemed to overwhelm the little beginnings of human society that struggled in its sombre wastes' (15).
And the deadness of the Nebraskan landscape, its frozen emptiness
in winter, brought to mind a world without man's presence:

> It is like an iron country, and the spirit is oppressed by its rigor
> and melancholy. One could easily believe that in that dead land-
> scape the germs of life and fruitfulness were extinct forever.
> (187–8)

I argued earlier that Cather was inspired by the historical examples of Rome and France. Yet, as we see here, Cather's imagination
was also drawn to a historiography founded on geology and
archaeology. Within this framework the recent examples of occidental empires were dwarfed. The cyclical model proposed that
empires would fall, but provided the consolation of other imperial
ascendancies in the future. Within *O Pioneers!* this confidence is at
times undermined. Imperial history, an anthropocentric account of
mankind's achievements, is eroded by the newly-perceived non-
human chronologies. Cather's comment on John Bergson's failures
is telling: 'The record of the plow', she writes, 'was insignificant,
like the feeble scratches on stone left by prehistoric races, so inde-
terminate that they may, after all, be only the markings of glaciers,
and not a record of human strivings' (19–20). Human presence is

successively eroded; the pioneer plough makes an insignificant impression; the traces of primitive man might prove to be natural and not man-made; only the impersonal movement of the glaciers can be guaranteed. These references (the 'geologic ages', 'dead landscape', 'sombre wastes') create an antiphonal voice in *O Pioneers!* that disrupts the more easily decoded surface of the novel (a simple tale of immigrant pioneer success).

'Of all the bewildering things about a new country', Cather writes, 'the absence of human landmarks is one of the most depressing and disheartening' (19). Ostensibly a tale of immigrant pioneer success, the novel makes repeated references to non-human timescales, thereby setting up a disquieting context where the achievements of mankind, however spectacular, are dwarfed by the enormity of 'geologic ages'. Alexandra, faced with a landscape which escapes the marshalling control of human effort, adopts a remarkably nonchalant attitude towards the land. She thinks that she could '"let the grass grow back over everything"' (16). For a pioneer, Alexandra can be remarkably *unconcerned*, as if all the effort of settlement might evaporate and nothing would matter.

This easeful attitude towards nature and the land emerges also in Cather's critical prose. She suggested in a letter that the lack of plottedness in *O Pioneers!* was analogous to the lack of definite form in the Midwestern landscape. To quote James Woodress's paraphrase of the letter:

> She agreed with Sergeant's one criticism that the book had no skeleton but defended it on grounds that the country she was writing about had no skeleton either. There were no rocks or ridges; its black soil ran through one's fingers. It was all soft, and somehow that influenced the mood and the very structure of the novel.[10]

Note Cather's acceptance of the shape of the landscape. Note, also, her willingness to take the softness of the soil as a guiding metaphor for her writing. What is important about these comments is not that Cather related land and novel – correspondences of this sort are common in American literature – but that she was utterly equable in the face of the wilderness. As Stephen Fender argues, American writers have often placed land and fiction in a kind of inverted relationship: the novel's plot becomes a compensation for the absence of formal structure in the wilderness. In Fender's words, 'the more plotless the landscape, the more plotted the writing'.[11] Cather, though, not only *does not* have the rage to plot; she accepts the plotless landscape and makes this a principle of novelistic composition. If Fender is right about writing and the West, then Cather is unusual for her acceptance of the land's plotless wildness. As with Alexandra's sense of a germination within her own body, so Cather's commentary on her novel envisages the earth acting upon the human rather than vice versa.

In order to understand the full significance of this strand in *O Pioneers!* we must consider Cather as a novelist who recasts the ideology of that most American principle of progress: westward expansion. What are the ideological implications of Cather's ecological interest in a world without humankind?

PROGRESS, PIONEERING AND THE WEST

Cather has been read as a novelist who straightforwardly depicted the pioneer settlement of the West and the triumphant imposition of civilisation on the wilderness.[12] The very title, *O Pioneers!*, quotes Whitman's exhortation to the frontiersman, placing the text within a tradition of pioneer eulogies. The text itself tracks the movement from wilderness to settlement, bare earth to tilled land. Nebraska evolves from a place where 'the germs of life and fruitfulness were extinct forever' to one where Alexandra felt 'the joyous germination in the soil'; from the wilderness of Part I ('The Wild Land') to settlement in Part II ('Neighbouring Fields') and on to wholehearted concentration on the human story (Part V, 'Alexandra'). Cather's characters, especially Alexandra, seem to embody the ideology that underpinned the movement west: self-reliance, hard work, faith in technology.

At times, however, the novel plays out various conflicts within that ideology, as when Alexandra and her brothers argue about their farm's future. Cather presents this debate as a clash between conservative, retrogressive pioneering and the more daring, experimental and ultimately successful pioneering of Alexandra. She borrows money to speculate in land:

'We borrow the money for six years. Well, with the money we buy a half-section from Linstrum and a half from Crow, and a quarter from Struble, maybe. That will give us upwards of fourteen hundred acres, won't it? You won't have to pay off your mortgages for six years. By that time, any of this land will be worth thirty dollars an acre – it will be worth fifty, but we'll say thirty; then you can sell a garden patch anywhere, and pay off a debt of sixteen hundred dollars. It's not the principal I'm worried about, it's the interest and taxes. We'll have to strain to meet the payments.' (66–7)

If we compare Cather's version of pioneering to historical accounts of Midwestern settlement, then her account emerges as broadly accurate. *O Pioneers!* is, to use Robert Clark's terms, on this issue more historical than mythical. Alexandra expands her farm by borrowing money and hoping that the revenue from the new land will be sufficient to pay off the interest. This speculation in land is in keeping with historical evidence about the development of Midwestern farms. Frontier expansion was carried forward less by the mythic homesteader staking his claim than by entrepreneurial landowners who bought up larger and larger estates. Some historical accounts envisage the land speculator as a ravenous capitalist; many small farmers, bought out by larger landowners, ended up as indigent tenants on land they formerly owned. But Alexandra represents a purified or honourable speculator whose deals cause no harm.[13]

She is a good pioneer, tending the land and making it fruitful; has a personal stake in the land; becomes a kind of mythic earth mother. Although Alexandra brings civilisation to the wilderness, she is insistently identified with nature: 'Her mind was a white book, with clear writing about weather and beasts and growing things' (205). This identification culminates in the last sentence of the novel, where Alexandra is absorbed into the land ('Fortunate country, that is one day to receive hearts like Alexandra's into its bosom'); but this mythic characterisation also transforms the historical detail of land speculation. Cather grafts an idealised mythic discourse onto her historical subject-matter. The land speculator was resented for his mercenary relationship to the land. The Jeffersonian ideal of a farmer working with the soil was supplanted by a commercial model where tenant farmers did the work. But Alexandra, a speculator, preserves the farmer's closeness to the land; the 'mother earth' idealisation, a mythic discourse, ties her to the land. It is almost as if Cather believed that mythic characterisation could offset the entrepreneurial basis of pioneering, where farming is simply a matter of cents and dollars. But, of course, *O Pioneers!* also illustrates that very entrepreneurial endeavour (the arguments with her brothers about borrowing money). Alexandra then becomes a conflation of two types of settler: the canny speculator and the idealised pioneer farmer.

The conflation is not easily achieved; the prose sometimes shows the tension between the two types rather than their marriage. Presenting Alexandra as a speculator and an idealised pioneer led Cather into convoluted, if not illogical, characterisation. Alexandra is depicted as a successful settler; but the obvious index of success, material wealth, suggests the speculator's greed. Cather's solution is to portray Alexandra as a woman whose life has the *potential* for material ease, even though she is pointedly unconcerned by materialism. Alexandra's house, therefore, is conspicuously grand, but Cather cannot allow her to furnish it – it then simultaneously represents the speculator's commercial success and the pioneer's dogged austerity. Approaching the estate the visitor sees 'a big white house', which with its outbuildings suggests 'a tiny village' (83). The impression of grandeur is undermined when one arrives at Alexandra's bizarrely furnished home:

> If you go up the hill and enter Alexandra's big house, you will find that it is curiously unfinished and uneven in comfort. One room is papered, carpeted, over-furnished; the next is almost bare. The pleasantest rooms in the house are the kitchen – where Alexandra's three young Swedish girls chatter and cook and pickle and preserve all summer long – and the sitting-room, in which Alexandra has brought together the old homely furniture that the Bergsons used in their first log house, the family portraits, and the few things her mother brought from Sweden. (84)

Alexandra *has* to be made uncomfortable with her own material success. Her domestic comfort is retrospective, resting in the continuity of tradition (European cooking, furniture from the old house) rather than new moneyed ways. Then, as if confirming the difficulty of imagining the amalgamation of pioneer and speculator, Cather's focus drifts outside:

> When you go out of the house into the flower garden, there you feel again the order and fine arrangement manifest all over the

great farm; in the fencing and hedging, in the windbreaks and sheds, in the symmetrical pasture ponds, planted with scrub willows to give shade to the cattle in fly-time. There is even a white row of beehives in the orchard, under the walnut trees. You feel that, properly, Alexandra's house is the big out-of-doors, and that it is in the soil that she expresses herself best. (84)

In the garden Cather projects an idealised conflation of pioneering and speculation, traditional agrarianism and innovative farming. The garden itself is a middle ground, positioned between home and prairie, civilisation and wilderness. Alexandra here achieves a self-expression harmonised with the natural world, a human order finely adjusted to the exigencies of animal life (the willows planted to shade the cattle). The development of the land is presented as a formalism that is an end in itself ('order', 'arrangement', 'symmetrical', 'row') or as a process dedicated to animals and plants. The financial rewards of farming are carefully excised or excluded. Alexandra's wealth becomes a happy accident, the fortuitous spin-off from sound pioneering.

Cather's family moved to Nebraska in the mid-1880s, a time when the notorious landowner William Scully was arousing animosity in that State and others for his aggressive acquisition of prairie lands. Scully, an Irishman who belatedly took out American citizenship, provoked enormous opposition to 'alien' landowners. The agitation was long-standing, spilling into the local press and politics (populism was in part a reaction against alien encroachments). Nebraska, along with other States, passed legislation during 1887 to prohibit 'aliens' from acquiring real estate. There is, of course, no reason why a novel written in 1913 should demonstrate absolute fidelity to life several decades earlier. But *O Pioneers!* never hints that Europeans might find it difficult to own American soil; the controversy about land dealing and 'aliens' is erased from Cather's account. She opts instead for a familial row about the tactics of development.[14]

This is undoubtedly a depoliticised representation of settlement, and one can easily imagine a critique that would attack Cather for erasing or displacing historical actuality. But we have to look at *O Pioneers!* from the point of view of 1913. Inaccurate as the novel might have been, the multicultural frontier of *O Pioneers!* is an example of 'innovative nostalgia', the projection onto a past decade

of a historical reading whose real relevance is to the period when
the novelist was writing. The novel's refutation of nativism, of
narrow or xenophobic provincialism is pertinent to the context in
which Cather wrote. Cather created an American frontier which
diverges from the actualities of the late nineteenth-century
Midwest; but her fictionalised frontier tells us a great deal about
her fascination with an open, pluralist, cosmopolitan culture of the
American plains. The frontier of *O Pioneers!* is at ease with itself,
and thus becomes a progressive 'good community' that rebuffs
the xenophobia implicit in the actual history of the Midwest.
O Pioneers! projects a wilfully distorted frontier not, as many critics
have suggested, because of an instinctive nostalgia in Cather's creative temperament, but because Cather is setting up fictionalised
communities of immediate relevance to an America that was becoming ever more marked by racial diversity.

Cather's unsettling and unconventional representations of landscape form part of a larger revisionary strategy in *O Pioneers!* The
novel is best understood, I believe, as a transformation of the conventions underpinning the pioneer myth. First, Cather recast the
gender of pioneering. *O Pioneers!*, as many commentators have emphasised, is a novel about female pioneering: Alexandra Bergson
explores, settles and develops the land, just as the archetypal male
pioneer had done.[15] The idiosyncrasy of deploying a female protagonist becomes evident when we look back over written accounts of
the pioneer effort. Annette Kolodny's survey of pioneering literature
from the colonial period through to the nineteenth century demonstrates the highly *sexualised* language of these letters, diaries and journals. The language of the pioneers encoded their experiences in very
gender-specific ways. Pioneers, usually men, insistently imagined a
male pioneer moving across a feminised landscape. That landscape,
Kolodny argues, is symbolised as either the virgin earth which the
pioneer ravishes, or as a mother, 'the total female principle of
gratification' promising 'a return to the primal warmth of womb or
breast in a feminine landscape'.[16] Kolodny's argument sometimes
becomes dangerously ahistorical – she posits a synchronic model
which appears to lie outside historical change. But the suggestiveness of her pattern is undeniable, enabling us to identify motifs and
symbols across a range of American texts. Using Kolodny's model
as a basis for exploring Cather's novels, we can discover how the
individual artist transforms and revises a cultural inheritance of
established metaphorical patterns.

A nice illustration of Cather's self-conscious use of motifs from the history of pioneering is her reference to *Robinson Crusoe*. Early in the novel Carl Linstrum carries a magic lantern whose wide range of pictures from the New and Old Worlds represents a masculine world of adventure: 'hunting pictures in Germany, and Robinson Crusoe and funny pictures about cannibals' (17). But several pages later we read this sentence: 'Alexandra often said that if her mother were cast upon a desert island, she would thank God for her deliverance, make a garden, and find something to preserve' (29). Mrs. Bergson here becomes a female Robinson Crusoe who brings to her catastrophe the practical domestic arts. The sentence demonstrates how in Cather's fiction the 'pots and pans' derided by Trilling are used to tease, if not subvert, the stereotyped image of the feminine sphere. Later in the book Alexandra reads 'The Swiss Family Robinson' aloud to an appreciative audience. This is another moment where Cather's pioneers take a self-referential pleasure in stories which reflect back their own experiences. Again Cather shifts the focus from masculine pioneering (so often imagined as the activity of the single male, the male duo, or the small posse of men) to a feminised pioneering. It is a family which settles the wilderness – and a family responds to the story: 'They were all big children together, and they found the adventures of the family in the tree house so absorbing that they gave them their undivided attention' (63).

Similar reversals occur in Cather's descriptions of the western land. Reading Kolodny's study, it becomes clear that the American land was symbolically fecund, a land of plenitude not only for its profusion of material goods but also in its supply of feminine imagery. The land could be imagined again and again as a configuration of the mother or the virgin. As Ellen Moers has brilliantly demonstrated, scattered throughout Cather's fiction are landscapes which appropriate the feminised landscape and renew its coded womanliness with a powerfully sexual symbolism. Moers draws attention to the South-western landscapes in *The Song of the Lark*. Discussing the feminine topography of the Panther Canyon, its grooves and recesses and exhilarating open spaces, Moers argues that the descriptive passages are 'concerned with female self-assertion in terms of landscape'.[17] *O Pioneers!* eventually forges such a self-assertion. The last passages of the book witness a fulfilled Alexandra received into the 'bosom' of the land (309). This reciprocity with the land has to be earned. At first Cather's native soil is stark and denuded, proffering little literally or symbolically. This bareness (the emptiness, as we have seen, of prehistoric ages) resists symbolising acquisitiveness. Whereas the pioneer appropriated the land by imaginatively converting it into a female body, in the opening chapters of *O Pioneers!* the emptiness of the land prevents this – there is nothing to symbolise. The pioneer is rebuffed by the land, but slowly becomes intimate with it and finds an austere consolation in nature's workings:

> It fortified her to reflect upon the great operations of nature, and when she thought of the law that lay behind them, she felt a sense of personal security. That night she had a new consciousness of the country, felt almost a new relation to it... She had never known before how much the country meant to her. The chirping of the insects down in the long grass had been like the sweetest music. She had felt as if her heart were hiding down there, somewhere, with the quail and the plover and all the little wild things that crooned or buzzed in the sun. Under the long shaggy ridges, she felt the future stirring. (70–1)

If this passage is not entirely successful ('The chirping of the insects...like the sweetest music'!), then this is because, first of all, Cather writes from the perspective of an imaginatively limited character (Alexandra is not given to reflection). Second, Cather awkwardly straddles several linguistic registers in this passage. Her writing turns from symbolism to a factual language, but she preserves the heightened rhetoric associated with the westerner's first energising encounter with the land. She grafts together a heightened, almost mystical language of pastoral bliss with microscopic observation of 'the little wild things' – the latter discourse reminding us of the prose of natural history.

Cather's second major revision of the pioneer myth stems from her doubts about American claims to represent the culmination of historical progress. A letter she wrote about *One of Ours* in 1922 shows that this scepticism derived from her readings of imperial history. Her startling interpretation of the First World War claimed that this conflict was essentially cultural; but the real clash was between unlettered America and sophisticated Europe, not Germany and the other European nations. She then compared the American endeavour to that of the crusaders, who also fought against a more cultivated people, the Arabs. Cather thus reverses the hierarchy implicit in ideas of historical progress. Instead of Arabic culture giving way to the crusaders, western Europe and then America, Cather privileges the earlier and supposedly more 'primitive' societies; the later a civilisation, in her model, the more inferior it is.[18]

Privileging an earlier civilisation is often an important tactic for conservative thinkers, and one acknowledges a reaction against modern civilisation in Cather's letter; but when her ideas about progress are placed in their American context a subversive meaning emerges. American social theory in the nineteenth century grew out of Enlightenment theories about the progress of civilisation. 'Stadialism', a constellation of ideas formulated by the Scottish Enlightenment philosophers and given a fictional representation in Walter Scott's novels, argued that society evolved through distinct stages: barbarian stages gave way to increasingly sophisticated cultures, agricultural then commercial, until our present-day civilisation was reached. America seemed to confirm this theory; the traveller, moving across the country, saw the stages spread out across the terrain. The stadialist model exerted a powerful grip on the American imagination. Thus Thomas Jefferson's famous panorama (1824):

> Let a philosophic observer commence a journey from the savages of the Rocky Mountains, eastwardly towards our seacoast. These he would observe in the earliest stage of association living under no law but that of nature, subsisting and covering themselves with the flesh and skins of wild beasts. He would find those on our frontiers in the pastoral state, raising domestic animals to supply the defects of hunting. Then succeed our own semi-barbarous citizens, the pioneers of the advance of civilization, and so in his progress he would meet the gradual shades of improving man until he would reach his, as yet, most improved state in our seaport towns. This, in fact, is equivalent to a survey, in time, of the progress of man from the infancy of creation to the present day.

The American patchwork of Indian, pioneer and urban settlements confirmed the stadialist thesis. The indigenous Indian population served as an index whereby the gap between earlier and later stages could be gauged; stadialism projected linear progress, carrying civilisation onwards towards ultimate perfectibility.

'Barbarism,' wrote Jefferson, has 'been receding before the steady step of amelioration', and soon will 'disappear from the earth'.[19]

What did novelists make of stadialism? George Dekker's study, *The American Historical Romance*, which covers writers from Scott up to Cather and Faulkner, proposes that the idea formed the historiographical matrix that underpinned the great tradition of American novels. Dekker claims that stadialism 'was not racist – quite the contrary', fostering a quasi-anthropological outlook. Believing that modern society emerged step-by-step from earlier civilisations, the stadialist was *de facto* interested in 'savage' peoples; the 'primitive' illuminated the modern. Moreover, Dekker points out that the novelist, an heir of Romanticism, often had a sympathetic concern for 'the savage and barbarian peoples doomed by progress'. Nominally siding with the progressive forces (the city-dwellers, the 'civilised'), the novelist found much to admire in outmoded cultures which seemed to retain an integrity and passion lost by later stages.[20]

When Dekker discusses Cather the intellectual grip of his stadialist model slackens. Dekker gestures towards the importance of progress to Cather (she is grouped with Melville and Twain as novelists 'who wrote during the decades when progressivism was most strenuous and self-confident'), but does not specifically define progress in an early twentieth-century sense.[21]

The underlying limitation of Dekker's thesis is that stadialism was essentially an eighteenth and early nineteenth-century paradigm; it provides a philosophical context for American fiction which undoubtedly existed around 1800, but became less relevant as the century wore on. By the twentieth century its configurations have drastically changed. These changes are evident if we reread the Jefferson piece to see what he *does not* tell us about American civilisation. Jefferson wrote before the transformation of the West and the massive immigration of Europeans. 'Let a philosophic observer commence a journey from the savages of the Rocky Mountains, eastwardly towards our seacoast': this is a journey from West to East, a journey *into* civilisation. As such, it reverses the quintessential journeys of nineteenth-century America, travels such as those of Lewis and Clark (whose 1803–6 expedition to the Northwest was authorised by Jefferson), or of Washington Irving's *A Tour on the Prairies* (1835) and Francis Parkman's *The Oregon Trail* (1849) – into the wilderness, westwards. With the movement west came a heightened sense of cultural and racial diversity, and not only because in the West the white American might meet the native American. The massive outburst of America westwards was in part powered by the explosion of immigrants through the eastern seaboard and across the continent. Ethnic diversity was at the heart of America's drive westwards. Jefferson's account, though, is untroubled by racial and cultural difference. The idea of different stages implies diversity, but the stadialist model, at least in Jefferson's vision, is conditioned by the assumption that the goal of historical progress is the modern society of the United States. There is an underlying homogeneity in Jefferson's America; it lacks the racial variety that came about later in the century in the wake of immigration; we are presented with a generic 'improving man' but little description of the specific, local cultures encountered in this panoramic sweep of the country. And, furthermore, Jefferson takes little account of the West itself. He reverses the usual trajectory of American journeys and in so doing overlooks the importance of the West as the territory into which 'progress' could be projected, as the culmination, the zenith of progress and its literal proving-ground. Crucially, Jefferson makes little of the West as the land in which Americans discovered the 'Other'. For in the very act of reaching their progressive ideals Americans encountered the radically different 'Other' excluded from their ideology; to push civilisation upwards was to encounter the beginnings of civilisation, the 'earliest stage' which progress claimed to have succeeded.

Jefferson, of course, could not be expected to have anticipated this encounter between progress and the 'savage' as early as 1824; but the intellectual milieu had changed greatly by the end of the nineteenth century, and it is for this reason that I want to introduce other analogues for Cather's fiction, sources outside the range of Dekker's stadialist reading of the historical romance. When we arrive at the twentieth century other ideas have been grafted upon stadialism, notably social Darwinism, which posited a different relationship between primitive and advanced societies. When Darwin's ideas were fed into social and political thought (often in a crudely simplistic way) they were developed in two directions. The Darwinist stress on the proliferation of species led to an appreciation of variety in itself. Furthermore, Darwin spurred on the burgeoning science of anthropology, the study of diversity in mankind. The word 'culture' was first used in its plural form around the year 1900: the shift from singular to plural marks a major intellectual reorientation as the ideal of a single and singular culture is overlaid by a myriad of differing cultures. From evaluation of cultures against the example of Europe or America there was a move towards an open-ended appreciation of different civilisations.[22]

But Darwinism also gave a harder and potentially racist edge to stadialism. Now the emergence of one civilisation (usually occidental and often specifically Anglo-Saxon) seemed as 'natural', and therefore incontrovertible, as the triumph of successful species in the animal kingdom. The progress of civilisation became an unremitting biological axiom. And while stadialism, at least as it was interpreted by novelists such as Scott, had not necessarily implied that later stages were superior to their predecessors, this supposition was explicit in social Darwinism. The comparative methodology of the stadialist becomes invidious, as cultures are compared to demonstrate the superiority of the Anglo-Saxon. As Richard Hofstadter has demonstrated, American social theorists and politicians posited such an Anglo-Saxon superiority at the very moment when the United States was faced with waves of Jewish, Slavic, and Asian immigration.[23]

In late-Victorian America numerous books promulgated these ideas, transposing ameliorative stadialism into a harsher key. John Fiske's *American Political Ideas* (1885) and Josiah Strong's *Our Country: Its Possible Future and Its Present Crisis* (1885) were popular summaries of the so-called 'Anglo-Saxon' thesis. One of the best known accounts of the movement westwards, Theodore Roosevelt's *The Winning of the West* (1889), begins with a racially-based review of imperial expansion: 'During the past three centuries the spread of the English-speaking peoples over the world's waste spaces has been not only the most striking feature in the world's history, but also the event of all others most far-reaching in its effects and its importance'. Ironically, Roosevelt's statement was made just when the mass of incomers to the US was *not* English speaking. His assertion links a Darwinist sense of racial advancement to a chauvinistic vaunting of his own language. By the time that Brooks Adams wrote *America's Economic Supremacy* (1900) imperial and racial advancement had been put into operation in the Philippines. 'The civilization which does not advance declines', wrote Adams, and, conflating history and natural history, 'From the dawn of history, nature has always preferred those organisms which worked most economically at the time her choice was made'.[24]

We can trace the gradual infiltration of this nexus of racial and nationalist notions through American culture during the first 40 years or so of Cather's life (from around 1880 to 1920). Three years before *O Pioneers!* was published Roosevelt, who by now had served a term as President, delivered his speech, 'The World Movement' (1910). Talking in Berlin, Roosevelt envisaged America as the highpoint of 'Civilization'; his unabashedly progressive thesis saw history as a steady ascent towards the zenith of the modern United States. 'Civilization' began 'with that series of bold sea ventures which culminated in the discovery of America'. America was then 'changing and developing every inheritance and acquisition into something new and strange' – having emerged out of Europe, America had radically transformed its inheritance. Comparisons with earlier cultures were now redundant. Roosevelt adduces a comparison with the Roman empire, only to prove the large-scale differences between America and Rome: 'it is well to emphasize in the most emphatic fashion (*sic*) the fact that in many respects there is a complete lack of analogy between the civilization of to-day and the only other civilization in any way comparable to it'. He concludes that 'the present civilization can be compared to nothing that has ever gone before'.[25]

The convergence of economic success, imperial expansion and a rhetoric of 'natural' supremacy derived from Darwin led to a renewed sense of American triumphalism and exceptionalism. There was an intensified sense of the nation's singularity; Roosevelt can find nothing to compare with his country. His argument is hardly a worked-out thesis, but this is partly because he felt it sufficient to allude to the academic historiography of the period, which similarly stressed the strength and the uniqueness of the United States. Roosevelt was indebted to the 'Frontier thesis' formulated by the historian, Frederick Jackson Turner, in the 1890s. Turner, whose work was enormously influential, directed historians away from the search for European sources of American culture, politics and society – earlier commentators had located these roots either in English institutions or even further back, in medieval Germany. Turner believed that America was societally and politically divorced from Europe. His seminal essay, 'The Significance of the Frontier in American History' (1893), emphasised the centrality of the westward movement and the frontier to the formation of a national culture that was unique. American exceptionalism arose from the unique geographical attribute of the frontier; analogies with Europe were irrelevant: 'Whatever be the truth regarding European history, American history is chiefly concerned with social forces, shaping and reshaping under the conditions of a nation changing as it adjusts to its environment'. For Turner, separation from Europe fosters cultural homogeneity. The frontier, the movement of the people, the drive to colonise the wilderness – in the very act of settlement the American people become one. His thesis is in many ways similar to Michelet's account of France – there is a shared insistence on the formative power of environment – but Turner is keener to look forward beyond the processes of amalgamation and assimilation to the point when the people are as one, an incorporated and homogeneous unity. *E pluribus unum* is the motto of both historians, but Michelet emphasises the *pluribus* and Turner concentrates on the *unum*.[26]

Not surprisingly, Turner disliked Cather's fiction. His criticism of *O Pioneers!* is an important but neglected moment in the reception of Cather's novels. It illustrates the gulf between her vision of a pluralist America still linked to Europe and the increasingly dominant historiographical views of Turner and Roosevelt, where America is exceptional, unique and culturally homogeneous. After reading *O Pioneers!* and *A Lost Lady* Turner expressed his dissatisfaction to Alice Hooper, claiming that Cather represented too sympathetically what he called 'non-English stocks' (that is, immigrants from Scandinavia and central Europe). Fascinated as he was by social mobility, this comment suggests that he was less enamoured of racial mixing and interfusion. The frontier thesis dealt with the trends of modern America – immigration, settlement, movement – and enlisted them to establish a historical theory of powerful simplicity. Turner's America was in essence a proleptic idealisation of a nation that he thought was coming into being; and the hallmark of that society was its homogeneity. Despite his interest in the culturally varied West it is clear that Turner's America was a nativist Utopia filled with immigrants of English and north European descent. Although Turner was anything but a racist, there is no doubt that he was happiest in envisaging an America made up of migrants from a relatively confined and traditional stock of origins.[27]

We can now see the importance of Cather's interest in Michelet. He presented a different clutch of ideas about immigration, race and progress from the American models immediately available to her; she could explore the ramifications of this model rather than subscribing either to social Darwinism or Turner's American exceptionalism. Her own understanding of empire drew on a plethora of examples; she did not single out America. Viewing Nebraska within a series of imperial migrations and foundations, she gained historical distance on her homeland. Cather famously declared that in order to know the parish one must know the world first. Although the statement implies a return to the locality, it places the 'world' first syntactically, establishing synoptic knowledge as the basis of the novelist's art. This wider, comparative perspective is more important in her novels than the regionalism, provincialism and 'local color' denoted by the 'parish'. When Cather portrays the parish, as in *O Pioneers!*, her native soil is variegated and cosmopolitan. The title *O Pioneers!* proffers nationalist triumphalism, Whitman's visionary future of westward colonisation; but this is offset by the novel's epigraph, drawn from a foreigner, the Polish poet Mickiewicz: 'Those fields, colored by *various* grain!' (my emphasis). The epigraph replaces the unitary native soil (an American land for a single American people) with a diverse, patchwork country. Turner hypothesised that the hegemonic power of the land would weld the diverse races together and create national coherence. For Cather, on the other hand, the soil is either polymorphous ('various grain') or tantalisingly bare ('an iron country'); her landscapes stand empty or swarm with a multitude of peoples. In both ways the pressure of nativism, of the *native* soil, of a land for one people, is resisted.

The narrator's timbre in *O Pioneers!* shifts from the intimate informalities of the 'parish' to the more impersonal tones in which Cather accounts for, and talks to, the 'world'. The narrating voice is pitched between easy familiarity and careful distance – she mimes amused intimacy and anthropological curiosity:

> The country children thereabouts wore their dresses to their shoe-tops, but this city child was dressed in what was then called the 'Kate Greenaway' manner, and her red cashmere frock, gathered full from the yoke, came almost to the floor. This, with her poke bonnet, gave her the look of a quaint little woman. (11–12)

Cather's tone (that of the local historian) and her fastidious specificity (noting the length of dresses) create an enquiring, annotating authorial voice. Yet there is also an ironic, amused knowingness to the writing; the distance never hardens into sneering at the foibles of provincial dress. The doubleness of the prose, the sense of being both within and without the scene, might remind the reader of Thomas Hardy, another provincial writer who maintained an ironic familiarity towards his rural material.

Throughout *O Pioneers!*, where the focus seems to be so narrowly upon the Midwest, she habitually mentions other cultures. There are passing references to Lombardy, France, Mexico. A typical sentence describes the French church, which 'reminded one of some of the churches built long ago in the wheat-lands of middle France' (211). The reader of Cather's novels becomes attuned to these windows into other times and places (often medieval and European). Memories or similes, the sentences broaden our perspective, displacing the reader, if only temporarily, away from regional America into another context. Cather turned an apprentice writer's tic – the need to seem *au fait*, conversant with culture (resulting in a gauche display of cultural reference) – into a strength. Her edgy desire to show herself knowledgeable led to a healthy interest in the outside world; to rebuff accusations of provincial ignorance she developed a style which, while concentrating on the parish, never forgot the world. Cather is one of the few modern Midwestern writers unaffected by that cult of insularity which seems to have stamped writers from Hamlin Garland and Sherwood Anderson through to Garrison Keillor. In their works the small town is everything; in Cather's fiction everything comes to the small town, filtered through memory, migration and cultural inheritance.

Cather's poise is largely dependent on the historical distance she keeps from the scene described: Alexandra is dressed in 'what was *then* called the "Kate Greenaway" manner'. Hints at chronological distance are small but important; they enable Cather to write about her home territory as if it were distant or foreign. It is to the question of time that I now want to turn.

AMERICAN TIMES

Time, time passing, make the parish into the world. If the past, even the recent past, seems strange to us, then our own native land can become a foreign land. And if this is the case, then time itself is the greatest rebuff to localism and regionalism: in time, all becomes foreign. Cather realised this as early in her career as *O Pioneers!*. Her later novels explore the ramifications of this insight. Imagining America historically (in *Shadows on the Rock, Death Comes for the Archbishop* and *Sapphira and the Slave Girl*), she came to know her native soil as if it were a foreign land. During the central period of Cather's career there is a conjunction of interests in the 'foreign': she fictionalised past America (foreign because it is now past); and she explored the foreign elements in modern America (immigration, cultural and racial pluralism). Imagining the past as a foreign land, she came to understand the foreignness in contemporary America.

Discrepant and divergent timescales are integral to *O Pioneers!*. The novel frequently juxtaposes different timescales. At the beginning of the text there is the geological chronology suggested by the landscape, but alongside this is the human history of John Bergson's failed attempt to settle the land: 'In eleven long years John Bergson had made but little impression upon the wild land he had come to tame' (20). Divergent chronologies, a feature of this novel from the opening pages, affect the novel's ending in particular. The last pages have puzzled readers. Hermione Lee, for instance, finds them 'strange and evasive'.[28] One reason for her disquiet might be the shifting tenses in these pages, as characters think back and look forward. The last sentence ties the end of the novel back to its beginning:

> Fortunate country, that is one day to receive hearts like Alexandra's into its bosom, to give them out again, in the yellow wheat, in the rustling corn, in the shining eyes of youth! (309)

Theories of historical recurrence from Virgil to Michelet inform this sentence; past, present and future coexist within the turning cycle of history. 'Shining eyes' echoes the introduction of Alexandra at the start of the novel, the girl with 'her clear, deep blue eyes...fixed intently on the distance' (6). The ending superimposes the earlier sense of juvenile potential upon the future, transforming Alexandra's prospective death into a fresh source of energy. Simultaneously, Cather coalesces the natural and human worlds: Alexandra received into the earth, her body given out again as corn and wheat. As we saw earlier, Cather could be sceptical about our expectation that the natural world will comply with human will; thus the fusion of Alexandra and the land is hard-won, a sign of the eventual successful settlement of the Midwest. The last sentence plays with conventional figurations of the land. 'Into its bosom': the land is gendered, is female, but we have a female pioneer, rather than the expected male. And, furthermore, the identification of the pioneer and the land comes at the very end of the novel. It is an *achieved* merging of the human and the natural, a symbiosis that has been accomplished during the course of the book. 'To receive hearts like Alexandra's': the idea of regression towards the welcoming earth is here, but this is offset by a counter-pointing sense of renewal and regeneration as the land gives out new crops, new pioneers. The various conflations (human and natural; past, present and future) constitute a subtle fictional analogy to the point that Cather made in her article on Nebraska, where she imagined the future revival of a past pioneer age. That revival also depended on numerous conflations: of different times, of humankind and the earth.

Conflation, but not merging. In Cather's cyclical historiography the basic movement is one of time turning; by situating ourselves at different points on the cycle we can contrast cultures, comparing ancient and modern, European and American. Hence Cather's well-defined references to time and place, her anthropological or histori-cal specificity. A comparison with one of her contemporaries, Scott Fitzgerald, throws into relief the careful specificity of Cather's historical imagination.

The Great Gatsby, like *O Pioneers!*, is a novel about settlement, time and America. Fitzgerald's novel ends with a similar coalescing of themes and timescales when Nick Carraway imagines how America greeted the first explorers:

And as the moon rose higher the inessential houses began to melt away until gradually I became aware of the old island here that flowered once for Dutch sailors' eyes – a fresh, green breast of the new world. Its vanished trees, the trees that had made way for Gatsby's house, had once pandered in whispers to the last and greatest of all human dreams; for a transitory en-chanted moment man must have held his breath in the presence of this continent, compelled into an aesthetic contemplation he neither understood nor desired, face to face for the last time in history with something commensurate to his capacity for wonder.[29]

Another long perspective through history, yet the effect is to produce a dehistoricised myth of America, a dream that exists outside time. Fitzgerald's historical imagination continually threatens to dissolve into an Emersonian ahistoricism; here it does just that. The prose gestures towards historical accuracy: the moment of discovery, the details of nationality and place. But this instant of historically-grounded experience is now lost (the wonder felt 'for the last time in history'), and Fitzgerald transfers that revelation, when America was discovered, into an enchantment outside historical time. The movement is from the objective and historical to the subjective and ahistorical. America is the 'transitory enchanted moment' that is recurrently captured, the epiphany extended into a 'reign of wonder' by the dreaming American. The passage deploys transcendental ideas: the collapse of the objective, external world into subjectivism; wonder; the replacement of historical time by a series of epiphanies; the shift from diachronic time to the synchronic extended moment. Carraway's vision fleetingly acknowledges the loss and destruction necessitated by the settlement of America ('the trees that had made way for Gatsby's house'), but then turns back to the endless dream of American plenitude. And how is that plenitude figured? It is, of course, a *feminised* fullness – the 'fresh, green *breast* of the new world' promises both sexual and maternal receptiveness in exactly the way described by Kolodny.

The last sentences of *The Great Gatsby* continue the processes of melting, merging, dissolution that started when 'the inessential houses began to melt away'. Gatsby, Carraway, the author and the reader are joined together in a collective dream – note the decisive shift of pronoun to 'us':

> Gatsby believed in the green light, the orgastic future that year by year recedes before us. It eluded us then, but that's no matter – tomorrow we will run faster, stretch out our arms further...And one fine morning –
> So we beat on, boats against the current, borne back ceaselessly into the past.[30]

Future events carry us back into the past; the superimposition of tenses is similar to the last sentence of *O Pioneers!*. Both Cather and Fitzgerald conclude their novels with heightened rhetoric, but here the similarities end. Cather's conclusion is firmly grounded within the matrix of her novel: the hope for a renewal of energy – natural and human – arises from the diminished energies that have been the subject of the last chapter (Alexandra's growing tiredness and disillusion). The counterpointing of past and future develops from previous passages where various chronologies were juxtaposed (geological and imperial time; Alexandra's proleptic vision and her brothers' quotidian routine). Cather's conclusion, therefore, sinuously grows from the novel's examination of American time and history. *The Great Gatsby*, a novel about the fabulist's desire to create a history in the image of his own dreams, steps away from historical time. At the end even the reader is enveloped by the dream, disengaged from his or her position in history, drawn into the vision of American plenitude, described here in rhetorically expansive but deliberately vague phrases, 'the green light, the orgastic future'.

Retrospection is not nostalgia; it can be the means to compare civilisations across historical time. Cather takes this analogical imaginative principle to an extreme, juxtaposing the drive towards civilisation (pioneer settlement) against a world without man, a world where human efficacy is undercut. Her cyclical models of history become in *O Pioneers!* the means to meditate sceptically on the linear, progressive, narrowly occidental ideas that had manifested themselves in American writing about race, progress and civilisation. Cather valued earlier stages of civilisation in themselves, not as mere stepping stones towards a supposedly 'higher' order. My later chapters examine her changing uses of this basic idea. The first stage of this development, in *My Ántonia*, was to explore further the cultural variety in the Midwest.

4

My Ántonia and the Americanisation Debate

THEORIES OF AMERICANISATION

'This passion for Americanizing everything and everybody is a deadly disease with us', announced Willa Cather during an interview in 1924. What did she mean by 'Americanizing' ? This chapter examines Cather's changing responses to what I will call the Americanisation debate; the aim is to read her novel *My Ántonia* (1918) in the context of the political, sociological and educational arguments which had developed early this century around the issues of immigration and assimilation. Cather made her own distinctive contribution to that debate: letters, journalism and fiction continually testify to her fascination with immigrant culture. Drawing on this material we can read Cather's novel within its historical context. We will then be able to understand the subtleties and shifts in her commentary on one of the United States's most urgent cultural problems. Writing *My Ántonia* during the First World War, Cather suggested that a liberal form of Americanisation could encompass a kaleidoscopic cultural variety. Between 1916 and 1918, when the Americanisation debate began to form, but before the issue was usurped by nativism, it was possible to imagine a multinational America in which different cultures co-existed. The war, the upsurge in patriotism, and the concomitant legislation to regulate immigration and foreign languages put an end to the idea that the America coming into being would be a multicultural Utopia. *My Ántonia* was written during this apparent new dawn; she crystallised in fiction the hopes for a pluralist community. From the hopefulness of 1916–18 Cather retreated to her denunciations of modern America made in the early 1920s. This essay follows the development of Cather's ideas about multiculturalism during the period, placing them within their cultural context and teasing out the paradoxes in her position.

I am particularly concerned with the issue of biculturalism, a topic which has recently and brilliantly been explored by Werner Sollors. Sollors describes a pattern of 'consent and descent' in American culture, as citizens identify themselves ancestrally with their ethnic community (descent) and culturally with their new families, new culture and political system (consent):

> Descent relations are those defined by anthropologists as relations of 'substance' (by blood or nature); consent relations describe those of 'law' or 'marriage.' Descent language emphasizes our positions as heirs, our hereditary qualities, liabilities, and entitlements; consent language stresses our abilities as mature free agents and 'architects of our fates' to choose our spouses, our destinies, and our political systems.[1]

I return at several points to the distinction made by Sollors, and use the concepts of 'consent' and 'descent' to examine the dilemmas facing Cather's heroine, Ántonia.

In *Americanization* (1916) Royal Dixon discussed 'hyphenates', the term he used for recent immigrants into the United States. Dixon felt that waves of immigration meant that America had lost the sense of itself as a nation; he urged his countrymen to 'Americanize America'. This could be achieved through the teaching of English: 'and we need only add that the wonder of it is that a step so simple as approaching the foreigner and teaching him English has not long before this been recognized and put in practice by law and by grace, since it is the logical and all-powerful key to the situation of converting the foreigner from an alien to an American'. 'Americanization' was the term used to describe this process: through the acquisition of English the immigrant would be acculturated and lose his or her foreignness. The immigrant was then an American rather than, say, a German-American. Contending his thesis on pragmatic grounds, Dixon stated that 'it is in the Babel of tongues that the alien is debased and defrauded'. But his underlying principles – indeed, the principles of Americanisation in general – were ideological: American English was the means to transmit the ideals of the United States, to inculcate citizenship and the 'American way'.[2]

Dixon, editor of *The Immigrant in America Review*, was one of a number of Americanisation pundits who debated this issue during and after the First World War. The theorists of Americanisation –

educationalists, social scientists, politicians – responded to the social upheaval brought about by wave upon wave of immigration. Rates of European immigration had at last begun to slow down in the post-war period: from 3 687 564 (1891–1900), to 8 795 386 (1901–10) and 5 735 811 (1911–20), the huge influxes of migrants had now passed their peak.[3] Legislative controls were brought in to regulate immigration. The 1924 Immigration Act, also known as the National Origins Act, controlled entry according to the origin of the prospective American citizen; quotas were set as a percentage of the number of each national group resident in the United States in 1890 (thus favouring immigrants from northern and western Europe, who were more numerous than immigrants from southern and eastern Europe at that time). The debate now shifted to the question of assimilation: how was America to deal with the foreigners it had already received?

Assimilation raised a central question, to which the Americanisation theorists provided a range of answers: should the immigrants adjust themselves to American culture, or should American national identity redefine itself in the face of a multicultural population? The English language is the hook on which this question is hung; and the English language becomes the symbolic centre of the Americanisation debate. One reason for the heightening of interest in Americanisation was the sharpened awareness that American English constituted an autonomous language, a language that could be used as the index of national identity. In 1919 H. L. Mencken published his first edition of *The American Language*; and in 1925 the magazine *American Speech* was founded. Using such works Americans could isolate their language from its European mother tongue; and this helped to weld American English onto a strenghtened sense of purely American identity.

For Peter Roberts, in *The Problem of Americanization* (1920), the argument could be stated simply: 'the alien who does not know the English language will never understand America'.[4] Several years later, George Stephenson, one of the first historians of immigration, also emphasised the centrality of English teaching: 'Speaking in sweeping generalizations, the Americanisation movement involves the teaching of English, cultivating a friendly feeling between natives and immigrants and between the various racial groups, giving instruction in the fundamentals of citizenship, preventing undesirable segregation in cities, and meeting the demand for immigrants in desirable locations and occupations.'[5]

But this was where the problems began. How, for instance, was Americanisation to be administered? Should the teaching of English be a matter for government, for the local state, or for the individual employer who took on the tongue-tied immigrant? And what happened to the immigrant's former language and, by extension, former culture: how desirable were old world customs in the new world? It was obviously impossible to prohibit a bilingual American/European culture in the home, church or temple; but was a dualistic culture practical in society as a whole?[6]

Broadly speaking, we can distiguish between hard-line and liberal Americanisationists. The hard-liners rejected 'alien' values and sanctioned a violent rupture between the immigrant and the old world. The melting pot idea had, of course, been canvassed somewhat earlier (Israel Zangwill's play, *The Melting Pot*, was published in 1909); but the war helped to stir the pot. Americanisation, in this view, was a homogenising process that would meld a nation out of disparate stock. Thus Roberts and Dixon allow for a degree of linguistic and cultural pluralism, but these traces become part of what Dixon termed the 'American epic consciousness': 'let us say that the ideal towards which Americanism must press is that in which epic consciousness of each nationality shall contribute to and find expression in the American epic consciousness'.[7] At the extreme wing of the hard-liners were those sceptical commentators who doubted the efficacy of Americanisation. Gino Speranza, despite a name which suggests a not entirely WASPish ancestry, gave a pessimistic account of assimilation in his article of 1920, 'Does Americanization Americanize?':

> To feel that the powers of attraction and assimilation of America are tremendous, is both true and patriotic; but to practise the belief that such powers can work miracles – such as the rapid conversion of the mixed and unstable immigrants of Europe into *real* American citizens – is sheer superstition and, as such, the child of ignorance... There cannot be two nationalisms even if one is major and one minor, even if one claims to be American first and German second... Yet the more 'raw' citizens (if I may use the term) you take in, helping the process by a veneer of Americanization, the more you threaten our characteristically American form of democracy.[8]

In the same issue, demonstrating that Americanisation stirred up a highly partisan debate, John Kulamer responded more sympathetically than Speranza (though he refused to support the legislative encouragement of assimilation): 'Liberal and generous treatment, in accord with the principles of Americanism, on the part of individuals in their daily contact with the foreigners will do more than volumes of laws.'[9]

On the other hand, liberal Americanisationists advocated a transfer or migration of old world culture from Europe; American life would benefit from the resulting pluralism. In this view America encompasses a variety of cultures rather than subordinates them to its own 'epic consciousness'. An example of this position was *Old World Traits Transplanted* (1921), a study produced by sociologists at the University of Chicago as one in a series of *Americanization Studies*. Robert Park and his colleagues pointed out that 'all emigration represents some crisis in the life of the emigrants' and proceeded to develop a psycho-pathology of immigrant life. They maintained that settled, assimilated Americans must respect the recent immigrants, and they showed how immigrant organisations aided Americanisation. Liberal thinkers defined America through the diveristy of its peoples, claiming that immigration made the United States unique:

Immigration in the form it has taken in America differs from all previous movements of population. Populous countries have planted colonies, states have been conquered and occupied, slaves have been imported. But when a single country is peacefully invaded by millions of men from scores of other countries, when there are added to one American city as many Jews as there are Danes in Denmark, and to the same city more Italians than there are Italians in Rome, we have something new in history.

Liberal Americanisation recognised that the new world could only be created with due appreciation of the European heritage. This leads the Chicago writers to esteem memory. The immigrant, they say, comes to understand America through similarities with the world that was left behind. Patriotism is cited as a devotion that is shared by American and immigrant: the immigrant understands patriotic allegiance because he has felt this emotion for his homeland; such a feeling could be regenerated in the new world. 'If we wish to help the immigrant to get a grip on American life, to understand its conditions, and find his own role in it, we must seize on everything in his old life which will serve either to interpret the new or to hold him steady while he is getting adjusted.' Memory, then, is politicised by the Americanisation debate; it is enmeshed in arguments about citizenship and patriotism.[10]

Interest in the European heritage also led Americanisation pundits to draw parallels between the United States and great European civilisations. The sociologist Carol Aronovici asserted in 1919 that 'Drawing from the example of Spain we might almost say that where race amalgamation and race assimilation stop, advancement stops'. Aronovici hoped that the European assimilative process would be accelerated in America: 'A synthetic process of social and national integration brought about by an intensified democratic state will merge the present heterogeneous masses of racial and national groups into one great people'.[11]

Sociologists and educationalists surveyed the overall picture, trying to evaluate America's progress towards 'one great people'; but Americanisation was not only a subject discussed by academics. Within the popular culture there were accounts of what it meant to be 'Americanized' – immigrant testimonies and autobiographies form a major genre in early twentieth-century America. The most famous of these were Jacob Riis's *The Making of an American* (1901) and *The Americanization of Edward Bok* (1920). The latter, a Pulitzer prize-winner, was a bestseller from 1922 to 1924.[12] Bok's success is entirely founded on his facility in English. An immigrant Dutch boy, Bok learns English, works for newspapers and becomes an important editor. The book celebrates in a reassuringly eulogistic manner the opportunities that America has given him, but the one moment of critical asperity occurs when Bok attacks his early education: 'if there is one thing that I, as a foreign-born child, should have been carefully taught, it is the English language'.[13]

WILLA CATHER AND AMERICANISATION

The burst of writing on Americanisation coincides with Willa Cather's interest in the subject. In 1918, two years after Royal Dixon's *Americanization*, Cather published *My Ántonia*, a novel which explores the same areas as the texts I have just adduced: immigration, settlement, memory, language-acquisition. And in the 1920s, when Americanisation continued to arouse controversy, Cather gave some of her rare public speeches on this topic. In 1921, during speeches in the Nebraskan towns of Hastings and Omaha, she attacked hard-line

Americanisation. The *Omaha World-Herald* reported that 'Miss Cather told her audience that one of the things which retarded art in America was the indiscriminate Americanization work of overzealous patriots who implant into the foreign minds a distaste for all they have brought of value from their own country.' She reiterated her case in a 1924 interview with Rose Feld for the *New York Times Book Review*: 'Social workers, missionaries – call them what you will – go after them, pursue them and devote their days and nights toward the great task of turning them into stupid replicas of smug American citizens. This passion for Americanizing everything and everybody is a deadly disease with us'.[14]

Americanisation brought out this urgent, impassioned and homiletic tone in Cather for several reasons. First, it was a major issue in her home state, Nebraska. As she herself pointed out, Nebraska had a large foreign population – the 1910 census recorded 900 000 foreigners to 300 000 native stock.[15] Many of these immigrants were from a Germanic background. During the First World War, which led to an upsurge in patriotism after America entered on the allied side, German-Americans became objects of suspicion, as did the German language: there was a campaign to drop German from school curricula. The teaching of languages became a much-debated point. Edward A. Ross, a prominent sociologist and political scientist, lectured an audience in 1924 that

> It is a burning shame that at present American-born children are leaving church elementary foreign-language schools not only unable to read and write English, but scarcely able to understand or speak it. That we should permit native Americans to receive all the schooling they will ever get in a foreign language is the pinnacle of imbecile amiability.[16]

Nebraska had already extirpated 'imbecile amiability'. Responding to this xenophobic *Zeitgeist* the state passed measures to prohibit the teaching of languages before the eighth grade. This in turn led to the Meyer v. Nebraska case of 1923: a teacher was convicted for giving German lessons, and although the Supreme Court overturned the conviction (citing the Fourteenth Amendment) it affirmed its resistance to foreign languages:

> The legislature had seen the baneful effects of permitting foreigners, who had taken residence in this country, to rear and

educate their children in the language of their native land. The result of that condition was found to be inimical to our own safety. To allow the children of foreigners, who had emigrated here, to be taught from early childhood the language of the country of their parents was to rear them with that language as the mother tongue.[17]

The Meyer case marked the culmination of a patriotic upsurge that began with the First World War. Nebraska had prohibited foreign-language teaching in 1919. The years 1919–20 saw a flowering of anti-Bolshevik agitation, a distrust of radicalism and 'Reds'. Cather's speeches on language and immigration (1921) are therefore placed in a period and a place dominated by Americanisation. A provincial state such as Nebraska, recently created (1867) and flooded with immigrants, was paradoxically at the centre of American politics with regard to this issue.

The other reasons for Cather's impassioned tone stem from her trenchantly-held view of an ideal American culture. The desire to proscribe foreign languages was a manifestation of what she termed 'standardization'; it smacked of the uniformity that seemed to be overtaking modern society. Americanisation undermined the European cultural legacy which Cather cherished. She believed, in fact, that a heterogeneous, Europeanised Midwestern society could nurture a cosmopolitan culture: 'it is in that great cosmopolitan country known as the Middle West that we may hope to see the hard molds of American provincialism broken up'.[18]

It needs to be admitted that Cather's heterogeneous, pluralist immigrant culture is, nonetheless, essentially white and of North European descent. The culture described in the letters, the speeches and the novels overlooks the immigration from Southern and Eastern Europe; it also omits the Chinese and the Jews who made up so much of the immigrant population. As I noted in the 'Introduction', there is extensive evidence in Cather's work of indifference to, if not hostility towards certain ethnic groups – notably, America's Jews. But I also noted a certain developing self-consciousness about this issue, as evident in Cather's revisions to her texts so as to remove anti-Semitic references. Cather, then, tends to display an attentive sympathy within the context of a circumscribed pluralism. That is, she does not write about such ethnic groups as the Chinese-Americans, but she does write about a greater variety of European peoples than many of her contemporaries. And within the framework of this localised ethnic spectrum, her fictions of race and multiculturalism can often seem strikingly receptive to difference. *My Ántonia*, as I will now show, is a major instance of this attentive sympathy.

My Ántonia, written at the end of the war, is noticeably reticent about a conflict which as Hermione Lee comments, 'makes the loudest silence in the book'; but the book has much to say about one of the effects of the war, namely the intensified Americanisation programme.[19] The military draft had revealed that of 10 million registrants, 700 000 were so illiterate that they could not even sign their names. Government agencies accordingly increased their work: the Bureau of Education published its *Americanization Bulletin* for the first time; Independence Day was especially directed towards the immigrant and a mobilisation of patriotism.[20] Against this background, Cather wrote a novel that reads as if it were a rebuff to the hard-line Americanisationists and a prescient commentary on Nebraska's rejection of foreign languages in 1919.

In *My Ántonia*, Cather describes lives that are shaped by the need to learn a new language and a new culture. The novel's heroine, Ántonia Shimerda, comes from an immigrant Bohemian family which at first knows no English: 'they could not speak enough English to ask for advice, or even to make their most pressing wants known' (20). Ántonia's friendship with Jim Burden is initiated by her desire to learn English (the oblique tentativeness of this romance might have more to do with cultural factors – learning a language – than with Cather's famous difficulties in representing successful heterosexual relationships). While she learns words and phrases, the Nebraskan landscape takes shape before us, described as if for the first time. The fresh and almost naive immediacy of Cather's descriptive passages is, in part, the result of the defamiliarisation of language that occurs when we are shown how English is learned:

Ántonia pointed up to the sky and questioned me with her glance. I gave her the word, but she was not satisfied and pointed to my eyes. I told her, and she repeated the word, making it sound like 'ice'. She pointed up to the sky, then to my eyes, then back to the sky, with movements so quick and impulsive that she distracted me, and I had no idea what she wanted. She got up on her knees and wrung her hands. She pointed to her own eyes and shook her head, then to mine and to the sky, nodding violently.

'Oh,' I exclaimed, 'blue; blue sky!' (26)

We have here the 'reign of wonder' that Tony Tanner has located as a central motif in American literature.[21] Words are used with novelty and wonder to describe the world. The most clichéd elements of our environment ('blue sky') are imbued with mystery when they are named afresh. Edenic analogues move within the comedy of this scene, suggested by the paradisiacal resonance of the act of naming. Some Americanisationists felt that the nation had lost its selfhood beneath a tide of immigration. Cather, however, demonstrates that immigration renews America's myths about its own identity. With each wave of immigration, America is once again perceived as paradise, as Eden; and through the Americanisation process the land is literally named for the first time.

To write at all about the English language and language acquisition was to enter into a highly charged discourse about American nationalism and immigration – indeed, a discourse about American culture itself. *My Ántonia* signals, from its very title, an engagement with the Americanisation debate. *My Ántonia*: a footnote guides us to the correct pronunciation of Ántonia, 'the Bohemian name' (3). Cather does not aim for a veneer of exoticism, the patina that could be achieved simply through the deployment of foreign names and strange words. Instead, she gives due respect to the alien name that her metic carries, and so carefully underlines her heroine's foreignness.[22]

This sympathy recurs throughout the novel; Cather's American characters are responsive to foreign cultures and languages. Jim Burden is intrigued when he hears Bohemian: 'I pricked up my ears, for it was positively the first time I had ever heard a foreign tongue' (6). There are moments when characters use foreign words without being aware of their meaning, but the power of a strange language nonetheless communicates itself. Jim's grandfather at one point reads from the psalms and says the word 'Selah': 'I had no idea what the word meant; perhaps he had not. But, as he uttered it, it became oracular, the most sacred of words' (13). The epiphany exemplifies Cather's ecumenical generosity: her characters find spiritual value even in experiences that are foreign to them and therefore baffling or opaque. Moreover, Cather shows how a commonplace devotion, a cornerstone of Protestant daily life, turns on a word that is unknown. Domestic religious life is made strange and made sacred by the admission of the foreign. Cather elliptically reminds us that American Protestantism inevitably incorporated elements of that 'alien' culture which hard-line Americanisation rejected. There is nothing melodramatic or confrontational in Cather's prose; one can easily read over these sentences without heeding their low-key subversiveness. But in her own distinctively oblique fashion Cather rewrites Americanisation rhetoric.[23]

My Ántonia is, above all, a novel about bilingual communities. Cather shows how the immigrant, accustomed to two or more cultures, uses different languages for different purposes. Otto Fuchs uses his first language when he writes to his mother: 'he spoke and wrote his own language so seldom that it came to him awkwardly. His effort to remember entirely absorbed him' (85–6). Fuchs has practically lost his European language; other characters absorb American English so readily that a similar slippage might occur. Ántonia herself is rapidly attuned to English: 'Tony learned English so quickly that by the time school began she could speak as well as any of us' (155). Cather observes that children do adapt linguistically much more readily and completely than adults. Fuchs and Ántonia are quickly 'Americanized', in the narrow sense of learning English. Yet, in Cather's liberal definition of Americanisation, this does not mean that the immigrant's earlier language and culture are forsaken. When Jim returns to look for Ántonia after 20 years he finds she is married to her fellow Bohemian, Cuzak. Their children speak Bohemian; the family have a domestic culture that is solidly European. We hear again the language-switching that prevailed at the beginning of the novel; 'Cuzak began at once to talk about his holiday – from politeness he spoke English' (357). The novel has turned full circle: the immigrant leaves her European homeland, becomes an American, but preserves European culture at home and in her language. Finally, Cather shows, there can be an amalgamation of Europe and America; the Cuzak children are at ease in both worlds. Ántonia's family stands as a repudiation of those Americanisation pundits who advocated the severance of ties with the old world. The Cuzaks are the culmination of many subtle and unexpected reversals in this novel: 'native' Americans are receptive to foreign cultures; the foreigners learn English; Ántonia fulfils the American dream of pioneer settlement even as she revivifies a European way of life.

Within the context of the Americanisation debate, these details add up to a radical commentary on what it is to be 'American'. Whereas Americanisation ideology sought to fix the meaning of 'American' (making it synonymous with 'Protestant', 'English-speaking', 'North European'), Cather's sense of the word is far more capacious and fluid. To return to the terminology I mentioned at the start of this chapter: Cather is interested in an American culture based on both 'consent' and 'descent'. The domestic culture of the Cuzaks, for instance its use of the Bohemian language, exemplifies descent. Ántonia preserves the language of her ancestors, and by marrying one of her countrymen the continuities of descent are further emphasised. However, in her pioneering endeavours and her settlement of the land Ántonia has lived out the principles of consent – hers is a thoroughly American life of autonomy and self-making. Indeed, in one memorable phrase Jim Burden explicitly sees Ántonia as the *originator*, and not the descendant, of a race: 'She was a rich mine of life, like the founders of early races' (353).

Readings of the novel, nevertheless, sometimes ignore the political intricacy of Cather's writing, particularly in the final Book, 'Cuzak's Boys'. James E. Miller in '*My Ántonia* and the American Dream' reads *My Ántonia* as a novel about disillusion: 'by and large, the dreams of the pioneers lie shattered, their lives broken by the hardness of wilderness life'.[24] He is correct to say that something has been broken. Cather describes the physical 'breaking' of her heroine, who now has hair 'a little grizzled' (310) and many teeth missing (335). But because he neglects the theme of Americanisation, Miller reads the latter section of the novel as bleaker than it really is. In counterpoint to disillusion, Cather writes of a creativity and renewal that is the result of her idiosyncratically pluralist version of Americanisation. Jim and Ántonia are in nostalgic mood, and they spend their time with old photographs or in reminiscence; but they are surrounded by children, many speaking Bohemian, who offset the melancholia with their vitality and joy. One of the most memorable scenes in the book – a scene that demonstrates Cather's sensitivity to physical energy, to light and to food – occurs when the children burst from the fruit cave, 'a veritable explosion of life out of the dark cave into the sunlight' (339). The fruit cave, where food is preserved during the winter months, cyclically returns us to the sod houses in which characters at the start of the novel lived – it is another domestic space hollowed out of the earth itself. But it is also an apt symbol of conserved energy; Cather shows immigrant life – a conserved European heritage – erupting from the American soil:

> We turned to leave the cave; Ántonia and I went up the stairs first, and the children waited. We were standing outside talking,

when they all came running up the steps together, big and little, tow heads and gold heads and brown, and flashing little naked legs; a veritable explosion of life out of the dark cave into the sunlight. It made me dizzy for a moment. (338–9)

Cather's first full-length interview was for the *Philadelphia Record* in 1913; in it she discussed the immigrant communities of Red Cloud and mentioned the narrative skills of the old women:

Even when they spoke very little English, the old women somehow managed to tell me a great many stories about the old country. They talk more freely to a child than to grown people, and I always felt as if every word they said to me counted for twenty.[25]

It is likely that the origins of *My Ántonia* lay in such a tale. Cather recalled that when she arrived in Nebraska as a girl the first thing she heard about was the suicide of a Mr. Sadalaak, even though he had died several years earlier. This story made a great impression on her, and she remembered that people never stopped retelling it. Cather claimed that having heard this repeatedly-told story she was destined to write *My Ántonia*. The novel is, then, the latest formulation in a series of tellings of the same tale.[26]

Immigrant life is oral and narrative, in spite of the old women's faltering knowledge of English. The immigrants are habitual storytellers, preserving memories of Europe through anecdotes and tales. *My Ántonia*, faithful to the immigrant experience, has an extraordinary multiplicity of voices. Cather deploys a series of discrete stories and anecdotes, many of which deal with the immigrants' lives in Europe, with language acquisition, with the making of new lives in America. The novel is a tissue of recollections of European domestic life, simple anecdotes about lost people and places, stray memories. Ántonia, for instance, tells Jim about her home country, about hunting badgers and 'Old Hata' who sang to the children (38–9).

Cather's perception of immigrant folk-culture affects the form of *My Ántonia*, a novel which she said seemed to lack typical novelistic features:

My Ántonia, for instance, is just the other side of the rug, the pattern that is supposed not to count in a story. In it there is no love affair, no courtship, no marriage, no broken heart, no struggle for success. I knew I' d ruin my material if I put it in the usual fictional pattern. I just used it the way I thought absolutely true.[27]

Cather's image for *My Ántonia* – the 'other side of the rug, the pattern that is supposed not to count' – hints at a Jamesian notion of the story as the woven pattern of a carpet; yet it also suggests parallels with popular women's crafts such as weaving or quilt-making. This conflation of Jamesian theorising and folk-art is analogous to the method of *My Ántonia* ; the novel's loose, barely plotted structure is an experiment in form *and* an embodiment of the Midwest's oral folk-culture. We find a similar synthesis of 'art' and 'folk-art' in Cather's comment that, when she listened to the immigrant women, 'I always felt as if every word they said to me counted for twenty'. The inability of the immigrants to express themselves fully means that the listener has to imagine a fuller, richer account behind their faltering, spartan English narratives. Words, Cather implies, can suggest or stand for many other words. Apparently limited or depleted accounts can paradoxically adumbrate a denser shadow-narrative. Her theory of composition was based on an analogous paradox: through selection and excision the writer can produce a prose of greater suggestive power than writing that is, superficially, more dense or rich. Compare the comment on the immigrant women (1913) to her dicta on writing (1922):

> If the novel is a form of imaginative art, it cannot be at the same time a vivid and brilliant form of journalism. Out of the teeming, gleaming stream of the present it must select the eternal material of art... Whatever is felt upon the page without being specifically named there – that, one might say, is created. It is the inexplicable presence of the thing not named, of the overtone divined by the ear but not heard by it, the verbal mood, the emotional aura of the fact or the thing or the deed, that gives high quality to the novel or the drama, as well as to poetry itself.[28]

'The thing not named': this shadow-presence is a feature of both immigrant culture and Cather's art. In writing, it is the suggested presence, 'the verbal mood', 'the emotional aura'. In immigrant culture it is the hinterland of the immigrant's past, that other life which is momentarily shadowed forth in fractured tales told in an alien language.

The open, receptive form of *My Ántonia*, then, allows Cather to weave into the narrative strands from the old world; the porous texture of the novel admits different stories. This narrative structure constitutes a commitment to a pluralist America: Cather's unplotted novel refuses to lay down a strong narrative line, a prescribed American story. Thus *My Ántonia*, with its lack of a strong narrative tug and its apparent formlessness, facilitates the democratic mingling of stories from the new and old worlds.

To construct a novel in this way entails risks: the novel can splinter into a series of episodes, losing all coherence. *My Ántonia* has been criticised for this very reason. Louis Auchincloss wrote of Peter and Pavel's wedding story that 'It is a brilliant and horrifying little piece that has nothing to do with anything else in the novel.' 'The action in *My Ántonia* is episodic, lacks focus, and abounds in irrelevancies (consider the inserted wolf-story of Pavel and Peter, for example)', commented James E. Miller.[29] The example adduced here – the wolf-story – typifies the digressive method of *My Ántonia*. Pavel tells a story from the European homeland: wolves attacked the sledges in which a wedding party was travelling, and in the chaos Pavel pushed the bride and groom off their sledge to certain death. *Pace* Miller, the wolf-story is relevant, and its relevance rests in its development of the Americanisation theme: Pavel's story extends Cather's examination of oral folk-culture, bilingualism and translation. European tales of ravenous wolves had spread, as the immigrants had spread, across the Midwest. Cather, either consciously or unconsciously, used a story that was popular in the folk-culture of the American Plains; and she set down the story to demonstrate the ways in which oral transmission had taken place.[30] The story is told by Pavel to Mr. Shimerda; Ántonia overhears the tale and then translates it for Jim Burden. At first Jim can only sense the excitement of the Europeans; he cannot understand the reasons for their agitation:

> Presently Pavel began to talk to Mr. Shimerda, scarcely above a whisper. He was telling a long story, and as he went on, Ántonia took my hand under the table and held it tight. She leaned forward and strained her ears to hear him. He grew more and more excited, and kept pointing all around his bed, as if there were things there and he wanted Mr. Shimerda to see them. (54)

The passage is full of different kinds of communication: whispering, touching, gesticulating. Jim, as yet, does not understand the subject of this story, 'the thing not named' in English. Eventually he is told about the wolves; the story appears as a translated inset in the narrative. The inset is clearly demarcated from the preceding text: there is an interruption in the narrative flow as Pavel's story is heard and translated; and Cather signals the interruption typographically by a paragraph break before the inset tale. Pavel's story, then, is 'framed'. Using the frame Cather places the Russian folk-tale within the American narrative, but she ensures that the tale preserves its old world autonomy. The frame is a technical response to the problems of Americanisation; it enables Cather to find an even-handed reciprocity between European and American cultures. She brings cultures together while emphasising their differences.

After he tells his story Pavel dies; his companion Peter moves away. Despite the break-up of this immigrant household, the story of the wolves continues to be remembered because Ántonia and Jim preserve the memory: 'for Ántonia and me, the story of the wedding party was never at an end' (61). The original story has a progressively wider audience as it moves from Pavel to Mr. Shimerda and then out to Ántonia and Jim. Simultaneously, the story binds Ántonia and Jim together: 'we did not tell Pavel's secret to anyone, but guarded it jealously' (61). Cather explores the ways in which a folk-memory develops, moving centrifugally and centripetally, spreading outwards even as it binds the listeners together in a community of memory. The proponents of Americanisation felt that the persistence of the old world heritage, with all its attendant memories, threatened America with cultural atomisation. Pavel's story posits an alternative hypothesis: through the transmisson of memories a sense of community is fostered. The wolf-story, in short, is not as irrelevant as James E. Miller contended. Rather, this episode articulates Cather's ideas about American nationalism and the American community: community instead of division; the merging of racial and national folk-cultures. For Cather, immigrant folk-tales represented the living, diverse culture she promulgated in her Americanisation speeches.

Cather's theories of art and her practice of fiction were conditioned by her upbringing in Nebraska; she seems to have understood the composition of fiction as a creative act analogous to the telling and retelling of folk-tales. Her approach to the actual business of writing turned on the different material incarnations of the same story. Her diligent revision of manuscripts and type-scripts involved changing the physical appearance of drafts; the draft would be written, typed, retyped in a different colour – the aim was to facilitate the revision of material, since the eye can discern solecisms more easily when the form of the text is altered. Writing, as Cather worked at her desk day after day, was essen-tially redrafting (she told Sinclair Lewis that she was unconcerned with preserving the first drafts of her work). And this technique, the keystone of her craft, evoked the tellings, retellings and repeti-tions-with-variation of the folk-tales she heard as a girl. As Cather wrote, her own work became, as it were, translated; the original, primary draft was lost within an accreting series of later versions. The drafts are rather like the later tellings and retellings of the Peter and Pavel story; they have an autonomous existence of their own, and come to replace the original tale.[31]

In translation, too, the basic story serves as a template for refor-mulations which are at once the same and different. For Cather, a much translated writer, the spread of her work into different lan-guages provided another opportunity to see transmission and retelling at work. She was, for instance, pleased with the foreign re-ception of *Death Comes for the Archbishop*, and she boasted that *My Ántonia* had been translated into eight languages. Gratified by the French thesis on her work by René Rapin, Cather wanted to have it translated for her American friends. The last example concludes a chain of transmissions: from America to France; from the novelist to the critic; and then the reversal of this process as Cather plans to have translated a French critical study for an American readership. It is also worth noting how, as with the wolf-story, we have differ-ent kinds of audience receiving the work (the author herself, the French scholarly community, the American circle of friends) – one story holds together different communities of listeners and readers.[32]

Cather understood from her Nebraskan youth that disparate aspects of her experience (translating Latin texts, listening to immi-grant women, writing fiction) were underpinned by the shared foundation of transmission. She interpreted a range of apparently unrelated cultural phenomena in this way, finding a common structure of transmission. The beginning of *My Ántonia* demonstrates this cultural anthropology in action. Jim Burden meets the unnamed narrator of the 'Introduction'. They talk about Ántonia Shimerda; Jim has written an account of her, which he later delivers to the narrator, scribbling on the front of his manuscript *My Ántonia*. Remembering, telling stories, writing, handing over the manuscript: the 'Introduction' is a glancing vignette, but it embraces a gamut of transmissions – it can be read almost as an overture, a prefiguring of the motifs developed in the main text. The similarities with the gossipy, folky intimacies of the immigrant women are striking, but Cather neatly updates the context, placing this moment of transmission in a railway carriage – the train compartment unobtrusively becoming the typical modern setting for recollection, gossip:

> Last summer, in a season of intense heat, Jim Burden and I happened to be crossing Iowa on the same train. He and I are old friends, we grew up together in the same Nebraska town, and we had a great deal to say to each other. While the train flashed through never-ending miles of ripe wheat, by country towns and bright-flowered pastures and oak groves wilting in the sun, we sat in the observation car, where the woodwork was hot to the touch and red dust lay deep over everything. The dust and heat, the burning wind, reminded us of many things. We were talking about what it is like to spend one's childhood in little towns like these, buried in wheat and corn, under stimulating extremes of climate: burning summers when the world lies green and billowy beneath a brilliant sky, when one is fairly stifled in vegetation, in the colour and smell of strong weeds and heavy harvests; blustery winters with little snow, when the whole country is stripped bare and grey as sheet-iron. ('Introduction')

The land takes shape as a memory, becoming focused before us. What happens here is a typically Catheresque moment of memory and repetitive recall. In a phrase that is picked up and echoed many pages later in the wolf-story, the narrator says, 'During that burning day when we were crossing Iowa, our talk kept returning to a central figure, a Bohemian girl whom we had both known long ago'. Talk keeps returning: Cather is intrigued by these moments when the loose web of chat and memory begins to tighten and centre around a figure, an episode. The major theme adumbrated here is, simply, transmission: Jim and the narrator share their memories of Ántonia, exchanging recollections. We know that Cather had at first tried to write the novel as a third-person narrative before opting for the first-person story with a male narrator. Cather discussed the implications of this gender shift (female author and male narrator) in her letters, and commentators have been quick to fit this compositional history into discussions of gender and sexual role-playing in the life and the fiction. But the effect of having a narrator in the novel is also to foreground the processes of writing and transmission. We see, quite literally, the text being created, named and handed over. Thus the effect of an overture, a pre-capitulation of the novel's fascination with all kinds of translation and transmission.[33]

At the end of the Pavel and Peter episode Jim dreams of a composite landscape through which he travels: 'At night, before I went to sleep, I often found myself in a sledge drawn by three horses, dashing through a country that looked something like Nebraska and something like Virginia' (61). Jim's memory transfers and fuses various terrains. The Ukraine becomes America; that America is, in turn, a composite of Nebraska and Virginia (Jim's home states and Cather's too). The landscape undergoes a process of amalgamation that is similar to the experiences of Cather's characters, who are also European *and* American, Southern *and* Western. Cather's American soil is here a shifting and various land, as much a patchwork terrain as her Americans are a patchwork people. Cather thereby fends off the American myth of a native soil on which a 'native' (that is, white, north European and Protestant) population lives.

To gauge the subtlety of Cather's method in *My Ántonia* we need to turn back to the Americanisation debate. Theorists of liberal Americanisation went beyond the question of language learning and used the basic idea of Americanisation as a vehicle to carry their speculations about other cultural matters. As we saw earlier, the Chicago sociologists were led to meditate about memory and its role in helping the migrant to adapt to a new land. *My Ántonia* works in a similar way. Cather deploys the fundamental stuff of Americanisation ('blue sky!'), but she then goes further and reflects on memory, on folk-art, on the very foundations of culture. Cather's descriptions of how a story is transmitted and how a novel of American life can be constructed further the insights of liberal Americanisation. It is to these broader cultural matters that I now want to turn.

AN AMERICANISED CULTURE: IDEALISM AND DISILLUSION

Two years before *My Ántonia* was published Randolph Bourne wrote his remarkably prescient article, 'Trans-National America' (1916). Bourne, a progressive, an opponent of America's entry into the War and a radical educationalist was also a sympathetic reviewer of *My Ántonia*.[34] He described a cosmopolitan America where what he termed, in typically progressive fashion, the 'Beloved Community' would grow out of multiculturalism. 'Trans-National America' was an attack on the authoritarianism of Americanisation ('We act as if we wanted Americanization to take place only on our own terms, and not by the consent of the governed') and an outline of a cosmopolitan Utopia, an America capaciously receptive to a variety of peoples. This piece, published before the First World War had precipitated an upswing in patriotic fervour and hardened attitudes against foreigners, opposed the conservatism of the Anglo-American establishment to an exciting racial heterogeneity. For Bourne, as for Cather, the recognition of America's failings is set against the potential cultural successes of a pluralist society ('America is a unique sociological fabric, and it bespeaks poverty of imagination not to be thrilled at the incalculable potentialities of so novel a union of men').[35] Again like Cather, Bourne despised the encroaching uniformity of America and sought a revitalisation through ethnic and cultural diversity:

> We have needed the new peoples – the order of the German and Scandinavian, the turbulence of the Slav and Hun – to save us from our own stagnation… What we emphatically do not want is that these distinctive qualities should be washed out into a tasteless, colorless fluid of uniformity.[36]

In Bourne's article the question of assimilation is used as a lever to prise open the extant American culture. Bourne wants to know what kind of a country America is, what its culture is like; 'Americanization' is used to interpret 'American'. His conclusion is that America needs to find a means to integrate its diverse constituent cultures while preserving their idiosyncratic differences:

> This is the cultural wreckage of our time, and it is from the fringes of the Anglo-Saxon as well as the other stocks that it falls. America has as yet no impelling integrating force. It makes too

easily for this detritus of cultures. In our loose, free country, no constraining national purpose, no tenacious folk-tradition and folk-style hold the people to a line... America is transplanted Europe, but a Europe that has not been disintegrated and scattered in the transplanting as in some Dispersion. Its colonies live here inextricably mingled, yet not homogeneous. They merge but they do not fuse.[37]

Bourne alighted in 1916 on a problem Cather had begun to explore in *O Pioneers!* and pursued in *My Ántonia*: how was this heterogeneously centrifugal society to find cultural coherence? Bourne understood that America risked fragmentation socially and culturally. The language he used sought to redeem a vocabulary of dispersal ('The influences at the fringe, however, are centrifugal, anarchical') with a diction of coherence ('impelling integrating force'). What was needed was a 'folk-tradition and folk-style'. When Bourne tried to imagine the cosmopolitan culture that would result he used images from the folk-arts of weaving and quilt-making:

America is coming to be, not a nationality but a trans-nationality, a weaving back and forth, with the other lands, of many threads of all sizes and colors. Any movement which attempts to thwart this weaving, or to dye the fabric any one color, or disentangle the threads of the strands, is false to this cosmopolitan vision.[38]

We can note here the congruences between Cather and Bourne. They used similar images of weaving: Bourne to envisage what a cosmopolitan America would be like; Cather, to describe the form her novel of cosmopolitan America took. For these writers images of weaving were suggested by the recognition that the culture of the new 'Trans-National America' would be a folk-art. It needs to be stressed that for Bourne and Cather a national folk-art was not already, as it were, out there, latent within the national life. Cather had glimpsed the shards of a now-disintegrated folk-culture in the tales told by the old immigrant women; but there is no suggestion that this oral tradition had a wider currency. America, though, *required* a folk-culture. Bourne suggested that America needed a folk-tradition by which to integrate itself; Cather's art attempted to work out how that American folk-art might develop. In the wolf-story she showed how community might be created by stories.

The wolf-story also demonstrates that Americanisation was complexly related to the status of artistry in America. The story, as it is told and retold, shifts from the communal to the individual and then back to the communal; it is inherited from European folklore, refashioned by the individual storyteller and returned to the burgeoning American popular culture. There is an interplay between individual and folk forms of art. Cather here displays a broader awareness of Americanisation than the professed Americanisation experts, for whom the transplanting of Europeans into the US was largely a matter of language acquisition and the sociology of settlement. In Cather's hands Americanisation pans out into wider reflections on culture itself. How do cultures evolve? Can they be transferred from one part of the globe to another? Is it possible to belong to two cultures? Does the novelist inherit a storytelling form with its origins in communal arts, or is the novelist's craft inevitably severed from folk-culture?

These questions were discussed in Cather's intellectual milieu. Louise Pound, one of Cather's oldest friends from her student days at the University of Nebraska, went on to become an eminent literary critic and folklorist; her work was often concerned with the survival of European oral culture in its new American home. The friendship between Cather and Pound is usually discussed in biographical terms: their meeting as students, a possible lesbian relationship, and the resentment and estrangement that disrupted their intimacy.[39] Such biographical investigation has its own validity, but it can lead to the occlusion of Pound's intellectual output, a body of work that was prolific and important (and eventually made her the first woman president of the Modern Language Association). Louise Pound's work on American folklore provides us with analogues to Cather's fictionalisation of this subject. And furthermore, in reading Pound's scholarship on folklore and cultural transmission we become aware of the contradictions and complexities of Cather's fiction. The scholar articulates a series of striking, assertive propositions; the novelist, in contrast, explores the ambivalences of the Americanisation debate.

Pound was a specialist in ballads and oral literature. She became an editor of *American Speech*, a journal that was started in 1926 and examined American etymology, dialect and folklore; it published pieces on the American transformations of transplanted European culture, for instance Herbert H. Vaughan's 'Italian and Its Dialects as Spoken in the United States'. Pound's own research traced the importation of European culture into America. In the first volume of *American Speech* she wrote a scholarly note on 'An American Text of "Sir James the Rose"' in which she discussed an eighteenth-century Scottish ballad that had made its way by oral transmission to Lincoln, Nebraska. And she argued that Walt Whitman, rather than being a demotically American poet, was a polyglot user of Romance languages in his verse. Pound wrote the entry on 'Oral Literature' for the Cambridge *History of American Literature* (1921), a piece that declared 'the main interest of oral literature is historical. From it may be seen how songs and verse tales develop, how themes and styles are transmitted from generation to generation, and from one region or land to another.'[40]

Pound speculates about cultural transmission: how are ballads communicated? Do they change as they filter down through the ages? Her hypothesis is that transmission – through time and across countries – produces artistic degeneration. In *Poetic Origins and the Ballad* (1921) Pound traced the American versions of ballads that had been collected by F. J. Child in his famous nineteenth-century anthology:

> Contrast, where dates are available, early pieces with late, or American versions with their Old World parents, and make inference from the mass. The crudity and the unliterary quality increase with the lapse of time, and by popular presentation. The epic completeness and effectiveness of the Child piece is likely to sink downward to simplicity or fragmentariness.[41]

Although Pound collected and wrote on American ballads, and was a contributor to the *Journal of American Folklore*, she often took a hard line on that material. 'Simplicity' and 'fragmentariness' are the fate of American oral literature, and the main reason for this is that the ballad in America exists 'by popular preservation' – that is, it is the product of *communal* artistic effort. Pound argues that the lack of individual creativity in the American ballads means that they are 'crude, structureless, incoherent, and lacking in striking and memorable qualities'. Earlier in *Poetic Origins* Pound had advanced the contentious theory that the ballad was, in its origin, the product of autonomous and solitary artistic endeavour rather than, as one might expect, a manifestation of collective creativity. Thus:

That it is an absurd chronology which assumes that individuals have choral utterance before they are lyrically articulate as individuals, seems – extraordinarily enough – to have little weight with theorists of this school. Did primitive man sing, dance, and compose in a throng, while he was yet unable to do so as an individual?[42]

And she concludes her first chapter with a trenchant rejection of communal artistic creativity: 'the assumption that group power to sing, to compose songs, and to dance, precedes individual power to do these things, is fatuously speculative'.[43]

Pound, then, revises the literary history of the ballad, undermining it as a group art and vaunting it as the expression of individuals. The ballad becomes a quasi-romantic form of self-expression. Poetic degeneration occurs in the shift from individual to wholly collective creativity; and this also happens in the cultural transmission from the old world to the new. The degeneration of the ballad presages further cultural disintegration, since communal art cannot survive for long: 'in general, real communalistic or people's poetry, composed in the collaborating manner sketched out by Professor Gunmere and Professor Kittredge, is too crude, too structureless, too unoriginal, too lacking in coherence and in striking or memorable qualities, to have much chance at survival'.[44] Working around the same issues that Cather had dealt with in *My Ántonia* – cultural transmission, individual as opposed to collective creativity – Pound reached pessimistic conclusions. To the central question of whether transmission inevitably entailed degeneration Pound could only answer that this was indeed the case. This makes her the overseer of the death of European folk-culture as it fades and disintegrates in its new home.

Comparing Pound's work on cultural transmission to Cather's, we can see the ambiguities and contradictions in the novelist's position. *My Ántonia*, published three years before the Americanisation speeches (and before nativism had a legislative impact in Nebraska), reads as a remarkably optimistic text about cultural transmission and continues to be relevant to America's ongoing controversies about assimilation and bilingualism. As we saw in the wolf-story – a tale that seems folkloric in its portrayal of lurid melodrama emerging from a humdrum, domestic context – in Cather's fiction the oral narratives of Europe continue to retain their power. Whereas Pound sees cultural transmission as a two-stage process of decline (individual creativity falling towards the communal; the old world becoming the new) Cather repositions these stages as a regenerative dialectic: folk-culture is renewed by being shunted to and fro between Europe and America, the individual and the community. The 'crisis in the life of the emigrants' diagnosed by the Chicago sociologists (1921) is, of course, present in the novel, but the crisis is also seen as a means to renewal: of folktales, of America, of the storyteller's art and, by implication, of the novelist's own creativity. She 'poeticized' the politics of Americanisation, taking the raw material (language learning, immigration, a multinational society) and showing how this all came down to the question of stories; and in so doing Cather showed that simply to *tell* a story can become a political act.

But at the same time there are foreshadowings of the failure of Americanisation. Intriguingly, while the wolf-story celebrates the communality of oral transmission, it also shows how the folkloric culture of shared storytelling must come to an end. After all, the story is *written*. We only know the story because Cather has preserved it for us in the written form of fictional prose. In this sense, Cather's novel ironically undercuts its own attempt to preserve an oral immigrant culture. The preservation of the wolf-story in Cather's text also confirms Pound's point that 'real communalistic or people's poetry' has little chance of survival. Just as Pound's work preserved an oral culture through the permanence of writing, so Cather fixes in print the ephemeral spoken words of the Midwest's folk-culture.

My Ántonia is increasingly overshadowed by these ironic contradictions. Ántonia's homestead already contains the seeds of its own failure. The homestead is isolated; only within Ántonia's homestead is the bilingual community firmly established at the end of the novel. It does not form part of a larger community of liberally Americanised families. Burden's journey to see Ántonia emphasises the remoteness of her home. Book V begins with a glancing account of the widely-separated community of old friends; there is a sudden rush of different places as the novel sweeps across the areas where its characters now live and work. Jim has travelled to Bohemia, Ántonia's old country; he meets Tiny in Salt Lake City; Lena Lingard now lives in San Francisco (327–8). Travelling first by train, Jim then travels by buggy (with a 'fairly good livery team' – Ántonia's house is obviously remote) and finally walks up to the house (329–30). His journey follows a path into America's past – away from modernity into an archetypal frontier scene: a homestead, the open prairie, a man walking down a path. Much of the power of the ending of *My Ántonia* comes from the mixed resonances of this scene. The novel began with the narrator talking to Burden during a train journey; now at the end of the book we return to the primal America of wandering, exploration and homemaking. It is the recovery of the ideals of an earlier age, suggesting that just below the surface of American life persists a still recoverable, pristine, frontier life; but it also covertly admits failure. The Americanisation of the new world is successful, but only within a radically atomised society – as if in the very act of becoming American the immigrant also became what Melville called an 'isolato'.

Writing in 1917 and 1918, Cather seems to have been presciently aware of the tensions inherent in the benign Americanisation she advocated. What I have termed liberal Americanisation is thus tempered and qualified by a sense that this variety of hyphenated identity might never achieve a broad cultural currency. Given the upswing of nativism after the war, and given our continued difficulties in accommodating ethnic and cultural differences, or reconciling 'consent' and 'descent', Cather was perhaps right to envisage such a circumscribed and cautious model of the Americanised bicultural identity. And yet, despite these qualifications, we must acknowledge Cather's commitment to biculturalism, a commitment enshrined in the small accentual mark in the title. Ántonia: in the very name of her novel Cather steers between the old and new worlds, between consent and descent, between the national and the trans-national.

5

One of Ours: The Progressive *Bildungsroman* and the Death of Idealism

NEBRASKA AND PROVINCIAL IDEALISM

Malcolm Cowley observed in his classic study of the 1920s 'lost generation' that the years of the First World War had caused them to 'fear boredom more than death'.[1] The 'death' here is easy enough to understand: death in the trenches. But what did Cowley mean by 'boredom'? As his study of the expatriate American writers of the 1920s makes clear, 'boredom' signifies the cultural barrenness of provincial America. It is this boredom which Hemingway and Fitzgerald grew up to fear, and in Cowley's account it is what drove them from the United States to Paris.

One of Ours depicts the 'boredom' and the 'fear' experienced by Cowley's lost generation. From the provincial mundanity of the Midwest, Cather's novel shifts to the deathly Europe of the trenches. Claude Wheeler, the protagonist, is a typical figure from the lost generation. He emerges from a background of provincial boredom; he seeks something greater; he is drawn to a code of stylised masculine heroism. He fervently desires an escape from the quotidian banality of his provincial life, and his idealistic hankering for something greater compels him into an acceptance of warfare as the vehicle for his idealism.

The novel begins with the historical sweep that Cather used in *O Pioneers!* and 'Nebraska'; the action is placed against the backdrop of the development of the state. The local colour is framed by a historical context, as the narrative surveys the growth of Midwestern civilisation. Nat Wheeler, the typical Cather pioneer and a first-generation settler, has seen the emergence of the land from nothing:

He had come to this part of Nebraska when the Indians and the buffalo were still about, remembered the grasshopper year and

the big cyclone, had watched the farms emerge one by one from
the great rolling page where once only the wind wrote its story.
He had encouraged new settlers to take up homesteads, urged
on courtships, loaned young fellows the money to marry on, seen
families grow and prosper; until he felt a little as if all this were
his own enterprise. The changes, not only those the years made,
but those the seasons made, were interesting to him. (6)

The bare stuff of Nebraska: this is the promising emptiness in
which Alexandra Bergson and Ántonia Shimerda built a life and a
community. Their counterpart in *One of Ours* is Claude Wheeler.
He shares their energy and idealism, their youthful potential. His
earnestness expresses itself as a yearning for something greater, as
a fervent desire for betterment, as an urge to escape the narrow
provincialism of Nebraska and what Lionel Trilling, reviewing *One
of Ours*, termed 'fat prosperity'.[2] The following exchange with
Ernest Havel, his doggedly earthy friend, could serve as an epigraph to the novel, catching as it does Claude's burning desire for
'something splendid': 'Well, if we've only got once to live, it seems
like there ought to be something – well, something splendid about
life, sometimes' (52). This phrase becomes Claude's signature. He is
seen later on meditating on the same theme: 'the conviction that
there was something splendid about life, if he could but find it!'
(103). And others sense this flame in Claude. His mother notices it
in his look, 'a quick blue flash, tender and a little wild, as if he had
seen a vision or glimpsed bright uncertainties' (69). He is inflamed
by a rhetoric of earnest idealism, personal commitment and
unspecified yearning (the 'bright *uncertainties*'). The novel, particularly in its early pages, is littered with expressions of Claude's
urgent and often gauche idealism.

Claude's ambitions set him apart from those who accept the limitations of their provincial culture, and for this reason critics have
read the novel as a critique of small-town tedium and a tale of
youthful revolt. Indeed, for Alfred Kazin this led to an utterly
clichéd novel: 'when she developed the theme of small-town boor-
ishness in *One of Ours* into the proverbial story of the sensitive
young man, she could only repeat herself lamely'.[3] Cather herself
encouraged such interpretations with her comment that this was a
'story of youth, struggle and defeat'.[4] But to read the novel as, quite
simply, a tale of youthful ambition and provincial insularity is to
neglect the specific historical context in which the text was

produced. For Claude's urge for splendour is a distinctively *progressive* desire. He is the progressive hero searching for a community of like-minded honourable progressives. He wants to move on, to move into a world of culture and refinement beyond the penny-counting of the humdrum agricultural world into which he has been born. Claude's progressive energy is focused in three ways. First, in his wish for education and for cultural advancement. Claude is the prospective member of the progressive middle class who is confronted with the provincial inanity of small-town America: 'Yet, as for him, he often felt that he would rather go out into the world and earn his bread among strangers than sweat under this half-responsibility for acres and crops that were not his own' (80). The yen to move beyond the parish and into the world is then focused on Claude's need for culture.

> He has no friends or instructors whom he can regard with admiration, though the need to admire is just now uppermost in his nature. He is convinced that the people who might mean something to him will always misjudge him and pass him by. He is not so much afraid of loneliness as he is of accepting cheap substitutes; of making excuses to himself for a teacher who flatters him, of waking up some morning to find himself admiring a girl merely because she is accessible. He has a dread of easy compromises, and he is terribly afraid of being fooled. (34)

The need for a community of like-minded souls; the moral fervour; the suspicion of that which is cheap; the refusal to compromise – the terms in which Claude's idealism is described are grounded in the rhetoric of American progressivism. Thus Claude's search for cultured companions is a variation on the progressive desire to create a beloved community. At the university he finds others like himself, notably his history professor. Teachers, singers, missionaries – Cather's novels feature knots of professionals who constitute embryonic progressive communities. Note the professor's passion: 'His lectures were condensed like a legal brief, but there was a kind of dry fervour in his voice, and when he occasionally interrupted his exposition with purely personal comment, it seemed valuable and important.' (37)

Second, the novel features a jeremiad against the sins of modern America; alongside the fervent, idealistic rhetoric sits a progressive jeremiad that catalogues contemporary woes. The tenor of this attack is anti-materialist and anti-consumerist. Thus Claude's need to escape from the provincial is often described as if it were an escape from the evils of consumer society. For instance, he attaches himself to the Erlich family because of their non-materialistic, cultured home life:

> They merely knew how to live, he discovered, and spent their money on themselves, instead of on machines to do the work and machines to entertain people. Machines, Claude decided, could not make pleasure, whatever else they could do. (43)

Cather's writing on these issues shades into a fuzzy indirect style which is pitched somewhere between the reported thoughts of her hero and a polemical authorial intrusion.

> The farmer raised and took to market things with an intrinsic value; wheat and corn as good as could be grown anywhere in the world, hogs and cattle that were the best of their kind. In return he got manufactured articles of poor quality; showy furniture that went to pieces, carpets and draperies that faded, clothes that made a handsome man look like a clown. Most of his money was paid out for machinery, – and that, too, went to pieces. A steam thrasher didn't last long; a horse outlived three automobiles.
>   Claude felt sure that when he was a little boy and all the neighbors were poor, they and their houses and farms had more individuality. (101)

The attack follows Cather's familiar assault on manufacturing and the standardisation of modern America. Moreover, it is a typical example of the nostalgia which was one aspect of the 'innovative nostalgia' of the progressives. The materialism of modern America is lambasted; the integrity of an earlier, purer America is held up as an ideal.

The third progressive element in Claude's life is his religious sensibility. Claude is often represented in terms of a generalised or non-specific rhetoric of faith; his idealism is the Christianised Utopianism of progressivism. His meditations emerge in a language of yearning idealism whose roots lie in the urgent desires of the American Awakenings and their impassioned pleas to create an earthly City of God. Cather is careful to delineate the idiosyncrasies of Claude's Christianity:

Though he wanted little to do with theology and theologians, Claude would have said that he was a Christian. He believed in God, and in the spirit of the four Gospels, and in the Sermon on the Mount. He used to halt and stumble at, 'Blessed are the meek,' until one day he happened to think that this verse was meant exactly for people like Mahailey; and surely she was blessed! (50)

Claude is a believer (the prose perhaps clumsily mimes an upswing in belief with its rhetorically raised exclamation mark) but he eschews theology. Claude's Christianity is carefully separated from any denominational allegiance. At one point Claude's all too Protestant idealism, a youthful fervour flavoured with the moral and quasi-religious earnestness of the progressives, is conflated with a rather Catholic interest in the idealism of the martyrs. As part of his European history course he writes an essay on Joan of Arc. Claude makes his martyrs into progressive idealists, seeing their heroism through the lens of his own desire for a cause: 'The martyrs must have found something outside themselves. Otherwise they could have made themselves comfortable with little things' (53).

In sentences such as these Cather attempted to reinstate a fervent or polemical Christianity which would transcend the contemporary, heterogeneous spread of churches. Claude's Christianity preserves an inspired but generalised spiritual power. As we shall see, this encompassing Christian progressivism was even to cover the Catholic Church in *Death Comes for the Archbishop*. The main threat to Cather's ecumenical sympathy seems to have been Protestant fundamentalism. Cather's own church, the Episcopalian church, toed a moderate line, but many American churches were caught up in the fundamentalist upsurge. That upsurge led to the partisanship that afflicted many churches – one of the main features of the break-up of progressivism was the splintering of the Protestant hegemony.[5] Through the figure of Claude Wheeler, Cather tacks her way between a benevolent and broad-minded Christian idealism, on the one hand, and a narrow fundamentalism on the other. The language of Claude's belief describes a generally progressive belief in Christ, even as it skirts adherence to one denomination or another.

One of Ours establishes the tone and tenor of Cather's response to the decline of progressivism. In its mixture of idealism and disillusion, fervour and pessimism, heightened rhetoric and flattened irony the novel establishes the ideological and stylistic heterogeneity that was to dominate Cather's major fiction of the decade. At the heart of Cather's project was the desire to resurrect or at the least continue the progressive mission. But progressivism was now cut back, curtailed, undermined by doubt if not disillusion. How, then, could Cather maintain a progressive idealism against the grain of the decay of progressivism?

We can see the problems that this caused when we read Cather's representation of the language of idealism. She attempted to replicate the naive rhetoric of progressivism and this led to the novel's extraordinarily gauche passages. We saw this gauche idealism emerging in some of the sentences I quoted earlier – in the rhetorical upswing of the sentence about Mahailey ('and surely she was blessed!'), and in Claude's jeremiad about machinery and industrialisation. One of the dilemmas posed by this novel is the question of how one can write about a naive culture without sounding naive. It is also difficult to decide *who* is naive. For in these gauche passages the inner voice of Claude and the narrating voice overlap:

> The farmer raised and took to market things with an intrinsic value; wheat and corn as good as could be grown anywhere in the world, hogs and cattle that were the best of their kind. In return he got manufactured articles of poor quality; showy furniture that went to pieces, carpets and draperies that faded, clothes that made a handsome man look like a clown. (101)

How was Cather to portray Claude's idealism while signalling her own authorial position towards the faltering ideology of progressivism? Her 'solution' in *One of Ours* was this free indirect style which blurs the relationship between Claude and the narrating voice. This discourse makes it difficult for the reader to locate the specific origin of the gauche idealism. The passion is unmistakable, but who is speaking? The recurrent problem of positioning an indirect discourse is here of pressing importance since it involves the construction of Claude's character and the narrator's intrusive voice. It is difficult to know whether the style simply enacts and reinscribes the progressive ideology (is it synonymous with, identified with, the authorial viewpoint or 'Cather'?) or whether the indirect style means that these statements are identified with Claude and thus, as it were, purely 'his' and to be read in inverted commas. We have to admit finally that the narrating voice of *One of Ours* is often pitched somewhere between Claude and Cather, between an intimate account of Claude's thoughts (with all its potential for irony and bathos) and an authorial complicity with Claude (so that his idealistic inner voice merges with the narrator's, shadowing if not echoing Cather's own idealism). The free indirect discourse, positioned as it is between narrator and character, irony and complicity, embodies Cather's divided response to progressivism's fading idealism. Cather's narrative voice is at once 'with' Claude in all his gaucherie and ironically distanced from him.

For this reason – the merging of the narrator's voice with that of the protagonist – Cather's vaunted artistic control seemed to have slipped in the composition of this novel. Edmund Wilson, in an unfavourable review of *One of Ours*, located this problem as one of characterisation, claiming that we are never sufficiently inside Claude: 'the emotions of the hero are not created: we do not experience the frustration of Claude when his wife will not return his love'.[6] The novel's ideological configuration created local disruptions in the text which were immediately sensed by the reviewers.

A second response to the problem of a naive progressive discourse was to play off different forms of idealism against one another. In so doing Cather criticised the elements of progressive idealism which she disliked while upholding a general idealism. The novel juxtaposes, through its characters and their various beliefs, the range of American idealisms at the time of the First World War. At moments, in fact, Cather's parallels and juxtapositions take on an almost geometric precision, as if she had schematically worked out a formula for evaluating the respective claims of different forms of moral fervour. Hence the time Cather devotes to Claude's marriage to Enid.

The second part of the novel's American section concerns the testing of Claude's idealism, especially during his marriage to the priggish Enid. The marriage is envisaged in Claude's language of indistinct fervency: 'Claude had seen the future as a luminous vagueness in which he and Enid would always do things together' (143). The marriage 'Would be the beginning of usefulness and content' (146). 'Everything would be all right when they were married, Claude told himself. He believed in the transforming power of marriage, as his mother believed in the miraculous effects of conversion' (176). But Claude's faith in transformation and miracles founders against his wife's austere beliefs. Her language is that of a high-minded idealism: 'It's terrible to think of all those millions that live and die in darkness' (125). She accuses him of not being 'willing to govern our lives by Christian ideals' (222). This is because Enid's ideals have become focused on one issue: Prohibition. Cather devotes much prose to descriptions of Enid's Prohibition activities, but this should not be read as simple period detail or window-dressing. Prohibition acts as an index of a particular form of provincial Christian idealism. It exemplifies insular Midwestern Christianity and stands for a pious, censorious moral fervour – the negative underside of Claude's idealism. 'Enid never questioned the rightness of her own decisions. When she made up her mind, there was no turning her' (219). She travels 'more than two thousand miles for the Prohibition cause' (209). Hers is a curious kind of bleached or emptied-out or desiccated idealism – an idealism which does not even have ardour ('she disliked ardour of any kind, even religious ardour' (210)).

Prohibitionist, prospective missionary and desexualised paragon of the fundamentalist values satirised by Harold E. Stearns and Sinclair Lewis, Enid represents another, if not the prominent form of Midwestern idealism. That idealism had come to concentrate on certain moral crusades: Prohibition; anti-evolutionism; a fervent Christian fundamentalism. In the marriage Cather contrasts a generalised progressivism (Claude's feeling that there must be 'something splendid' in life) with these localised Midwestern crusades. The contrast enables Cather to separate American progressivism into two main currents. Claude and Enid, husband and wife, stand for the dialectical impulses of American progressive idealism; they exemplify the warring drives towards, first, a generalised redemptive fervour and, second, a localised moral crusade which attempted to cleanse the United States through specific campaigns.

The contrast of husband and wife enables Cather, through the figure of Claude, to pursue an idealism which is distinguished from, if not privileged above, idealism's specific local configurations. Claude refutes Enid but commits and recommits himself to his own idealism. Other contrasts help to delineate the specific configuration of his beliefs. He is not as stuffily pious as his wife, but neither is he as resignedly cynical about faith as his friend, Ernest Havel. The following exchange between Ernest and Mrs. Wheeler is one of those conversations in the novel that is carefully coded to demonstrate the varieties of Midwestern idealism. Note how Mrs. Wheeler responds to Ernest's gloomy prognosis about the war:

'The war will be over before Washington can do anything, Mrs. Wheeler,' Ernest declared gloomily, 'England will be starved out, and France will be beaten to a standstill. The whole German army will be on the Western front now. What could this country do? How long do you suppose it takes to make an army?'

Mrs. Wheeler stopped short in her restless pacing and met his moody glance. 'I don't know anything, Ernest, but I believe the Bible. I believe that in the twinkling of an eye we shall be changed!'

Ernest looked at the floor. He respected faith. As he said, you must respect it or despise it, for there was nothing else to do. (227–8)

The apparently casual and informal tone of this passage is deceptive. What Cather is doing is to portray the spectrum of American idealism. Mrs. Wheeler is as fervent as Claude and the turns of her speech ('I believe the Bible') pinpoint again Cather's insightful equation between Christian idealism and enthusiasm for the war. Ernest and Mrs. Wheeler establish positions on the idealistic spectrum: Ernest as the disenchanted recusant; Mrs. Wheeler as the straightforward believer. As with Enid's Prohibition work, Cather is deploying further varieties of belief against which Claude's idiosyncratic energies can be gauged.

In his interlarded complexity, his overloaded and layered richness, Claude is a precursor of later Cather heroes such as Tom Outland in *The Professor's House*. These figures possess a density and width of character that seems disproportionately complex in comparison to the other figures in the novels. What happened in the creation of these characters is that Cather forsook realist tenets of composition and used her hero as a vehicle to carry the weight of cultural and political ideas. The character becomes a means to explore the cultural terrain, rather than remaining in the province of 'convincing' or 'rounded' characterisation. This is the main way in which *One of Ours* indicates the strain of its attempts to absorb and reconcile the conflicting forces that bear down on the text. Claude is a projection of the warring cultural forces of the time; he absorbs a plethora of cultural imperatives. Those critics who had experienced the war at first hand, or felt that they understood the war through 'realistic' accounts such as Dos Passos's *Three Soldiers*, could only decode Claude in terms of a prescriptive theory of truth to life. Thus Mencken's accusation that 'Its American soldiers are idealists engaged upon a crusade to put down sin.'[7] In this criticism, castigating Cather for a lack of realism and the privileging of simplistic idealism, Mencken ironically alighted upon the real theme of the book: the progressive crusade.

'He was deeply hurt, – and for some reason, youth, when it is hurt, likes to feel itself betrayed' (113). From this very Conradian sentence grows a series of hurts as Claude's youthful idealism breaks against the disappointments of adult life. The question is now whether Claude can preserve his youthful beliefs without succumbing to the cultural provincialism of the Midwest. What direction can idealism take, if it is not to collapse into the crude crusade of the Prohibitionist? Cather conflates fear of cultural torpor (American society, as seen by Claude, is similar to that portrayed in *Main Street* – a small-town environment with few opportunities for cultural enrichment) with a keen sense of the deadening effects of Christianised idealism. Gladys Farmer reflects that 'Claude would become one of those dead people that moved about the streets of Frankfort; everything that was Claude would perish, and the shell of him would come and go and eat and sleep for fifty years… She wanted him to be more successful than Bayliss *and still be Claude*' (154–5). Similarly, Ernest Havel sees Claude's marriage as a failure of principle: 'When he married Enid, Claude had been false to liberal principles, and it was only right that he should pay for his apostasy' (226).

Will it be possible for Claude to redeem himself? Can he atone for his apostasy? The war is to be the setting of Claude's idealistic journey, the apotheosis or nemesis of his sense of 'something splendid about life'.

THE WAR

The First World War came as a great shock to many Americans. The rapacity and brutality of the conflict were seen as far removed from America's enlightened culture. A *New York Sun* editorial declared that 'There is nothing reasonable in such a war…and it would be folly for the country to sacrifice itself to the frenzy of dynastic policies and the clash of ancient hatreds which is urging the Old World to destruction'.[8] But under Woodrow Wilson's leadership this superior insularity was supplanted by a vision of a solution to this war and all future conflicts: a community of nations. Historians stress Wilson's personal idealism. Daniel Smith writes:

> He was deeply moralistic in his approach, the result of being steeped in Calvinistic piety and training during his youth. Idealism usually meant for him, however, not the ignoring of practical considerations but the exalting of noble purposes and goals.[9]

Brought up in a culture of piety and committed to 'noble purposes', the President was a counterpart to Cather's fictional idealist. Arthur S. Link characterises Wilson's vision in a thoroughly Claude-like manner: 'It was a clarion call to the Old World to shake off war's stupor before European civilisation was destroyed, and many men of good will in all the Western nations were intoxicated by the President's vision of a postwar order founded upon the principles of Christian love, rather than upon the precepts of Realpolitik'.[10] These principles would lead to a world community rather than the 'ancient hatreds' now dominating Europe.

When war breaks out few of Cather's Americans have any awareness of where the conflict is happening (Claude does not know where Luxembourg is and his mother has to search the attic for a map of Europe (161)). The war is portrayed as a sudden intrusion into the American provincialism depicted in the opening 150 pages (the provincialism against which Claude has struggled and which only the educated really escape). There is a shocked response from Cather's Nebraskans, an appalled realisation that the world is not as committed to goodness as they had imagined. Claude says of the Germans that 'It's as if we invited a neighbour over here and showed him our cattle and barns, and all the time he was planning how he would come at night and club us in our beds' (170). The naivety is well observed. Historical accounts of the war stress the enormous shock felt in America at the savagery of the conflict, a shock heightened by the insular innocence of the States at the time. Simply stated, an inturned and self-scrutinising nation, deeply involved in its own projected progress towards societal goodness, was suddenly confronted with its antithesis. From the American stage to a worldwide conflict; from innocence to corruption; from redemption to purgatory.[11]

When the war comes Claude's gauche rhetoric of wishful idealism is shifted towards the conflict; he dreams of a valiant place in the defence of Paris. He superimposes the language of American progressivism on the European conflict:

> There was nothing on earth he would so gladly be as an atom in that wall of flesh and blood that rose and melted and rose again before the city which had meant so much through all the centuries – but had never meant so much before. Its name had come to have the purity of an abstract idea. In great sleepy continents, in land-locked harvest towns, in the little islands of the sea, for four days men watched that name as they might stand out at night to watch a comet, or to see a star fall. (173)

At first this might seem like authorially-sanctioned warmongering. However, we need to set this rhetoric in its cultural context. 'Purity of an abstract idea': Claude's fascination with Paris is with an idea, an abstract idea, and this phrase continues the idealism that has been associated with Claude. He simply continues earlier ways of thinking, turning his fervent need for a cause towards the conflict. The war is, quite literally, the answer to Claude's prayers. His is a Christian warrior idealism, a romance of personal and cultural redemption through conflict. 'To older men these events were subjects to think and converse about; but to boys like Claude they were life and death, predestination' (229). The conflict is for Claude an imaginary construct, a fantasy: 'His power of vision was turned inwards upon scenes and events wholly imaginary as yet' (237).

To map the ideological contours of Claude's progressive idealism we can compare his thoughts with those of a real-life idealist, the President, Woodrow Wilson. Wilson broke with American neutrality in 1917 and took his country into war. He published in that year a small book, *Why We Are At War*, which contained his messages to Congress and the Proclamation of War. This text is Wheeler-like in its urgent desire to impose a crusade upon the conflict. Wilson sought a world alliance, a league of nations, a Utopian community on a grand scale. Only within this framework, he argued, could the territorial acquisitiveness which had caused the war be eradicated. Essentially, Wilson tried to project American principles of democratic fraternalism on to world politics:

> These are American principles, American policies. We can stand for no others. And they are also the principles and policies of forward-looking men and women everywhere, of every modern

nation, of every enlightened community. They are the principles of mankind, and must prevail.[12]

'Enlightened community': the progressive communitarian ideal here becomes the basis of international relations. Wilson continually skips between 'American' and 'mankind' in his speeches. His speeches mark a break with the ideology of American exceptionalism that I discussed in Chapter 3, but only to replace exceptionalism with a hegemonic idealism in which national differences are subsumed within the American democratic Utopia:

> But the right is more precious than peace, and we shall fight for the things which we have always carried nearest to our hearts – for democracy, for the right of those who submit to authority to have a voice in their own governments, for the rights and liberties of small nations, for a universal dominion of right by such a concert of free peoples as shall bring peace and safety to all nations and make the world itself at last free.[13]

The heightened rhetoric is the most obvious point of contact between Wilson's speech and Wheeler's meditations. But there is also the elision of America and the world, the shift from the national to the international or, in Cather's terms, from the parish to the world. Reading *Why We Are At War* we understand the dynamic of the conflict for Wilson: a shift outwards from American insularity; the attempt to conflate national and international interests. We can also see why the war held such fascination for Cather. She also attempted to maintain an idealism which, as we saw in the last chapter, would encompass the new and old worlds. In Claude she created a Wilsonian idealist, an American progressive with dreams of a multicultural enlightened community.

The two sections of the book are bridged by Claude's idealism. The European war is the moral crusade that Claude had been looking for in his Nebraskan youth. Nonetheless, some of the harshest criticism of this novel turns on the perceived split in the text. In Mencken's analysis the division then prompts a further denigration: one part of the novel is better than the other:

> Willa Cather's *One of Ours* divides itself very neatly into two halves, one of which deserves to rank almost with *My Ántonia*,

and the other of which drops precipitately to the level of a serial in the *Ladies Home Journal*. It is the first half that is the good one.[14]

The attack on Cather is, as usual, couched in the familiar short-hand of cultural tokenism (the *Ladies Home Journal* standing for a whole world of feminised culture which the sympathetic Mencken sees Cather as momentarily submitting to). But the structural problem of *One of Ours* lies not so much in the division of the text, since a web of thematic continuities helps to bind the two sections together, as with the moment of transition between the two sections. Book Four, 'The Voyage of the Anchises', is the bridge from America to Europe. These pages are not reticent in their commentary on the themes of migration and cultural displacement – the Anchises was the ship on which Aeneas sailed and through this allusion Cather places Claude's journey in a tradition of wanderings. But, apart from this reference, it is hard to see the significance of the Book. Once we are beyond the references to migration and transference we realise that this chapter is about relatively little apart from the mundanities of life aboard the ship. Claude makes friends with a dissolute airman; outbreaks of pneumonia kill numerous sailors; there are descriptions of the seascape and the first sighting of France.

Closer reading, however, reveals two important issues at stake in Book Four. First, the awkwardness of this Book tells us much about Cather's difficulties in bridging the two worlds of Europe and America. This is a transitional chapter, and we are continually aware of the difficulty of that transition. At this point in her career Cather writes into the text the moments of change, the tempo changes and the bridges between worlds. Later in her career Cather would simply go ahead with the key change without worrying too much about the consequences. For this novel is broken-backed in a way that we will become familiar with. The wrenching of the text, the asymmetry, lack of balance, disjointedness, lopsidedness or fissuring result from Cather's attempt to encompass in one novel environments that are radically disjunctive. In *One of Ours* this wrenching is caused by the attempt to hold America and Europe together in one novel. The length and awkwardness of Book Four testify to the difficulties of creating a bridge between the two worlds.

The question of form, as we saw in the last chapter, is central to Cather's ideological response to her context. In the case of the wolf-story we saw how the digressive or 'framed' nature of the inset story enabled Cather to accommodate Europe and America. But as her career evolved, the polarities encompassed by her fiction became more and more extreme, and the narrative's ability to hold those polarities together became progressively strained. In *The Professor's House* and *Death Comes for the Archbishop*, as we shall see, the text is fractured or warped by the enormous pressure of the competing ideological significances that it attempts to contain. Intimately related to this problem is Cather's decision to favour, as her career developed, sparer narrative forms. She eschewed the baggy forms that dominated the beginning of her career (*The Song of the Lark, Alexandra's Bridge*) and opted for stripped and leaner fictional forms. The paradox of this is that Cather's novels simultaneously moved towards a tighter narrative shape even as they attempted to widen their cultural scope. Cather's multicultural, varied America is, then, embodied in a series of texts that are increasingly narrow even in terms of their simple word-length. There is an inverted relationship between form and content: the form is narrowed as the material that goes into the narrative is widened. In the later novels the effect of this reduced narrative style is to create abrupt fissures and disruptions in the text. Cather moves from one area of her polymorphous America to another, hardly heeding the transition between one zone and the next. But in the ampler format of *One of Ours* there is room to negotiate the movement between worlds. This leads to the extended and superfluous scenes on the ship, Book Four.

The second way in which the Book is significant is in its portrayal of masculinity. This theme is discussed more fully in the next section of my chapter.

MASCULINITY

The novel represents a revised American masculinity. Not only did Cather trespass on the masculine terrain of warfare and soldiery but she also revised or modified the heroic endeavours of wartime, softening and, as it were, feminising the war. The feminising of Claude is evident from the start, for example in his comic concern about his appearance and his name:

He was exactly the sort of looking boy he didn't want to be. He especially hated his head, – so big that he had trouble in buying

his hats, and uncompromisingly square in shape; a perfect block-
head. His name was another source of humiliation. Claude: it
was a 'chump' name, like Elmer and Roy; a hayseed name trying
to be fine. In country schools there was always a red-headed,
warty-handed, runny-nosed little boy who was called Claude.
His good physique he took for granted; smooth, muscular arms
and legs, and strong shoulders, a farmer boy might be supposed
to have. Unfortunately he had none of his father's physical
repose, and his strength often asserted itself inharmoniously. The
storms that went on in his mind sometimes made him rise, or sit
down, or lift something, more violently than there was any
apparent reason for his doing. (17)

Claude is discomfited with his own masculinity, a masculinity
which has traces of stereotypical manliness (energy, power) but is
never unabashedly manly. Claude is recurrently placed in conjunction with the feminine or even identified with the womanly. The
long and apparently superfluous chapters in the middle of the
book, when the troops sail from America to Europe, are used
mainly to demonstrate the feminised qualities of not only Claude
but also his comrades. Life on the ship is co-operative, supportive,
mutually comforting. One somehow cannot believe that a group of
conscripts would behave like a branch of the local men's group, but
Cather uses this episode to position Claude in increasingly feminised situations. Waves of illness sweep the ship and Claude
becomes a carer, a nurse. The narrative admits in a footnote that
this outbreak of influenza distorts the historical sources from which
Cather was working: 'The actual outbreak of influenza on transports carrying United States troops is here anticipated by several
months' (292). Cather anticipates the historical actualities because
in her rewritten version of the war she needs to transpose the feminised activities of nursing onto her community of men. Claude has
to be seen volunteering for war as soon as he can, but he also has to
be positioned as a carer, and this means that Cather brings forward
the date of the influenza attacks which devastated the troopships.
We see Claude sticking thermometers in mouths (295) and learning
from Doctor Trueman how to give a patient an alcohol bath (296).
However, Cather is careful to fend off hints of effeminacy. The text
rebuffs its own suggestiveness with sentences such as this: 'He
began to see that the wrist watch, which he had hitherto despised

as effeminate and had carried in his pocket, might be a very useful article' (297–8).

The feminisation of Claude and his fellow soldiers is linked to Cather's interest in the cultural ambitions of provincial Midwesterners. Her soldiers are as interested in the arts and culture of Europe as they are in fighting in Europe, and this again seems to qualify or complicate their masculinity. The troops might be fighting men, but Cather never allows warfare to become the sole index of their masculinity. Instead, there are passages describing the interests of her soldiers which frequently read far more bizarrely than Cather probably intended. Cather's troops are archaeologists, musicians and dilettantes. Thus Captain Barclay Owens:

> He was an engineer by day and an archaeologist by night. He had crates of books sent down from Paris, – everything that had been written on Caesar, in French and German; he engaged a young priest to translate them aloud to him in the evening. (369)

David Gerhardt, Claude's friend who is later blown apart in battle, studied the violin in Paris (in one unlikely scene Claude hears a record of one of Gerhardt's violin solos). He might be thinner than the other officers and less 'roughly bred' than his colleagues, but in Cather's cultured army he is admired for simply being a violinist and sticking with the training:

> He was as tall as Claude, but he weighed only a hundred and forty-six pounds, and he had not been roughly bred like most of the others. When his fellow officers learned that he was a violinist by profession, that he could have had a soft job as interpreter or as an organizer of camp entertainments, they no longer resented his reserve or his occasional superciliousness. They respected a man who could have wriggled out and didn't. (357)

It is this respect for culture that powers Cather's narrative and makes *One of Ours* such a strange war novel. Until the last chapters Cather uses the French setting as a context for her multicultural and feminised progressive idealism rather than for what we might expect, for instance details of military preparations. Only *One of Ours* could feature the following sentence during the run-up to war: 'He wished he could ever get David to talk about his profession, and wondered what he looked like on a concert platform, playing his violin' (372). In many tangential details the novel makes claims as a catalogue of cultural references rather than as a text that straightforwardly deals with *combat:* 'He withdrew as far as possible out of her path and picked up a book from the table, a volume of Heine's *Reisebilder* in German' (385).

These details feed back into the critical debate about masculinity and culture that I explored in my second chapter. I argued that critics worked out a pathology of cultural crisis to explain their own threatened masculine status within a national life supposedly dominated by scribbling women and pioneering men. *One of Ours* reflected back at readers such as Hemingway their own writerly dilemma. Thus Claude's anguished envy of Gerhardt and his violin:

He was torn between generous admiration, and bitter, bitter envy. What would it mean to be able to do anything as well as that, to have a hand capable of delicacy and precision and power? If he had been taught to do anything at all, he would not be sitting here tonight a wooden thing amongst living people. He felt that a man might have been made of him, but nobody had taken the trouble to do it; tongue-tied, foot-tied, hand-tied. If one were born into this world like a bear cub or a bull calf, one could only paw and upset things, break and destroy, all one's life. (418)

'Admiration' and 'envy', 'delicacy and precision' contrasted to the 'wooden thing': this is the bifurcated world analysed by Van Wyck Brooks and Harold E. Stearns in their commentaries on the gendered divide of America. It is here that the disquiet of Hemingway can be traced to its origin in the text. Ostensibly, Hemingway complained that a woman had had the gall to write about the war. But the resentment Hemingway felt might well have been provoked by Cather's meditations on masculinity and culture. She placed at the centre of the story a young man who, in his fervent desire for culture and for Europe, became a fictional precursor of the American expatriate writers of the 1920s. The troubling conflations of the novel, especially this conjunction of a feminised sphere of culture with the sphere of stylised combat, are closer to Hemingway's confused masculine ideology than most readers, including Hemingway himself, have been prepared to admit.

This association between Claude and the feminine continues through the book. Billeted with a French family, Claude sinks back into a replica of the domestic warmth of his life in Nebraska – he is utterly happy with the 'pots and pans' of domestic life (this identification probably annoyed Hemingway and other male readers since it confused the cultural codes within which and by means of which Claude is characterised: he is a domesticated warrior):

> It was good to lie again in a house that was cared for by women. He must have felt that even in his sleep, for when he opened his eyes he was thinking about Mahailey and breakfast and summer mornings on the farm. The early stillness was sweet, and the feeling of dry, clean linen against his body. There was a smell of lavender about his warm pillow. (350)

The 'smell of lavender' is, in the novel's own terminology, a sissy touch (on the next page Claude's name is referred to as 'sissy'). Here we encounter one of the major problematic areas in *One of Ours*. Cather has feminised her hero but she cannot allow Claude to become *too* dangerously feminine. Details of hearthside comfort and lavender-scented linen are familiar to Cather, and she places Claude within that domestic sphere, but she then faces the problem of how to distance Claude from the implications of that identification. He is allowed to have a 'sissy' name, but he cannot be allowed to become a 'sissy'.

Cather thus has to imply that her feminised, cultured heroes are not really 'sissies'. She needed to define Claude's feminised masculinity against less worthy varieties of masculinity. 'Feminised' needed to be defined in a way that did not imply 'effeminate'. Cather's solution to this problem is the figure of the German officer killed by Claude and his men when they storm a sniper's nest. From the details given it is clear that the German is an effete and effeminate figure. The officer speaks English, which places him in the group of multicultural sophisticates already seen in the novel, but his sophistication is coded critically. 'His linen and his hands were as white as if he were going to a ball' (430). He has a manicure set to keep his nails 'so pink and smooth' (431). He is surrounded by tokens of a decadent luxury, including a chain with a miniature: 'Around his neck, hung by a delicate chain, was a miniature case, and in it was a painting, – not, as Bert romantically hoped when he opened it, of a beautiful woman, but of a young man, pale as snow, with blurred forget-me-not eyes' (431). Putting a figure like this into the novel, a figure loaded with androgynous and decadent associations, enables Cather to counter the implications of Claude's cultural enthusiasm. Claude's naive response to the miniature ('It looks like a poet, or something. Probably a kid brother, killed at the beginning of the war') further distances him from this suggestively effeminate character.

THE WAR AND IDEALISM

It needs to be stressed how strong Claude's idealism is, continuing as it does to flourish even within war. It leads Claude to the extraordinary reflection that the war might be catastrophic, but it is not as bad as a world in which the values of his brother Bayliss (provincial, insular, narrowly pragmatic, the absolute negation of Claude's multicultural idealism) hold sway: 'No battlefield or shattered country he had seen was as ugly as this world would be if men like his brother Bayliss controlled it altogether' (419). The rhetoric of idealism, which we first encountered in Claude's visions of splendour on the Nebraskan prairies, erupts again, as gauchely fervent as it was before. Even the sound of artillery is for Claude a sign 'that men could still die for an idea' (419). 'Ideals were not archaic things, beautiful and impotent; they were the real sources of power among men' (420). Again we note the use of free indirect discourse in many of these passages, blurring the line between the narrating voice and the inner reflections of Claude.

The setting for this idealism is Europe. Europe, the repository of the evils of war, the place where American progressivism foundered, is in Cather's novel the vehicle for, the home of cultural idealism. The slant of Cather's progressivism, which I discussed in my opening chapter, was towards a multicultural progressivism. Often that idealism was Eurocentric. In the following passages, which occur towards the end of the novel, Claude's idealistic sense of the 'something splendid' explicitly shifts from its American context to a setting in France:

As for him, perhaps he would never go home at all. Perhaps, when this great affair was over, he would buy a little farm and stay here for the rest of his life. That was a project he liked to play with. There was no chance for the kind of life he wanted at home, where people were always buying and selling, building and pulling down. He had begun to believe that the Americans were a people of shallow emotions... Life was so short that it meant nothing at all unless it were continually reinforced by something that endured; unless the shadows of individual existence came and went against a background that held together. (406)

He knew that nothing like this would ever come again; the fields and woods would never again be laced over with this hazy enchantment. As he came up the village street in the purple evening, the smell of wood-smoke from the chimneys went to his head like a narcotic, opened the pores of his skin, and sometimes made the tears come to his eyes. Life had after all turned out well for him, and everything had a noble significance. (411)

The first passage contains the sour and disillusioned tones of the jeremiad. But Claude's idealism persists, shifted sideways onto a vision of a traditional pastoralism in France. The 'little farm' here reminds us of the Nebraskan farmland that Claude has just left. Claude's France, a pastoral and anti-materialist community proudly rooted in its cultural tradition, is a variant of the Utopia projected in *My Ántonia* and *O Pioneers!*. The second passage, a classically 'American' moment in its conflation of pastoral enchantment and mystical elevation, maps a recurrent and mythic sense of the idyllic onto specific historical contingencies. Claude's sense of splendour will have to find a European home, but even there a rushing sense of the loss of wonder threatens to engulf the Utopian moment ('nothing like this would ever come again'). Now, in the wake of the war and the reassertion of a narrow American nativism, Cather cannot maintain her idealistic vision of America. Instead, her American idealist transfers his Utopian visions onto Europe. Robert J. Nelson, writing about the second of these passages, is clearly puzzled by the erasure of 'French' features in this description. He writes: 'Claude's France is not the France of high culture, of art, of fashion; in fact, it is not the France of the French language'.[15] The answer to Nelson's puzzlement is that Cather's France is an idealised America transposed geographically to Europe. In Claude's idyllic vision an Edenic America, originally projected by Europe onto the new world, is reprojected by the wondering American onto France.

The difficulty is that Cather wants to preserve a progressive idealism which is set in the very historical context where progressive idealism had reached its nemesis. How could Cather transfer Claude's idealism onto France while acknowledging the simple historical fact about the war and American idealism, namely that the war was responsible for the splintering of that idealism? For here in France, where Cather's multicultural Utopianism finds a home, Utopiahism had died in the trenches.

The slanted gendering of Claude, Gerhardt and other soldiers removed one route to explore the disillusioning effects of the war. Making Claude kind, sympathetic and cultured, Cather makes his activities much more acceptable; and by feminising her troops she presented the war in a way that can seem conservative and uncritical. For the softening of the American troops removed a potential channel for satirical evaluation, the avenue that would explore the brutalising effects of the war and the degradation of conflict (such an exploration would probably begin with an emphasis on, if not an exaggeration of, the 'masculine' traits of brutality and violence).

Cather's solution to this difficulty – how to represent the nemesis, the catastrophe of war – was to set alongside each other two discourses: her own progressive discourse (a language of cultural advance, of an elevated Christian Utopianism); and the language of war, a language culled from the extant literature of combat. Cather does not mince words when it comes to the war. If anything, her prose is too keen on the bloodiness of the war. Within the space of a few pages there is a host of injuries. When Claude is injured he 'seemed to be bleeding from the nose and ears...he felt as if he were full of shell splinters' (398). We then see a doctor, his groin and abdomen torn open; his wound 'supported a mass of dark, coagulated blood that looked like a great cow's liver' (400). The doctor 'began to vomit blood and to strangle' (401). During a sniper attack a little girl is shot, 'blood and brains oozing out in her yellow hair' (428). A dead body is entombed in sandbags, 'the five fingers, well apart, looked like the swollen roots of some noxious weed' (447).

The gore and nastiness of these descriptions provides evidence that many of the assumptions about *One of Ours* are in fact incorrect. Strictly speaking, the war is not idealised in *One of Ours*. Cather does not idealise war, but an idealising discourse is presented closely enough to the battle scenes for this to appear to be the case. The problem here, of course, was the difficulty diagnosed by Hemingway: having no experience of the war Cather had to take her material at second-hand, and this leads to a clichéd grimness in her pages about combat. She relied on a learned or derived language. Her first readers sensed this problem. Sinclair Lewis complained: 'Except for the arousing scene on the army transport, with influenza stalking, her whole view of the war seems second-hand and – for her – second rate'. (Interestingly, Lewis picks up on the novelty of Cather's feminised scenes on board the ship.) Mencken unfavourably compared Cather's account of war with the innovative approach of Dos Passos, who in *Three Soldiers* had 'disposed of oceans of romance and blather' and forged a new style of 'bold realism'.[16] Compared to Dos Passos her accounts of war were written in a language bleached of any personal or idiosyncratic tone. Often, the detail moves towards a lurid grotesquery whose main purpose seems to be to impress us with Cather's knowledge of wartime. The gap between Cather's diligent, researched knowledge of the war and the transfer of that knowledge into convincing prose is evident in the next embarrassing passage:

> While the two officers stood there, rumbling, squirting sounds began to come from this heap, first from one body, then from another – gasses, swelling in the liquefying entrails of the dead men. They seemed to be complaining to one another; *glup, glup, glup.* (446)

This awkward language of documentary gore is a failure, but it was necessitated by Cather's desire to offset the rhetoric of idealism which, I have argued, is her main interest in the novel. It is as if, having written of the horror of war, Cather can then present the idealistic glory of war without apology. So at the end of the novel, when Claude dies in battle, the 'something splendid' of the novel's early pages re-emerges. Claude's own death is remarkably clean, as Cather distances him from the bloodiness that has dominated her writing. 'He was not bleeding very much...three clean bullet holes – one through his heart' (453). This signals the shift back to the pristine glory and splendour which Claude dreamed of in Nebraska and which now envelops his death. The ending of the novel moves back to Nebraska, where the memory of Claude continues to reverberate. 'By the banks of Lovely Creek, where it began, Claude Wheeler's story still goes on' (457). The novel has turned full circle; we are back in the fount of Claude's idealistic visions. His mother's reflections play again on the familiar theme of idealistic fervour:

> When she can see nothing that has come of it all but evil, she reads Claude's letters over again and reassures herself; for him the call was clear, the cause was glorious. Never a doubt stained his bright faith. She divines so much that he did not write. She knows what to read into those short flashes of enthusiasm; how fully he must have found his life before he could let himself go so far – he, who was so afraid of being fooled! He died believing his own country better than it is, and France better than any country can ever be. (458)

The problematic idealism of the novel is here bafflingly presented. Is this full-blooded patriotism? Susie Thomas thinks so. In a fascinating discussion of Cather's ruminations on the title (Cather thought of calling the book *Claude*), Thomas argues that we are encouraged, perhaps unintentionally, to read the novel as a celebration of soldierly solidarity: 'Claude may not have been an inspired appellation but *One of Ours* is disastrous; inviting precisely the reading she was so dismayed to receive'.[17] *Ours*: Thomas takes this as a key to the martial idealism of the latter part of the book. She implies that we are being too easily committed to an unreflecting patriotism. My own analysis suggests that this phrase denotes a progressive collectivism, a communality that has less to do with military ardour than with the Utopian bonding illustrated in Claude's earlier experiences in the university and on board the ship. The title of Book Five, drawn from Vachel Lindsay ('Bidding the Eagles of the West Fly On'), underlines the specifically Midwestern context of this idealism. For this quote comes from Lindsay's elegy on William Jennings Bryan, a poem about Midwestern Utopianism and the Nebraskan politician's crusading campaigns. Intertextually, this Book is placed in the context of Midwestern politics.[18]

Claude's story is that of an American progressive. He moves from idealism into the disillusioning violence of war. His story has an almost allegorical force, following as it does the curve of American internationalism from naive idealism through to the brutal encounter with European savagery. The representative significance of the novel was sensed by some of the reviewers. Edmund Wilson:

The publishers hint that Claude Wheeler is a symbol of the national character, and one can see that Miss Cather has aimed to make her people American types: the money-making farmer father, jocular and lacking in intelligence; the sympathetic religious mother; the son made wretched by passions which are outlawed among his neighbours and for which he can find no fit objects, which he is finally obliged to extinguish in the dubious crusade of the war. And this theme might indeed have served for a tragedy of national significance.[19]

'A tragedy of national significance': this indeed was what Cather tried to write in *One of Ours*. The unevenness of the text, the technical failures and clashing discourses, testify to Cather's difficulties in gauging the true 'national significance' of the war. Caught as she was between an endorsement of Claude's visions and a savage undercutting of his illusions, Cather's text attempted to maintain a progressive momentum against the weight of historical experience. In its qualified idealism the text echoed President Wilson's own experiences of the war. His plans for a progressive internationalism failed when the European nations reforged their old territorial *Realpolitik* at the Treaty of Versailles. Insular American progressivism could not be exported to Europe; the 'something splendid' of multicultural brotherhood vanished. Perhaps for this reason – its fictionalisation of a progressive decline and fall – Cather's novel achieved popular acclaim and the Pulitzer prize. The novel reflected back at its readership their own journey from insular idealism to disillusioned internationalism while preserving the vision, if only in memory, of splendour.

6

The Professor's House and the Incorporation of America

THE AMERICAN MUSEUM

My Ántonia and *O Pioneers!* demonstrated Cather's willingness to represent the varieties of American experience. The clearest form that this variety takes is racial and cultural heterogeneity: the cosmopolitan European peoples on the Nebraskan prairies, the varied languages of the pioneer settlements. It is tempting to read Cather as a liberal multiculturalist attuned to the American plethora, sympathetic to difference in all its forms; but we must also recognise the dangers of this diversity – incoherence, fragmentation, disunity. Cather's problem is a recurrent dilemma in American culture: how to create coherence out of diversity? In *The Professor's House* and *Death Comes for the Archbishop* Cather tried to reconcile the competing, if not centrifugal, tendencies in her culture. The next two chapters investigate the ways in which these novels attempt to incorporate or harmonise conflicting aspects of America and its past: the Pueblo's ancient culture and modern science; business and art; religious ritual and pioneer settlement. The settings of *The Professor's House* reveal a patchwork diversity: mesa settlement and university campus; the home of the title and the Smithsonian Institute; the West discovered by the explorer, Coronado, and contemporary commercial suburbia. And diversity is also present, most strikingly, in the notorious narrative shape of the novel: the text consists of a third-person narrative which frames an interpolated first-person section, 'Tom Outland's Story'. Even the narrative point-of-view is varied.

This novel poses particularly tricky problems for criticism that seeks to relate texts to contexts. Does *The Professor's House* embody, in its ruptured and divided form, a culture similarly afflicted by

124

division and fragmentation? Or does the text master or reconcile such divisions? For fragmentation is at the very heart of Cather's work during this period. She claimed that the world 'broke in two' around 1922. We then have to ask whether her fiction remains fractured, as if reflecting a broader cultural disintegration, or whether the text effects a cementing together of divergent cultural forces. During this essay I will suggest that *The Professor's House* can be read as working in both ways. 'Tom Outland's Story' marks a literal breaking of the narrative line, and creates profound discontinuities in the book; but the central character of the novel, Tom Outland, is a figure who somewhat improbably reconciles or incorporates divergent cultures. He is scientist, mystic, scholar, Pueblo-dweller and modern technologist. Depending on where we look at this complex, kaleidoscopic text, we find evidence of both divergence and reconciliation, integration and disintegration.

The endeavour to absorb incompatible cultural energies is most evident in Cather's creation of Tom Outland, her most unusual character. Outland is a remarkable and preposterous figure. Scientist and artist, 'savage' and technologist, he straddles two American worlds: the ancient cliff-dweller homes which he discovers on the Blue Mesa; and the technology of the jet engine which he designs at Professor St. Peter's university. His very name encapsulates this dualism: the 'outland' is the wilderness, the west, the primal American frontier where Outland lives for a summer; and it is the outland of the jet engine which he designs – beyond the edge of known science, outlandish. The sheer range of Outland's interests deserves note. He designs a jet engine; learns Spanish grammar and Latin poetry; explores the Blue Mesa and searches for Pueblo pottery; works on the railroads and in a university. He also represents the continuity of transcendental experience in America; he is a scientist but also a childlike conduit for those feelings of wonder which have so often coursed through the American hero:

> I remember these things, because, in a sense, that was the first night I was ever really on the mesa at all – the first night that all of me was there. This was the first time I ever saw it as a whole. It all came together in my understanding, as a series of experiments do when you begin to see where they are leading. Something had happened in me that made it possible for me to co-ordinate and simplify, and that process, going on in my mind, brought with it great happiness. It was possession. The excitement of my first

discovery was a very pale feeling compared to this one. For me the mesa was no longer an adventure, but a religious emotion. (250–51)

This language of wholeness and fulfilment, of possession and completion ('all of me', 'a whole', 'It all', 'possession') places Outland's communion with the landscape and himself in the fictional tradition of mystical, pastoral enrichment. Behind Outland's words lie the experiences of Thoreau at Walden Pond, Huck Finn on the raft, Queequeg as he gazes into the ocean. And yet Outland's reverie is markedly different from those earlier dreams. 'A series of experiments': the outside world, a world of science, is admitted through this analogy. Outland's pastoral mysticism is combined with, conjoined with, his scientific endeavours. He might, to use Leo Marx's formulation, be outside the 'machine' (that is, the mechanical, technological and industrial world of the city) but even here, immersed in memories of the 'garden' (the pastoral, Edenic wilderness), his thoughts carry traces of the pragmatic world.[1]

The character of Outland exemplifies that thickened, layered and knotted discourse I discussed in my first chapter. He is too complex for the transparencies of conventional character-analysis. Cather's conventions of character-creation were broadly realistic, to the extent that she admitted to using herself and others as touchstones, templates or prototypes for fictional characters.[2] But in creating Outland she went way beyond her own suggestions about character: if Outland *is* a conflation of real people, then he must carry with him the aspects of some half-dozen individuals, such is his polymathic diversity. Outland is better understood as an example of that layered writing which Cather shifts into when her fiction encounters the recalcitrant complexities of early twentieth-century America. For Outland is made to incorporate the centrifugally incompatible ideals of his age: pastoralism, modern science, 'savagism' and technology. It is to these strands that I now want to turn. What exactly were the cultural forces that formed a character like Outland? And why should Cather have wanted to run together so many divergent characteristics in one figure?

Early in her career as a journalist Cather visited the Carnegie Museum in Pittsburgh, writing an article about her trip for the March 1897 issue of *Home Monthly* magazine. The museum, one in a series of public endowments from the millionaire benefactor, contained a wealth of exhibits from natural history through to modern technology, and was designed to encourage self-education. 'The people', wrote an enthusiastic Cather, 'have taken hold of the museum and claimed it for their own'. She then described the exhibits and the design of the museum: prehistoric skeletons, replicas of the cliff-dweller homes which had recently been discovered in the South-west, models of the latest steamships; a series of rooms devoted to different epochs and cultures. The museum was a celebration of modern America's engineering skill and a recovery of the past through anthropology and archaeology. To enthuse about a museum, especially within the pages of the *Home Monthly*, seems rather odd – that is, until we consider how the Carnegie anticipated the intellectual sweep of Cather's novels. Her approving tone is unmistakable, even within the context of a quotidian article, and the reason for this is probably that at the Carnegie she found a symbolic counterpart to her own vision of America and its past. The chronological spread of the museum is suggestively similar to the encompassing timescales of *O Pioneers!* And the museum's representation of heterogeneous societies or cultures again foreshadows the patchwork variety of her major fiction.[3]

The museum is an example of what Alan Trachtenberg has called the 'incorporation of America'. His phrase refers to the business and administrative centralisation of the United States during the Gilded Age, but it also has a more general and almost figurative sense. 'Incorporation' applies to what Trachtenberg calls 'the processes of secularization, bureaucratization, and professionalization'; it describes the financial, administrative and social integration of America as a modern industrial society. The term could also, I suggest, be used to describe a transformation in historiographical discourse. At the end of the nineteenth century, Darwinist evolutionary theory posited new models of interconnectedness: apparently unrelated species could be linked through the evolutionary chain, and likewise human civilisations could now be thought of in terms of ancestry and connection. The Carnegie Museum, with its juxtaposition of rooms (cliff-dwellers and steamships) illustrated the new interconnectedness, showing that in spite of the diversity of the exhibits here was an incorporated vision of America beneath one roof: *e pluribus unum*. Moreover, the museum could be 'read' as a historical narrative, extending backwards in time and proleptically anticipating future technological advances. Darwinist time, as seen in the museum, had a range beyond the history of one's own culture. History was now the history of mankind, and to understand modern man and his achievements it was necessary to juxtapose contemporary exhibits against artefacts drawn from the ancient or even prehistoric world.[4]

The Professor's House addresses itself to the historical transformation wrought by Darwin's modification of time itself. If we think of the Carnegie Museum as a kind of narrative about America, we can obtain a useful frame within which to read *The Professor's House.* Both the museum and the novel allow different environments and epochs to jostle together; they are predicated on a multifarious America at once technologised and antediluvian. One of the implications of this juxtaposition was that technologised America and 'primitive' America might in some ways be linked. Outland, the engineer and archaeologist, exemplifies this linkage. His fascination with Pueblo culture is an instance of the extension of historical time before the European colonisation of America. Both Outland and his mentor, St. Peter, are intellectually fascinated by pre-Puritan America. Outland is most pleased by the *old* pottery: 'I think the very best is the old, – the cliff-dweller pottery' (118). St. Peter, himself a historian, is interested in the early history of America – his work is on the Spanish explorations of the New World. At one point the fictional historian is compared to an actual historian, the famous late nineteenth-century writer John Fiske, whose style is recommended to the Professor as 'more even and genial' (32) than St. Peter's own. The allusion to Fiske is significant. Fiske, an enthusiast for the new Darwinist historiography, called for more work on the so-called 'lower' civilisations. In his essay 'Old and New Ways of Treating History', he castigated 'the distortion caused by supercilious neglect of the lower races' and celebrated the 'vast extension of the comparative method' brought about by the anthropological interest in savagism. Another essay, 'Evolution and the Present Age', explicitly noted that evolution changed our historical perspective:

> Here we come upon one of the things which the doctrine of evolution is doing for us. It is altering our perspective; it is teaching us that the whole of recorded history is but a narrow fringe upon the stupendous canvas along which the existence of humanity stretches back; and thus it is profoundly modifying our view of man in his relations to the universe.[5]

By referring to John Fiske, Cather places Outland and St. Peter in the context of his historiography, his comparative methodology.

The Carnegie Museum showed how the new anthropological and archaeological sciences provided models of connexion and interrelatedness, models suggestively adumbrating an innovative historiography. Evolutionary sciences were not, however, always so easily absorbed in the United States. The year 1925, when Cather published *The Professor's House*, also witnessed the infamous 'monkey trial' in Tennessee. John Scopes, a biology teacher, was tried for teaching Darwin's ideas in a local school. State legislation, responsive to the upsurge in Christian fundamentalism sweeping America, had outlawed Darwin from the curriculum. Scopes was found guilty and fined, but the trial was regarded as a victory for the scientific and liberal intellectual communities because it exposed fundamentalist beliefs. The Scopes trial marked the last public performance of the Nebraskan politician and Christian evangelist, William Jennings Bryan, who failed to make the oratorical impact expected of him when he questioned Scopes for the prosecution. Bryan claimed that 'The contest between evolution and Christianity is a duel to the death'. Willa Cather, we may remember, had interviewed Bryan many years before; she was also to mention his famous 'Cross of Gold' speech, the oration which brought him great fame during the Free Silver campaigns, in a story.[6]

The Scopes trial demonstrated how disturbing Darwinist theory could be to some Americans. At the centre of the case against Scopes was the accusation that evolution destroyed the God-given hierarchy of man and animals. The prosecution displayed school textbooks illustrating the evolutionary tree from primates through to man: how, they asked, could God have allowed man to derive from a monkey? The kingdoms of man and animal were now shown to be in kinship and not in opposition. At its most simple, Darwinism posited a subversive *linkage*; it fostered a discourse of association and analogy, a form of intellectual 'incorporation'. It was this incorporation that disturbed Bryan and his fellow evangelists. Furthermore, the language of Darwinism, a 'language' seen in the design of the Carnegie Museum and the biology textbooks, was a deeply unsettling discourse. It disrupted established intellectual structures because its very premise was that life was governed by the ceaseless movement of evolution. It is not surprising that some

Americans, often progressives, themselves products of an unsettled and mobile society, warmed to the disestablishing implications of Darwin. John Dewey, commenting in 1909 on 'The Influence of Darwinism on Philosophy', noted that Darwin attacked 'the sacred oak of absolute permanency'. Darwin was 'treating the forms that had been regarded as types of fixity and perfection as originating and passing away'.[7]

Dewey's level-headed acceptance of Darwin exemplifies a certain strain in American thinking which was keen to develop his theories in a variety of intellectual disciplines. Such work provides a counterpart to Cather's Darwinist cartography in *The Professor's House*. There are striking parallels between Cather's mapping of America and that undertaken by her near contemporary, Thorstein Veblen. Veblen, the polymathic economist, political scientist and anthropologist, had, in his post-Darwinist project to understand modernity, arrived at an enmeshment of science, savagery and faith. Veblen argued that in order to understand modern civilisation we should look at its origins in primitive societies. Thus 'The Place of Science in Modern Civilisation' (1906):

> By force of the protracted selective discipline of this past phase of culture, the human nature of civilised mankind is still substantially the human nature of savage man. The ancient equipment of congenital aptitudes and propensities stands over substantially unchanged, though overlaid with barbarian traditions and conventionalities and readjusted to the exigencies of civilised life.[8]

Stadialism leaves its traces in the vocabulary of this passage: 'savage', 'barbarian' and 'civilised' are stages in the development of society; but Veblen's sense of continuity is stronger than a stadialist's would be. He is keenly aware that there might have been different stages, but emphasises a subsisting common humanity: 'the human nature of savage man'. Whereas the notion that human nature remains the same throughout the ages might seem conservative (because it presents an unchanging, static humanity), in Veblen's usage the idea has a potentially radical application (we are the same people as the savages, we share their humanity). If 'savage man' subsists in us, then it follows that Veblen is claiming a respect for the savage as the key to ourselves and our civilisation. John Fiske, in a discussion of the Washington Bureau of Ethnology, made a similar claim for the importance of the 'savage':

It is proved beyond a doubt that the institutions of civilized society are descended from institutions like those now to be observed in savage society. Savages and barbarians are simply races that have remained in phases of culture which more civilized races have outgrown; and hence one helps to explain the other.[9]

In Cather's fiction the persisting 'human nature of savage man' is frequently referred to. In *The Song of the Lark* and *The Professor's House*, characters who are superficially adjusted to what Veblen terms 'the exigencies of civilised life' discover a need to regenerate themselves in environments redolent of 'savage man'. Thea Kronborg and Tom Outland, an opera singer and an engineer (examples of professionalised modern America), rediscover themselves amongst the Pueblo settlements of the South-west. Their careers, like Cather's own, are revitalised by trips into a primordial environment (Elizabeth Sergeant recalled that Cather felt a new 'integration and tranquillity' after her trip to the South-west in 1912).[10] Tom Outland's stay on the mesa is a two-fold exploration, outwardly of the Pueblo culture and inwardly of his own elemental nature. His life on the mesa simplifies into a mystical communion with the environment; civilisation falls away and Outland becomes a creature interested only in light and warmth:

> Every morning, when the sun's rays first hit the mesa top, while the rest of the world was in shadow, I wakened with the feeling that I had found everything, instead of having lost everything. Nothing tired me. Up there alone, a close neighbour to the sun, I seemed to get the solar energy in some direct way. And at night, when I watched it drop down behind the edge of the plain below me, I used to feel that I couldn't have borne another hour of that consuming light, that I was full to the brim, and needed dark and sleep. (251–2)

It is a primitivist plenitude. He finds everything, and that everything is what the Pueblo-dweller would have had: warmth, light, sleep. Civilisation's excrescences are stripped away. Outland is then 'full to the brim'. The phrase is an odd one, unidiomatic, uncharacteristically obtrusive in Outland's well-caught American English (Cather's excellent ear for the rhythms and phrases of the vernacular was not the least of her writerly attributes). One can be 'full', but people are not said to be 'full to the brim'; and we would use such a phrase in connection with food and drink, not light. Outland, in fact, here imagines himself as if he were one of the water-carrying Pueblo vases which are strewn around the mesa. When Outland arrived at the Professor's house he carried an Indian vase (118–19). He also took a vase to the Smithsonian to be examined by unhelpful scholars. To imagine himself 'full to the brim' is thus to continue an association that has recurred throughout the novel, a coupling of Outland and the humble artefacts of Pueblo culture. But the phrase also develops that association. Outland *internalises* the ancient culture; he not only carries Pueblo pottery – he thinks with a metaphorical language derived from that culture. His language, in Veblen's words, demonstrates the persistence of 'the human nature of savage man'. The culture of the Pueblo becomes the warp and woof of Outland's thinking.

Later in the book St. Peter reflects on the formation of personality. His account of the personality's inner core, a latent childhood self that lies within the encrustations of adult experience, resembles Veblen's durable 'human nature':

The Professor knew, of course, that adolescence grafted a new creature into the original one, and that the complexion of a man's life was largely determined by how well or ill his original self and his nature as modified by sex rubbed on together.

What he had not known was that, at a given time, that first nature could return to a man, unchanged by all the pursuits and passions and experiences of his life; untouched even by the tastes and intellectual activities which have been strong enough to give him distinction among his fellows and to have made for him, as they say, a name in the world. Perhaps this reversion did not often occur, but he knew it had happened to him, and he suspected it had happened to his grandfather. He did not regret his life, but he was indifferent to it. It seemed to him like the life of another person. (266–7)

The Professor's psychic disturbance has been described by some critics as a form of Freudian regression. Leon Edel suggested that St. Peter and Outland were bound together by a shared regressiveness: 'He seeks stubbornly at least to preserve the memory of days with mother (the mesa, etc.) even as the Professor cannot leave his cubbyhole study and would not want the dressmaker's dummies removed'.[11] Edel describes emotional compulsion and obsession; but the phrases Cather uses describe the 'return' of a 'first nature', a renewed sense of self. The sense of an earlier stage returning in the present is closer to the primitivism of the post-Darwinists than it is to Freudian psychology. It also resembles the cyclical historiography favoured by Cather in O Pioneers!. Indeed, in St. Peter's plight Cather found a psychological equivalent to the historical recursions and cycles she had already written about. She then mapped this cyclical psychology onto an America of scientists and savages, professors and Pueblo-dwellers. The professor returns to an earlier self; Outland returns to an archaic terrain; modernity turns back towards primitivism. The congruity between Cather and Veblen is striking; in both writers a post-Darwinist appreciation of the primitive is given a psychological slant, becoming a means to think about 'mind' and 'character'.

But this appreciation is also a means to reflect, often caustically, on modernity. Cather and Veblen were satirists who illustrated the materialist inadequacy of contemporary America by juxtaposing their society against an idealised, earlier civilisation. Outland's primitivism is immediately evident when he meets the Professor's family. On the mesa he lives rough, reads poetry, communes with nature. Back in the world, in society, in the Professor's house, he is uneasy with manners – in fact, he is shown to be utterly unfamiliar with the customs of bourgeois domestic life, be they table manners or formal clothes or polite conversation. When Mrs. Peter invites him in for lunch, 'Outland started and looked with panic toward the door by which he had come in; but the Professor wouldn't hear of his going, and picked up his telescope to prevent his escape' (116–17). Wearing clumsy new shoes, he immediately trips up (117). The scene is played out in terms of slapstick comedy, but through these social gaffes and gags Outland's distance from the 'civilised' is intimated. The most pointed moment occurs when Outland eats potato off his knife, immediately after having 'warmed up in defence of Indian housewifery' (118) – his enthusiasm for indigenous culture exceeds his understanding of modern manners.

In The Professor's House Cather created a new genre, the primitivist comedy; but because the novel embeds its post-Darwinist exploration of American cultures within comic episodes like this one, it is easy to overlook the relevance of such terms as 'primitivism' and 'Darwinism'. When the novel is read in this way, as in J. R. Bash's thesis on Cather and 'primitivism', the approach draws on European intellectual history to locate Tom Outland as another instance of the 'noble savage'.[12] Yet to read the novel within the context of Enlightenment and Romantic thought is to neglect Cather's engagement with her American milieu. Veblen's work provides a crux for this engagement, a specific illumination of ideas abroad in early twentieth-century America, and a source of analogues for Cather's fiction. Broadly speaking, for these twentieth-century post-Darwinists the concept of evolution did not sanction the triumph of the white American over the indigenous American (as it did for the 'social Darwinists' who formulated a quasi-evolutionary theory of ineluctable racial advancement). Veblen and Cather investigated 'primitivism' for its own sake; the savage becomes an object of interest or even veneration, and in place of cultural hierarchy these writers undertake an open-ended and comparative evaluation of ancient and modern civilisations. The main result is that the ranking of 'primitive' and 'advanced' tends to be thrown into question; the primitive begins to gain in value, and the superiority of modern civilisation is then queried.

Cather in this novel is interested in the contrast between business America and scientific America. She explores this dichotomy by reference to the indigenous culture symbolised by the Pueblo mesa. Outland, the engineer-to-be, is at home on the mesa; he is repeatedly associated with Pueblo culture. He is then contrasted to other characters whose lives seem to be motivated by acquisitive rapacity: Fechtig, Louie Marsellus, St. Peter's daughter Rosamond. Many incidents in the novel delineate acquisition and greed. Consumption for its own sake is epitomised by Kathleen's decision to 'glass-knob' her bungalow. St. Peter's daughters are cantankerously at odds because of their different financial positions; and he is shocked by the encroaching commercialism of academic life, trying to resist the young professors who are 'farming the whole institution out to athletics' (58). At home or at work, St. Peter casts a jaundiced eye on the inadequacies of consumer society. This widespread greed is contrasted to disinterested intellectual endeavour, as seen in the research of Outland and St. Peter. Thus, Outland's discovery of the relics exemplifies a disinterested fascination with the Pueblo past, whereas Fechtig's theft of those relics is an act of cynical commercialism. Through these similitudes and contrasts, these geometric parallels and oppositions, Cather develops an allegiance between the modern scientist and the Pueblo Indian, and she then suggests an antithesis between these figures and the modern businessman.

When we turn to Thorstein Veblen we discover a remarkably similar jeremiad on 'conspicuous consumption' and, furthermore, a constellation of characters which Cather also deployed: disinterested scientist, peaceable Indian, greedy businessman. Veblen's classic critique of consumer society, *The Theory of the Leisure Class* (1899), opposed a stale and vacuously avaricious modernity to the creative and spiritually wealthy organic communities of the 'savage'. Veblen outlined the characteristics of the latter: 'These traits are truthfulness, peaceableness, good-will, and a non-emulative, non-invidious interest in men and things.'The modern leisure class, in contrast, is notable for its 'conspicuous waste' and 'conspicuous consumption' (phrases that nicely sum up the activities of several characters in *The Professor's House*).[13] In his 1906 essay, 'The Place of Science in Modern Civilisation', Veblen exempted one aspect of modernity from his strictures: scientific enquiry. The integrity of scientific enquiry rested in a disinterest compared by Veblen, in a highly revealing phrase, to that of the 'Pueblo mythmaker'. The scientist and the Indian share an 'idle curiosity' that distinguishes their creativity from more utilitarian intellectual endeavour. Only through 'habituation' to modern society, and to its technological aims, does the scientist's work become useful:

> The reason why scientific theories can be turned to account for these practical ends is not that these ends are included in the scope of scientific inquiry. These useful purposes lie outside the scientist's interest. It is not that he aims, or can aim, at technological improvements. His inquiry is as 'idle' as that of the Pueblo myth-maker. But the canons of validity under whose guidance he works are those imposed by the modern technology, through habituation to its requirements; and therefore his results are available for the technological purpose.[14]

The mention of the 'Pueblo myth-maker' here is not an isolated instance of the coupling of 'savage' and 'modern', 'primitive' and 'technological' in Veblen's work. Darwinist social theory, with its suggestive continuities across eras and civilisations, offered him the means to establish a variety of parallels, analogies and conjunctions. Veblen uses the notion of 'instinct' to propose a human continuum. Since, he argues, certain instincts persist beneath the shifts of societal and human evolution, then archetypal modern figures (for example, a scientist) can be understood in terms of their latent instincts. The technologist is revealed, as it were, to be a 'Pueblo myth-maker' in disguise. In *The Instinct of Workmanship and the State of the Industrial Arts* (1914) he suggested that there are subsisting, latent human motivations which manifest themselves in different ways as civilisation develops: 'Nothing falls within the human scheme of things desirable to be done except what answers to those native proclivities of man'. Veblen identifies two 'instinctive dispositions': 'the parental bent' and the 'sense of workmanship'. The latter is 'one of the integral hereditary traits of mankind'. He defines workmanship in operation in early herding societies, but then goes on to make comparisons with technological society:

> Here as ever the instinct of workmanship was present with its prompting to make the most of what comes to hand; and the technology of husbandry, like the technology of any other industrial enterprise, has been the outcome of men's abiding penchant for making things useful.[15]

Note the deliberate crossing of categories here: animal husbandry suddenly becomes a 'technology', enabling Veblen to erase the troubling opposition between pastoral and machine societies.

Through the identification of this schema we can see how Cather deploys representative figures, character types who were already present in American intellectual culture. Working closely in time, Veblen and Cather thought about a nexus of themes and characters (primitivism and technology; the scientist, the savage and the businessman) and created fables of America that bear comparison. Veblen outlines a Pueblo Indian community anthropologically and Cather fictionalises it; Veblen attempts to yoke modern science and primitive culture together, and Cather searches for a similar incorporation. Moreover, Cather shares with Veblen a desire to redeem science by squaring it with pastoralism; and for both writers the means to achieve this was through an 'archaeology' of technology which allowed its honourable roots in early society to become clear.

The labyrinthine contortions of Veblen's argument show how difficult it was to achieve this incorporation. In Cather's novel the idealistic yearning for a reconciliation of science and pastoralism results in similarly complex argumentative patterns – patterns which are often against the grain of what the novel is *overtly* or *explicitly* saying. Outland is the symbolic incorporation of cultural tendencies which are described elsewhere in the novel as irreconcilable. Contrast Outland's scientific curiosity with the ideas outlined in the lecture which we overhear St. Peter giving:

> I don't myself think much of science as a phase of human development. It has given us a lot of ingenious toys; they take our attention away from the real problems, of course, and since the problems are insoluble, I suppose we ought to be grateful for distraction. (67–8)

Polemically dismissive, the crystallised and epigrammatic certitudes of St. Peter provide one of the novel's voices in the debate about science. It is tempting to read this passage as the 'authorial' voice, or as a narrative voice that is close to Cather. These sentences are, after all, set within the classroom, and this encourages us to take St. Peter's comment as an authorised statement about America's scientific endeavours. But we have to set these comments against the condensed, ambiguous and layered writing which Cather employs in 'Tom Outland's Story'. Here, St. Peter's certainties are replaced by complexity and thickening of the prose. It is here we find details such as the punning on Outland's name. Here, also, we find St. Peter's colleague Dr. Crane. Crane is the only academic with whom St. Peter has a friendly relationship. He is a physicist, a scientist who works on the 'limitations of space' (87). Outland, too, worked on a form of space. He 'discovered the principle of the Outland vacuum, worked out the construction of the Outland engine that is revolutionizing aviation' (41). We could dismiss this strange reverberation in the novel, this recurring interest in space, in emptiness and in conquering space which preoccupies the scientists; but their experimentation does constitute one of the text's 'narrative secrets', necessitating in Frank Kermode's words an 'abnormally attentive scrutiny'.[16] What is the scientific investigation of space doing in this novel? There is, surely, no accident in the coincidence in this novel of so many different kinds of space. First, Cather establishes a leitmotif about domesticity and space through the proliferation of houses in the novel: the Professor's house; the new family home; Marsellus's Norwegian house; the cabin shared by Outland and his friends on the mesa. The scientists' interest in space thus continues, in an oblique fashion, the novel's fascination with different forms of space. But their interest also couples the laboratory and the mesa, the university and the frontier. Both places, Cather implies, are devoted to the exploration and management of space. What is suggested by this verbal echoing is a congruity between the laboratory and the wilderness, the scientist and the frontiersman. Outland's vacuum is counterpointed against the 'vacuum' of the West, another empty space with enormous commercial potential. Outland and Crane pursue their research, but their science echoes and continues the basic work of Americans on the frontier.

The exploration and development of the wilderness was, in essence, the management of space. The historian Richard Slotkin, in examining the myth of the frontier, came to a conclusion that is of great relevance to *The Professor's House*. He argued that the myth of a virgin land was a necessary myth because it justified capitalist expansion:

> Behind the mystique of the 'virgin land' lay the principle of the 'resource Frontier': the economic doctrine which holds that the Frontier is the discovery and conquest of new lodes of valuable resources – precious metals, industrial ores, supplies of cheap labor, 'virgin' markets among the masses of Asia or Europe.[17]

Slotkin describes a mythic discourse which replaces and displaces history. The actual frontier has vanished; a mythic frontier provides a means to project a limitless capitalist expansion. *The Professor's House* works in a similar way. A mythic register, a frontier myth of space, becomes the means to unite apparently irreconcilable aspects of America. In so doing, a Utopian America is projected, an America where the savage and the scientist are as one in their shared spatial explorations. It is to the Utopianism of the novel that I now want to turn.

PRIMITIVE UTOPIAS

In *The Instinct of Workmanship and the State of the Industrial Arts* Thorstein Veblen condemned the earlier primitivist theories of writers such as Thomas Hobbes:

> It will have been noticed that through all this argument runs the presumption that the culture which included the beginnings and early growth of tillage and cattle-breeding was substantially a

peaceable culture. This presumption is somewhat at variance with the traditional view, particularly with the position taken as a matter of course by earlier students of ethnology in the nineteenth century. Still it is probably not subject to very serious question today. As the evidence has accumulated it has grown increasingly manifest that the ancient assumption of a primitive state of nature after the school of Hobbes cannot be accepted.[18]

Veblen, a self-conscious radical if ever there was one, was keen to distance himself from 'the traditional view' – here an ethnology which regarded 'savage' early societies as just that : nasty, brutish, and short-lived. Veblen's agrarian, peaceful early society refutes the Hobbesian primitivism implicit in stadialist models, where mankind 'advances' from a 'barbarian' way of life. Veblen's savage Utopia strikingly anticipates Cather's Indian culture. While he imagines 'tillage and cattle-breeding' she describes landscapes strewn with shards of pottery (another peaceably un-Hobbesian art). Furthermore, the ideological use which Veblen puts his Pueblo Utopia to sheds light on the political configurations of Cather's imagined mesa community. Veblen used Pueblo culture as a mirror in which to reflect his modern political agenda; the rejection of Hobbesian primitivism is part of an ideological manoeuvre to present a progressive image of human potential. Human nature, Veblen says, is in its original state peaceful and egalitarian. There are continuities between the 'savage' mind and ourselves, he argues, and thus the Pueblo ideal can be reconstructed today. Veblen's argument thus becomes a form of progressive primitivism where the progressive hope for a cleansed society, an American good community, is projected through the new disciplines of archaeology and anthropology.

There are striking passages in Veblen's work where he seems to deploy idealised images of American democracy, refracting them through the lens of anthropology. Thus Veblen's Darwinist narrative encourages him to think back to the origins of society, but his search for an origin uncovers a society strongly reminiscent of a more recent American community: the Jeffersonian agrarian community pacifically at one with the virgin soil. Savage society therefore becomes American democracy *in utero*:

This savage mode of life, which was, and is, in a sense, native to man, would be characterised by a considerable group solidarity within a relatively small group, living very near the soil, and unremittingly dependent for their daily life on the workmanlike efficiency of all the members of the group.[19]

This is the organic, agrarian community beloved of American pastoral idealists from Jefferson through to the Fugitives. Yet, intriguingly, Veblen's agrarianism also embraces technology: the 'workmanlike efficiency' of the savage suggests technological discipline, making his primitives into early exemplars of modern America's business-like, industrial proficiency. This society holds together agrarianism and business.

The progressive Utopia of Veblen – at once archaic and forward-looking, innovative and nostalgic – provides a key to understand the central section of *The Professor's House*, where Tom Outland discovers on the Blue Mesa an earthly heaven which is also an incorporation of the 'savage mode' and modernity, of agrarian life and 'workmanlike efficiency'. 'Tom Outland's Story' imagines a wilderness Utopia. Here, Cather has created one of her most complex and fully-realised pictures of an idealised American settlement. The miniature community created by Outland and Rodney Blake is notable for the sheer amount of prose that is devoted to explaining its quotidian routines. Cather expansively and lovingly delineates an American communitas to place alongside Ántonia's homestead or Alexandra's farm. Three features of Outland's settlement are particularly important: communal collectivism; the merging of nature and man-made space; the drawing together of different historical epochs. First, the lives of the men are structured by co-operation and mutuality. Outland and Blake establish a reciprocal pattern of cattle-management: 'Rodney and I could take turn about, one camping near the cattle and one sleeping in a bed' (190). The foreman is interested in Outland's project and sells him horses cheaply as a favour (206). Bill Hook, the liveryman, also gives assistance (211). To begin with, all is co-operation and trust. As if to indicate how perfect their community is, there is an intriguing allusion to contemporary political problems: 'Blake brooded on the injustices of his time', including the hanging of the Chicago anarchists and the Dreyfus case (187) (these details set the action in the late 1890s). Second, the environment, the space in which they live, is one in which the demarcations between man and nature, home and wilderness, are utterly eradicated. The cabin shared by Blake and Outland is so integrated into the surrounding landscape that there is no clear border between house and nature: 'The gamma grass grew right up to the door-step, and the rabbits were running about and the grasshoppers hitting the door when we pulled up and looked at the place' (189). The mesa erases territorial demarcations – internal and external spaces fuse. Distinctions collapse: 'There was no litter around, it was as clean as a prairie-dog's house' (189). They live in a space that is both nature and civilisation; the barriers, divisions and hierarchies of normal societal organisation have now fallen away. Third, the mesa, in its amalgamation of primitive and modern, its incorporation of the Pueblo and scientific America, its straddling of eras, is another instance of Cather's remarkable ability to fold into one another different historical periods.

The fascination of 'Tom Outland's Story' does not stop here. For 'Tom Outland's Story' is also an enigmatic narrative which crosses over from Utopia to dystopia. Outland lives for a while in an idyllic community, just as the Pueblo Indians had done in their own world; but greed and aggression destroy both communities. Outland finds fragments of Pueblo pottery; but when he reports his discovery to the Smithsonian Institute, he is cold-shouldered by the frosty patriarchs in charge. After the exhilarating fusions of the mesa, a place without barriers, Outland now discovers fences, barriers and divisions. Excluded from the offices of the academic experts, Outland 'used to walk for hours around the fence that shuts in the White House grounds' (233). Back at the mesa, greed erupts. Outland's archaeological finds are appropriated by the rapacious German merchant, Fechtig. One of the relics, the mummified corpse named Mother Eve by Outland and his friends, never leaves the mesa because the mule on which she is being carried falls into a canyon (244–5).[20] In earlier chapters I discussed the pull-and-push of Cather's fiction as it moved between Utopianism and idealism, at one pole, and disillusion and dystopia at the other. In *The Professor's House* this polarisation is exacerbated. The heightened experiences of Outland on the mesa sit alongside moments of great darkness, savagery and greed. Perhaps the most horrific incident in 'Tom Outland's Story' concerns the female corpse, Mother Eve. Outland discovers the remains of a community which is essentially Veblen's enclosed and harmonious primitive culture; but then he finds a mummified body – 'not a skeleton, but a dried human body, a woman':

She was lying on a yucca mat, partly covered with rags, and she had dried into a mummy in that water-drinking air. We thought she had been murdered; there was a great wound in her side, the ribs stuck out through the dried flesh. Her mouth was open as if she were screaming, and her face, through all those years, had kept a look of terrible agony. (214)

Father Duchene, Outland's mentor at this stage, believes that Eve, as they suggestively name the corpse, was murdered for some sexual impropriety: 'In primitive society the husband is allowed to punish an unfaithful wife with death' (223).

At this moment Outland's idealising speculation about the Pueblo community is abruptly checked, and the image of this ancient culture becomes suddenly ambiguous. Can we reconcile this culture of pottery with the agonies inflicted upon one of its members? The Mother Eve incident is certainly a sardonic rebuff to those who would naively project their own societal ideals onto communities separated from us by centuries. Veblen was one such idealist. He wrote that the mesa habitat would not have been liable to 'notable differential advantages' or 'segregation of the population within the pueblo'.[21] But this must be an instance of Veblen's wishful thinking. Veblen's primitivism is itself, a myth; his Pueblo communities are idealised projections from a factual basis of archaeological and geological research. He rejects 'the school of Hobbes' for its characterisation of a brutal primitivism, but his peaceful savage is just as much a fiction. Cather's Utopia is undermined by the realisation that segregation and advantage were as likely in ancient societies as in modern communities. Eve is found 'in a little group of houses stuck up in a high arch we called the Eagle's Nest' (214). That is, she is on the fringes of the settlement. As a transgressor she has to be relegated to the community's margin. This detail, alongside the description of Eve's wound, indicates that Cather is making a very precise point about the social organisation of the Pueblo. The anthropological specificity of this account adds up to an oblique but nonetheless powerful reminder that to construct unduly peaceable images of early society is as much a distortion as to follow the Hobbesian model. There is no reason to suspect that the Pueblo would have been any less prone to jealousy, vengeance and aggression than other societies.[22]

It is intriguing that this key moment should turn on an issue of gender and, more specifically, on violent conflict between men and women. The story of cruelty towards Eve could hardly be more suggestive! One way to think about Mother Eve is as a commentary on images of primitive communities as essentially *feminised* cultures. In Veblen's writing the goodly community is usually a feminised idyll. He described the Pueblo Indians as a peaceful, domestic and agrarian civilisation. He pictures 'such sedentary agricultural communities as the Pueblo Indians' in 'that state of peaceable, non-coercive social organisation, in which they were found on their first contact with civilised men, with maternal descent and mother-goddesses, and without much property rights, accumulated wealth or pecuniary distinction of classes'.[23] In several ways Cather at first continues the association of the Pueblo with a feminised culture. This is evident in her coupling of the mesa with the feminine art of pottery. It is the discovery of irrigation channels and shards of pottery which encourages Outland to explore the mesa, and he returns to the city bearing Indian earthenware. Pottery has often been regarded as an expression of female creativity. Adrienne Rich cites the work of the anthropologists Robert Briffault and Erich Neumann 'to show that the deeply reverenced art of pottery-making was invented by women, was taboo to men, was regarded as a sacred process'.[24] And within the Veblen-esque scheme of the novel we can see pottery as one of the sedentary and peaceable arts of his feminised communities. It is this world which is rudely disrupted by the attack on Mother Eve, as the culture of pottery is undercut by sexual jealousy and retribution. One might also note that the feminine art of pottery is associated with the male protagonist, Outland. When Outland meets St. Peter, for instance, he carries a water jug within his telescope case. He takes Pueblo pottery to Washington for scholarly examination. This linkage creates a cross-current, a complication, a tension in the gendering of both Outland and the primitive world he encounters on the mesa. In Veblen's analysis, on the other hand, issues of gender are both prominent and remarkably unproblematic. Primitivism is linked to matriarchy, and Veblen eschews further analysis.

Again we might note that Outland seems to move within fundamentally different or even opposed cultures, as if he could bring them together or, in Trachtenberg's phrase, 'incorporate' them. Outland is insistently identified with the peaceable feminine art of pottery; but his basic mission of exploration of the mesa might seem a bluntly masculine exercise. 'Tom Outland's Story' is a tale of adventure and discovery, an exploration narrative which might remind us of other classic American wilderness tales. When Cather's hero travels to the mesa he enters a familiar manly environment. Sharon O'Brien writes that 'at first it seems we are in the classic masculine wilderness of the American novel'. Nina Baym, in a key essay on fictions of the wilderness, coined the term, 'melodramas of beset manhood'.[25] Baym meant by this phrase the classic American texts which pit a beleaguered male hero against an untamed wilderness. The hero, seen in the work of Fenimore Cooper, Twain and Hemingway, stands outside a society which is often represented as claustrophobic, repressive and feminine. Isolation and survival are the essence of his existence. The community of the frontier, where it exists, is built on the male pair: Ishmael and Queequeg, Natty Bumppo and Chingachgook, Huck and Jim. Westward expansion and the settlement of the wilderness were, in historical actuality, achieved by families. As Stephen Fender pithily noted, 'The more children you had, the more land you could clear for eventual farming, and the more firmly you established yourself'.[26] But American fiction separated the women from the men, pushing the men into an excitingly heroic confrontation with the frontier while the women stayed at home in civilised domesticity.

'Tom Outland's Story' conforms on first reading to the masculine wilderness myth. It almost seems to be a pastiche of that myth, such is the precision of Cather's usage of motifs like wilderness, male bonding, wondering communion with nature. Outland and his friend Blake live, after all, beyond female company. As if to underline the men's isolation from women and families, the two books which they have on the mesa are *Robinson Crusoe* and *Gulliver's Travels*, books about leaving home, about leaving the feminised world of society for masculine adventures in distant worlds (188). And not only does Cather follow the patterns of a locally *American* mythography: she also deploys the motifs of the masculine wilderness as they have been understood by anthropologists. Peter Schwenger has identified a four-part rite of passage:

> First, the boy is removed from society and taken into the wilderness. Second, he receives instruction on the lore and myths of the tribe. Third, he passes through an ordeal: he may undergo a simulated death; or endure pain, as in circumcision; or hunt and kill a dangerous animal. Fourth, the initiate returns to society and is welcomed as a man.[27]

The four-part structure of the masculine journey into the wilderness provides the paradigm of 'Tom Outland's Story': removal from society; education in pioneering and backwoodsmanship; ordeals (crossing rivers, hunting); the final return to society. However, these elements are significantly modified so that 'Tom Outland's Story' becomes an adjusted wilderness myth whose central character is something less than a beset hero. Outland, as we have seen, takes pleasure in pottery, a craft that is traditionally bracketed as feminine. The men do hunt, but they are compromised and conscience-ridden hunters: they refuse to shoot mountain sheep because of the animal's nobility and instead shoot a wild cow whenever they need fresh meat (214). And whereas the classic American hero is isolated on the margins of society, an escapee from the pressures of home and community, Outland is a markedly domestic, collectivist hero. 'It was the sort of place a man would like to stay in forever', Outland says about the cabin he shares with Rodney Blake by the Cruzados river (189). Outland's domestic, co-operative routines are lovingly and extensively described: 'I helped Rapp open the wooden shutters and sweep out the cabin. We put clean blankets on the bunks, and stowed away bacon and coffee and canned stuff on the shelves behind the cook-stove' (189–90); 'Rodney and I could take turn about, one camping near the cattle and one sleeping in a bed' (190).

What Cather does to the classic masculine wilderness myth is to *feminise* it. Veblen had used primitivism in *The Theory of the Leisure Class* to attack modern society; and Cather works in a similar but more roundabout manner, using the Pueblo's culture to query and then revise the masculine narratives of American literature. In fact, her questioning is at its acutest when she is dealing with subject matter that can broadly be encompassed by the term 'gender'. It is as if Cather's imagination was given an unusual torque by this sensitivity. The masculinist wilderness myth is feminised; the feminised community collapses into violence and segregation. But this torque, generating as it does skewed or revisionist readings of America, also disturbs the structure of the novel. The turns of logic and representation are fascinating, setting up powerful cross-currents in the novel; but they also threaten to disrupt the novel's homogeneity. To use the phrase that I introduced earlier in the chapter – they are difficult to 'incorporate'. This difficulty leads to the idiosyncratic structure of the novel, the distinctively broken shape of *The Professor's House*. In particular, it leads to the dislocation of the text by the intrusion of 'Tom Outland's Story'. In the next section I consider this question of form and incorporation.

THE STRUCTURE OF *THE PROFESSOR'S HOUSE*

We have seen how *The Professor's House* attempts to enmesh radically disjunctive cultural forces such as technology and pastoralism. When we move to the narrative structure of the novel we can see how problematic the *embodiment* of these ideals was. The logical strain, already present in Veblen's prose, leads to the warping and fissuring of Cather's text.

'Tom Outland's Story', the inserted tale at the centre of *The Professor's House*, violently disrupts the geographical and chronological unity of the text, giving the book its distinctively broken-backed shape. 'Tom Outland's Story' had its origin in a piece called 'The Blue Mesa' which Cather worked on in 1916. *The Professor's House* thus incorporates passages that were composed at different times, but Cather made no attempt to harmonise the disjointed narrative that resulted.[28] The novel shifts in terms of geography, time and narrative point of view: we move from Professor St. Peter's cramped household to the open spaces of the mesa; we travel back to an earlier stage in Tom Outland's life and to a previous epoch in America's history, as represented by the archaeological relics that litter the landscape. Whereas the rest of the novel is a third-person narrative, in 'Tom Outland's Story' we are given a first-person account which could almost be a diary or memoir, or even, given its informal spoken quality, a written transcription of an oral tale (making Outland into a cousin of Conrad's Marlow – the teller of a tale whose story is embedded in a fractured modernist narrative). St. Peter, we know, has a copy of Outland's diary, leaving the reader with the unconfirmed suspicion that Book II is in fact part of that document; but the novel steadfastly refuses to tell us with certitude the provenance of Outland's story.

Critical discussion has sought to overcome the problems posed by the multiform text. The critic seeks to make all of the narrative cohere. Leon Edel, for instance, contends that Tom Outland and Professor St. Peter are afflicted by parallel forms of regression: Outland's attachment to the Blue Mesa, where he spends an idyllic summer beyond societal responsibilities, is infantilely regressive; likewise, St. Peter's loyalty to his study is an evasion of adult, familial responsibilities.[29] Edel's alignment of one strand of narrative with another imposes coherence on the text, but in so doing the structural oddity of *The Professor's House* is overlooked. For the interpolation of 'Tom Outland's Story' is so striking in itself that it deserves attention as a meditated experiment in form: what did Cather aim to achieve by admitting such disjointedness into her novel and why did she structure the book around this startling juxtaposition?

Cather's own analogy for the effect of 'Tom Outland's Story' was drawn from art. She compared the effect of 'Tom Outland's Story' to the impression given by the window view in Dutch interior paintings. There is, she wrote, a glimpse from a cramped room into the liberating world outside:

> In many of them the scene presented was a living-room warmly furnished, or a kitchen full of food and coppers. But in most of the interiors, whether drawing-room or kitchen, there was a square window, open, through which one saw the masts of ships, or a stretch of grey sea. The feeling of the sea that one got through those square windows was remarkable, and gave me a sense of the fleets of Dutch ships that ply quietly in all the waters of the globe...[30]

These sentences seem to me more useful as art criticism or as testimony to Cather's cultural knowledge than as a gloss on the narrative construction of *The Professor's House*. Discussing an American novel, Cather swerves into a commentary on Europe and painting. There is something touching about her employment of an analogy from painting, almost as if she were gauchely demonstrating the range of her knowledge outside literature. Her comparison certainly conveys the painterly contrast between the worlds of St. Peter's study and Outland's mesa, but Cather's explanation also underplays the force of that contrast. In the Dutch paintings there is a shift in perspective, but the living-room and the sea finally remain part of the same world. The passage underlines this by referring to the 'fleets of *Dutch* ships' – the interior and exterior views are indissolubly linked as aspects of the same civilisation; the views of interior and exterior Dutch scenes complement one another. But in *The Professor's House* we are given far more violent contrasts; the shift in perspective is used to juxtapose conflicting orders of American civilisation. The wrenching of the narrative results from the enormous disjunctions between the various 'Americas' which Cather has let in to her narrative.

Cather, in her attempts to 'incorporate' America, constructed a novel whose fault-lines followed the rifts in her culture. I discussed earlier the ways in which Cather, working in a Veblen-esque way, created parables of America to conflate and amalgamate different cultural forces. But the radical split in the novel testifies to the difficulties in achieving that incorporation. The novel *formally* remains unincorporated. And the reasons for this formal disintegration can be found in the whirling, centrifugal historical forces which make *The Professor's House* – and then break it.

Here we can turn again to Leo Marx's analysis of the machine in the garden. Marx delineated a typical journey which the hero of classic American fiction makes in order to encompass the polarities of his culture: the hero leaves the city (the machine) and enjoys an idyllic, mystical, pastoral interlude (the garden), but then he has to return to the urban world. This, in essence, is Outland's journey and that journey provides the basic structure of *The Professor's House*: 'Tom Outland's Story' is the pastoral interlude, flanked on each side by episodes describing the worlds of the city and technology.[31] But the violence of the shifts between 'Tom Outland's Story' and the other Books – geographical, temporal and narratorial shifts – indicate the acuteness of the fissures in 1920s America. The novel thus comes to demonstrate the Marx thesis about the machine and the garden, but it demonstates that thesis *in extremis*. Leo Marx argued that the structures of American fiction embody the cultural tensions of the United States, and he implied that fiction could accommodate and absorb those divisive, disparate energies. Marx's model represents the myth and symbol school of American literary studies at its most elegant and also its most fallible. He accounts for the cultural dynamic of American civilisation, but he also irons out the *historical* clashes between pastoralism and technology. The idea of 'the machine in the garden' transcends history by positing a literary realm in which conflicting historical pressures are resolved in the aesthetic balance of opposites. Marx's New Critical reading contains the pressures which, in *The Professor's House*, tear the text apart.

Repeated close reading of her novels shows that Cather could not seamlessly absorb the jostling complexities of progressivism into her fiction. As early as *My Ántonia* it was evident that issues such as Americanisation brought with them bristling difficulties that disrupted and fissured the narrative. Cather's texts do not simply 'mirror' the ambiguities in her political, social and cultural context; the novels encode them, and encode as well Cather's own mixed reaction to her culture. What happens to Cather's novels illustrates what happens to a writer who chooses *not* to reinscribe the dominant ideology. Having rejected a hegemonic ideology (Bercovitch's 'American ideology'), Cather then found herself amidst a multi-layered, proliferating series of ideal 'Americas' (a primitivist America, a Catholic America, an Old World America). But there remained the desire to impose some sense of order – to say what her nation was. Hence the need to reconcile and incorporate competing or even opposed national cultures (the scientific or technological with the primitive or religious). The push-and-pull between a dispersed series of ideals and an incorporating, unifying discourse is present throughout Cather's career, but the tendency towards dispersal becomes more prominent at the end of the 1920s. In *My Ántonia* the tensions were tangentially present. In *The Professor's House* the structure of the novel is dominated by those tensions. In *Death Comes for the Archbishop*, as we shall see in the next chapter, Cather wrestled again with the legacy of progressivism, seeking another formalistic answer to its paradoxes.

7

Death Comes for the Archbishop: the Ideology of Cather's Catholic Progressivism

HISTORY AND COMMON SENSE

Death Comes for the Archbishop (1927), Cather's fiction about the Catholic mission in the Hispanic South-west, is a historical novel, but one that approaches its subject in an elusive, teasing manner. The story begins in the aftermath of the Mexican War (1846–8), victory in which enabled the United States to annex California and New Mexico, an area that had constituted half of Mexico's territory. The conflict cost 13 000 American lives and nearly 100 million dollars. It epitomised the nascent imperialism encouraged by the doctrine of 'Manifest Destiny', presaging future wars in the decaying colonies of the old Spanish Empire. Mexico also focused the burgeoning debate over slavery, as politicians argued over whether or not the new territories should become 'Free Soil' or slave states. Emerson, conscious of this sectionalism (the beginning of the conflict that led to the Civil War), remarked with uncharacteristic pessimism that the United States would conquer Mexico, 'but it will be as the man who swallows the arsenic, which brings him down'. 'Mexico will poison us.'[1]

Melodramatic details of political and military history are, however, largely absent from Cather's eirenic novel. Although historical figures who featured in the war and its aftermath appear in the book, either under their own names (Kit Carson) or fictionalised under another (Father Latour represents Lamy, the first Archbishop of New Mexico), Cather eschews the dramatic foreground of history. Her novel portrays the hinterland of history; it covers the quotidian background, the everyday ministrations of Fathers

150

Latour and Vaillant as they reform and strengthen their Church. The priests, in fact, see themselves as men on the fringes of history: 'As Father Vaillant remarked, at Rome they did not seem to realize that it was no easy matter for two missionaries on horseback to keep up with the march of history' (199). With characteristic Cather-esque deflation Latour's next ride to an important clerical conference is cut short by illness; he returns to his garden in Santa Fe, turned back again from the 'march of history'. When major historical incidents are mentioned, for instance the infamous Bent massacre or the expulsion of the Navajo from their lands, Cather's prose is laconically subdued. Her plain style is notable in a passage where the Church leaders discuss the results of the war:

> They were talking business; had met, indeed, to discuss an anticipated appeal from the Provincial Council at Baltimore for the founding of an Apostolic Vicarate in New Mexico – a part of North America recently annexed to the United States. (4)

The annexation is undemonstrably mentioned at the end of the sentence as if it were an aside or an item of interesting but minor news. A flattened tone is typical of the novel's recording of history: an almost parodically 'objective' style that gives terse details of time, place and event. The novel's opening phrase, 'One summer evening in the year 1848', is a good example of this, as is the similar beginning to Book One, 'One afternoon in the autumn of 1851'. Carefully encapsulating three timescales (year, season, time of day), these sentences seem to be a self-conscious pastiche, a stylised mimicry of historical fiction's claim to give accurate details of where and when the action took place. This historical positioning means that the reader without contextual knowledge can proceed unimpeded, but it also deploys a recognisable discourse: the precise, factual, rigorously empirical prose of nineteenth-century American 'Common Sense' writing.

'Common Sense' philosophy underpinned this prose. Adopting the work of the Scottish Enlightenment philosophers (Thomas Reid, Dugald Stewart, Thomas Brown, Alexander Gerard), the American educational and critical establishments were schooled in Common Sense principles: the primacy of facts and common sense, observation as the basis of knowledge, careful inference as the extension of that knowledge, and, above all, a distrust of speculation.[2] Recent work on Cooper, Hawthorne and Melville reveals the troubled and ambivalent response of these writers to Common Sense. Faced with a readership of Common Sensibility, the writer was to be confined to what was known and what was logically inferable from that factual basis.[3] Thus the pressure on Melville to write travelogues (a record of what actually happened, guaranteed by the foregrounded presence of an observing, testifying chronicler) and his reactions to the interdictions against speculation ('Benito Cereno' turns on Delano's Common Sense belief that the situation can be entirely comprehended through what he sees and hears, but a speculative leap of imagination is needed to pierce through to the reality). Thus also Hawthorne's critique of Common Sense in his Prefaces, where the speculative play of the novelist's imagination is defended:

> When a writer calls his work a Romance, it need hardly be observed that he wishes to claim a certain latitude, both as to its fashion and material, which he would not have felt himself entitled to assume, had he professed to be writing a Novel. The latter form of composition is presumed to aim at a very minute fidelity, not merely to the possible, but to the probable and ordinary course of a man's experience. The former – while as a work of art, it must rigidly subject itself to laws, and while it sins unpardonably so far as it may swerve aside from the truth of the human heart – has fairly a right to present that truth under circumstances, to a great extent, of the writer's own choosing or creation.[4]

The phrase 'historical romance' suggests a dialectic between empiricism and imagination, an oxymoronic combination of fact and fancy. Cather polarises these tendencies in the genre. On the one hand, there is the novel's basis in historical actuality, the incorporation of 'real' figures such as Kit Carson and the deployment of a Common Sense discourse to record the minutiae of history. On the other, Cather encompasses experiences outside the range of Common Sense: mystery, miracle, transcendence. Numerous episodes revolve around a sudden insight, the illumination of everyday (Common Sense) reality by what one can only call a spiritual or mystical light. When Latour hears the angelus the timbre of the bell transports him to a different time and place:

> Before the nine strokes were done Rome faded, and behind it he sensed something Eastern, with palm trees, – Jerusalem, perhaps,

though he had never been there. Keeping his eyes closed, he
cherished for a moment this sudden, pervasive sense of the East.
Once before he had been carried out of the body thus to a place
far away. (43)

If Common Sense style is metonymic, logically moving along a
chain of inferable propositions, then the style here is metaphorical:
one sensation replaces another, immediate reality dissolves into
another time and place. And that reality might be wholly
imaginary – the sense of something Eastern, the intimation of a
place never visited. The oxymoronic combination implicit in
Hawthorne's Preface is here pushed further; a character grounded
in historical reality is pictured in a moment of extreme imaginative
speculation.

Critics, uncomfortable with the contrasts of this shifting text,
have attempted to reconcile these conflicting elements. Early
readers were intrigued by the novel's generic ambiguity and strove
to place it as history, biography or fiction; one reviewer even
created the hybrid genre 'historical biography'.[5] Later critics
studied Cather's sources to illuminate the factual basis of the novel,
and then analysed the 'romance' aspects of the text, Cather's spiritual and imaginative insights.[6] The result is a Cather who
harmonises contradictory creative impulses and conflates polarities, the writer summed up in Hermione Lee's balanced phrases:
'both pioneer and historian, actor and author, female and male
voice, receiver and rewriter of history'.[7]

Behind these phrases lies the recurrent critical wish to find that
either organic synthesis or the yoking together of contraries is the
essence of art. However, Cather's texts can equally be read as in-
consistent, disrupted or fractured. Throughout her major novels
there is, if anything, an increasing 'gappiness' as the texts move
towards ever-increasing formal disintegration. My Ántonia (1918)
employed the inset story of Peter and Pavel, a digression away
from the New World to the European folk-memory of the immigrants. The Professor's House (1925) is broken structurally by the interpolation of 'Tom Outland's Story', a tale which is temporally,
geographically and narratologically separated from the rest of the
novel. Increasingly, Cather showed scant regard for preserving
unities, whether of place or time or point of view. Death Comes for
the Archbishop continues the disintegrative process, collating a
heterogeneous range of discourses: folk-tale, historical detail,

anecdotes about Mexican and Indian life, the spiritual biographies of Fathers Latour and Vaillant. The novel eschews a strongly plotted narrative line as Cather instead juxtaposes one discourse against another within a loose, discontinuous format. Constructing her novel in this way, Cather seemed to have strained the definitions of the novel. In fact, she was eventually to defend the form of *Death Comes for the Archbishop*, which seemed to many to have no form at all, on the grounds that this was a *narrative* not a novel. Her defence, written as a letter to the *Commonweal* in 1927, extrapolated from Hawthorne's account of the historical romance's imaginative freedom. She displaced his plea for speculative liberty into a discussion of narrative form, claiming for herself absolute compositional freedom:

> I am amused that so many of the reviews of this book begin with the statement: 'This book is hard to classify'. Then why bother? Many more assert vehemently that it is not a novel. Myself, I prefer to call it a narrative. In this case I think that term more appropriate.[8]

A novel's form is not, however, simply that – a question of form. The structure of the novel is deeply related to its embodiment of ideological issues. Her experiments with novelistic form have major implications for the ideological meanings of the texts: structure, the architecture of a novel, help to define its ideological configuration. Narratology has taught us to read for the oddities in the construction of a text; we now search for moments of incoherence or asymmetry rather than formal coherence, organic wholeness or symmetry. At these cruces the text's engagement with ideology is to be found as ideology erupts into the text or is silenced and suppressed. To use a geographical metaphor: we can think of the gaps in her novels as fissures or rents in the terrain of the text.

I have suggested already that in *Death Comes for the Archbishop* Cather deploys some of the codes and contracts of the historical romance but does so only to undermine them. In the rest of this chapter I will suggest how and why Cather fractures the historical romance; will outline the new historiographical currents which inform the novel; and will argue that the text takes in competing strands of American history which it cannot finally reconcile.

'PRIMITIVISM', CATHOLICISM

Death Comes for the Archbishop, a novel about the South-west and its Pueblo cultures, extends academic efforts to understand Hispanic and Indian America. Turn of the century anthropologists and archaeologists undertook some of their most pioneering work in this hinterland. Cather was familiar with studies by Charles Lummis (whose 1892 text *Some Strange Corners of Our Country* was published as the enlarged and suggestively retitled *Mesa, Cañon and Pueblo* in 1925) and Adolph Bandelier, the early explorer of the Santa Fe region which she adored. One can follow the cultural osmosis whereby this academic primitivism seeped into the culture at large. After universities established departments of anthropology in the 1880s and 1890s, popular magazines responded to public interest in the subject with photographic essays on the dwindling Indian tribes. The 'Pasadena Eight', a group of Californian photographers, had explored Arizona and New Mexico from the 1870s onwards, recording the Hopi Snake Dance. In Cather's lifetime Edward S. Curtis's massive 20-volume record, *The North American Indian* (1907–30), was widely celebrated. Emphatic racial, cultural and geographical divisions encouraged works that were analogously divided, as if the South-west was too diverse for the encompassing imagination and disrupted efforts to enclose the local culture in unified narratives. Thus Lummis's *A New Mexico David* (1891) is subtitled 'Stories and Sketches of the Southwest' and brings together anecdotes, travel sketches and tales. In *Notes for a New Mythology* (1926) and *Mornings in Mexico* (1927) Haniel Long and D. H. Lawrence eschewed conventional genres, creating instead a *bricolage* of personal reflection, travelogue, history and anthropology. *In the American Grain* (1925), William Carlos Williams's iconoclastic history, is another such work: heterogeneous, experimental, a freeing of the mutiple voices of American history. As a new area of America (the South-west) and other peoples (Indians, Mexicans) became part of the American story, writers and artists developed new forms which were increasingly polyphonous and 'open'.[9]

Cather explores this new openness. She exploited Hawthorne's pledge of authorial autonomy (the Romance obeys 'circumstances...of the writer's own choosing or creation'), capitalised upon the polyphonous breadth of other South-western works, and in so doing enlarged the range of her fiction to include a subject normally on the fringes of American culture: Catholicism. Catholicism was an unusual subject for an American writer, especially in the 1920s. Traditional Protestant suspicions about the authoritarianism of the Papacy (indicated by the Church's links with feudal governments) placed Catholicism and American democracy at opposite ends of the political spectrum. Anti-Catholic feeling went through one of its periodic revivals during the 1920s.[10] Add to this opprobrium and misunderstanding the low regard in which Christianity itself was held by critics and novelists in a period when America's literary intellectuals were alienated from the fervent Protestantism sweeping the country and one begins to see how idiosyncratic an achievement Cather's novel is. For the Protestant Utopianism of progressive social reformers does not seem to have been widely shared by novelists. When Christianity was written about, it was the object of satire, not celebration. A genre of anti-evangelical fiction runs from Harold Frederic's *The Damnation of Theron Ware* (1896) (a novel that Cather admired) through Howells's *Leatherwood God* (1916) and on to *Elmer Gantry* (1927), the latter a bestseller in the year when Cather's own Christian novel was published.[11] Harold E. Stearns couldn't find a contributor to write about religion for his 1922 symposium on America, *Civilization in the United States: an Enquiry by Thirty Americans*, and attacked Christianity in 'The Country versus the Town' (1921): 'our own rural Middle West is to-day too largely led by the broken-down evangelical cretinism so well exhibited in Mr. Howell's last novel'.[12]

'Evangelical cretinism' was also mocked by Cather, both in her private and public writing. A letter of 1896 scoffs at Presbyterian Pittsburgh, the town where, she writes, every girl has her church work in the way that other young women have fans or powder boxes. An early story, 'Eric Hermansson's Soul' (1900), satirised fundamentalist Free Gospellers. In 1907–8 Cather undertook for *McClure's Magazine* the editing and rewriting of Georgine Milmine's biography of Mary Baker Eddy, the founder of Christian Science; the series of articles was taken as a satirical attack by church leaders (and the book remains proscribed by Christian Science).[13]

Cather was received into the Episcopalian Church in 1922, and much of the creative energy that went into *Death Comes for the Archbishop* arose from a radical transformation in her religious feelings. She wrote about Catholicism when she herself had recently joined a Protestant Church, but the reasons for Cather's attraction towards Rome probably lay in the faith's cultural and historical significance. Catholicism for Cather was not the monolithic autocracy caricatured by American nativists; it was instead a repository of European culture, endlessly adapting itself to alien environments. The Church, therefore, is akin to the immigrant peoples celebrated in the early novels and has a similar ideological significance, representing an enriching cultural pluralism.

Cather's Catholicism is a faith of amalgamating, incorporating power, a church founded on the benevolent axioms of cultural heterogeneity and racial difference. Even Catholicism is transformed and hybridised in the new land – Cather is as ever interested in the quickening effect of transporting a culture – and in *Death Comes for the Archbishop* she shows how the Church itself changed for the better. The Church becomes a medium for the reform of the backward Mexican territories. The Church in its transported form is a progressive force. The novel begins in Europe, in Rome, and follows the transplant of modern Catholicism into America; it charts the replacement of a feudal despotism by the benevolent autocracy of Rome. Latour, another wanderer, brings a moderate clerical authority to Mexico, supplanting the corrupt priests Martinez and Lucero who, cut off from Rome, have drifted into petty tyranny. An absolutely deracinated Church, Cather suggests, lacks the tolerance gained from strong ties with Europe; but, as the Cardinals' conference implied, a wholly rooted one is moribund. In the Midi Romanesque church which Latour builds in the New Mexico wilderness Cather symbolises the harmony of Catholicism and America, the middle way between stasis and movement, rootedness and migration.

Catholicism is an amalgam of different cultures, as Latour realises when he hears the angelus rung:

> The Bishop smiled. 'I am trying to account for the fact that when I heard it this morning it struck me at once as something oriental. A learned Scotch Jesuit in Montreal told me that our first bells, and the introduction of the bell in the service all over Europe, originally came from the East. He said the Templars brought the Angelus back from the Crusades, and it is really an adaptation of a Moslem custom.' (45)

Cather exploits cultural fusion to witty effect here; the casual reference to a 'learned Scotch Jesuit in Montreal' could only occur in one of her novels. She relativises Christianity, placing it in conjunction with other religions and unravelling the various cultural skeins in Catholicism. The bell results from a chain of artistic transfers: '"The Spaniards handed on their skill to the Mexicans, and the Mexicans have taught the Navajos to work silver; but it all came from the Moors"' (45). Spaniards, Mexicans, Navajos, Moors: Cather's cultural archaeology finds a cosmopolitan mix of races behind the manufacture of the bell. Cather frequently interprets events through a multiracial or multicultural stencil. At the start of the novel, when the Mexican mission is being discussed in Europe, the Catholic clergy is presented as a spread of cultures. As the reader's eye moves down the passage a characteristic mixture of races stands out:

> They were talking business; had met, indeed, to discuss an antici-
> pated appeal from the Provincial Council at Baltimore for the
> founding of an Apostolic Vicarate in New Mexico – a part of
> North America recently annexed to the United States. This new
> territory was vague to all of them, even to the missionary Bishop.
> The Italian and French Cardinals spoke of it as *Le Mexique*, and
> the Spanish host referred to it as 'New Spain'. Their interest in
> the projected Vicarate was tepid, and had to be continually
> revived by the missionary, Father Ferrand; Irish by birth, French
> by ancestry – a man of wide wanderings and notable achieve-
> ment in the New World, an Odysseus of the Church. The lan-
> guage spoken was French – the time had already gone by when
> Cardinals could conveniently discuss contemporary matters in
> Latin. The French and Italian Cardinals were men in vigorous
> middle life – the Norman full-belted and ruddy, the Venetian
> spare and sallow and hook-nosed. Their host, García Maria de
> Allende, was still a young man. He was dark in colouring,
> but the long Spanish face, that looked out from so many canvases
> in his ancestral portrait gallery, was in the young Cardinal
> much modified through his English mother. With his *caffè oscuro*
> eyes, he had a fresh, pleasant English mouth, and an open
> manner. (4–5)

These paragraphs reveal a profusion of national or provincial identities: Italian, French, Spanish, Irish, English, Norman, Venetian. An apparently simple exercise in physiognomic description, the passage counterpoints accuracy about racial origin against a fondness for the hybrid – Father Ferrand, 'Irish by birth, French by ancestry' and García Maria de Allende, the Spaniard with the English mother. Cather discriminates amongst her priests with an anthropological precision, defining them through racial and geographical origin as if they were members of different tribes. Fundamentally, Cather revises difference and categorisation. She applies to her European tribes an anthropologist's discrimination; difference is here affirmed for its own sake. Indeed, Cather's hierarchy is a hierarchy of cultural relativism; individuals and races are evaluated according to their ability to migrate, transplant themselves, and absorb foreign influences.

In one section Latour meets the old Mexican woman, Sada, who has been prevented from entering the local church by her Protestant Anglo master (the unflattering picture of Protestantism continues Cather's early satires). Latour takes Sada into the church:

> Never, as he afterward told Father Vaillant, had it been permitted him to behold such deep experience of the holy joy of religion as on that pale December night. He was able to feel, kneeling beside her, the preciousness of the things of the altar to her who was without possessions; the tapers, the image of the Virgin, the figures of the saints, the Cross that took away indignity from suffering and made pain and poverty a means of fellowship with Christ. (217)

The epiphany occurs at night, in December, in the company of an apparently mundane character; the scene exemplifies Cather's interest in the transcendental insight emerging out of the ordinary moment. Latour, God's vicar, himself experiences God's presence vicariously through Sada (and the setting is cluttered with other examples of the vicarious: the Virgin, saints, the Cross). Cather provided a gloss on the scene in her *Commonweal* letter:

> But a novel, it seems to me, is merely a work of imagination in which a writer tries to present the experiences and emotions of a group of people by the light of his own. That is what he really does, whether his method is 'objective' or 'subjective'.[14]

Or, as Cather wrote in a letter late in her career, stories are made from the grafting of an outside figure onto part of the writer's self.[15]

Cather's aesthetic principles predisposed her to a favourable
view of Catholicism; an art based on empathy resembles a faith of
vicarious spirituality. Both require a broadening of the imagination
as the consciousness extends itself beyond the self into the sensibility of another. Furthermore, her notion of empathy is transformed
into an ideological principle; she developed empathy into a form of
'only connect' liberalism attuned to moments when cultural or
racial gaps are at least temporarily bridged. This notion is not given
an explicit formulation, but neither is it projected as watery, vague
sentimentality. In brief, parable-like vignettes such as the story of
Sada the novel indirectly builds up a composite and detailed fresco
of the varieties of empathy. When the European priest empathises
with the Mexican peasant the difficulties and rewards of crossing
cultural and personal barriers are movingly intimated. The bridging takes place in silence; Latour and Sada arrive at mutuality, an
unspoken communion, through the objects in the church: tapers,
Madonna, cross. Cather here seems presciently sensitive to language and to the potentially binding, authoritarian power of a discourse that attempts to comprehend and explain alien cultures or
the 'Other'.

As Edward Said's *Orientalism* famously demonstrated, Western
observers, in the very act of creating a discourse to understand the
Orient, effectively appropriated those foreign civilisations with a
subjugating, colonising langue. Said asserts that there is no 'such
real thing as "the Orient"' since it has been 'excluded, displaced' by
the written statements of Orientalists; that 'both learned and imaginative writing are never free, but are limited in their imagery, assumptions, and intentions'; and, therefore, that every nineteenth-
century European 'in what he could say about the Orient, was con-
sequently a racist, an imperialist, and almost totally ethnocentric'.[16]

Before we reach the episode about Sada we read passages describing the angelus, the casting of the bell and the conflation of
Christianity and Islam. Cather has already demonstrated the ways
in which western faith has been touched upon and changed
by the 'Other'. The Sada incident deepens these observations,
teasing out the implications of multiculturalism at the level of personal encounters (the effect is similar to that in *My Ántonia* where
the issues of immigration and assimilation – the so-called
'Americanization' process – are grounded in comic scenes about
language learning). Latour, faced with an enigmatic and alien
culture which demands interpretation, is in a position very much

like Said's Orientalists. But what is notable in the Sada episode is the creation of a discourse, a medium for understanding, *outside* of European written or spoken language. The symbols of the Catholic Church are by usage European (though Cather shows how even a Catholic ritual like the ringing of the angelus has its origin in the oriental religion of Islam); but the gist of the passage is that these objects can be appropriated by Sada and transferred from Europe to Mexico. Empathy and cultural transmission reverse the usual trend of European encounters with the 'Other'; Sada masters the presiding language (here, the symbols of Catholic worship) and Latour becomes a passive recipient (it is 'permitted him to behold').

In Cather's intellectual milieu there were similar attempts to explore the problematic relationships between colonist and colonised, civilised and 'primitive', European and Indian. Comparison with these other texts enables us to position *Death Comes for the Archbishop* and to evaluate what I have called its 'only connect' liberalism. Cather researched the novel after a stay with the ubiquitous Mabel Dodge Luhan in Taos, New Mexico in 1925. D. H. Lawrence was the most famous guest at the artists' colony Luhan had established; the two novelists met in New Mexico and each worked on books about the indigenous Indian culture of the area.[17] Lawrence's *Mornings in Mexico* (also published in 1927) celebrates the utter difference or otherness of the Indians. At the start of the book Lawrence watches a monkey but rejects the evolutionary connection between it and him:

> He's different. There's no rope of evolution linking him to you, like a navel string. No! Between you and him there's a cataclysm and another dimension. It's no good. You can't link him up. Never will. It's the other dimension.[18]

The 'other dimension' is at the heart of Lawrence's thoughts about race and culture; he founds his theories on this idea of radical otherness. He then tries to understand Indian culture without subsuming it into the western order of things, meanwhile castigating other European observers for the sentimentality of their writing about primitivism. Sentimentality hints at a reconciliation of the Indian and the European, but for Lawrence there can be no such *rapprochement*. He endlessly reiterates the point that Indian and European mentalities are utterly divorced:

The Indian way of consciousness is different from and fatal to our way of consciousness. Our way of consciousness is different from and fatal to the Indian. The two ways, the two streams are never to be united. They are not even to be reconciled. There is no bridge, no canal of connexion.[19]

The difficulty with this is that the more Lawrence insists upon difference, the more he writes the Indian into his own discourse; the separateness which Lawrence insists upon is bridged by his need to mobilise the Indian for didactic purposes. Because Lawrence continually uses primitivism to attack atrophied civilisation the reader is always aware of his vatic, intercessionary voice. No matter how much we are told 'There is no bridge, no canal of connexion', this voice constitutes that very connection; Lawrence cannot resist positioning himself as someone who *knows*, who has the privileged inside knowledge and is able to describe Indians to the ignorant European. And in the moment of positioning himself Lawrence undoes his own claims to distance and disconnection.

Lawrence is trapped in the interpretative cul-de-sac described by Edward Said: attempts to understand the Other are acts of power, and the discourse itself is so ridden with the coloniser's ideology that it becomes another form of colonisation. Said's analysis presents a traditional humanist hope – that works of art enable the artist and reader to enter into or understand cultures other than their own – as ultimately futile. The upshot of Said's argument is, first, to devalue the power of local or individual resistance to the dominant ideology (we are all ineluctably conditioned by an *a priori* discourse) and, second, to present cultures as essentially insular and atomised. Cather, on the other hand, anticipates the issues dealt with in Said's work (the collision of cultures, the decoding of the Other) but holds back from endorsing his extreme conclusions. Her fiction dramatises the act of knowing; her characters are shown in the process of exploring alien culture; the dominating Orientalist discourse is deferred. Characters are likely to be mystified by what they find or to lapse into silence; Cather suggests that a productive nescience, a profitable bewilderment, occurs when the western intelligence meets Indian or Mexican culture. Latour realises that the Indians' religious inheritance cannot be abruptly erased by receiving them into the Church; there are areas beyond empathy and outside the range of cultural transfer:

The Bishop seldom questioned Jacinto about his thoughts or beliefs. He didn't think it polite, and he believed it to be useless. There was no way in which he could transfer his own memories of European civilization into the Indian mind, and he was quite willing to believe that behind Jacinto there was a long tradition, a story of experience, which no language could translate to him. (92)

Translation was important to Cather as proof that people can transmit their language and literature to other nations and races. For Cather, a much translated writer, the spread of her work into different languages provided another opportunity to see transmission and cultural reformulation at work. She was, for instance, pleased with the foreign reception of *Death Comes for the Archbishop*, and she boasted that *My Ántonia* had been translated into eight languages.[20] Thus to admit that translation is not possible might at first seem to signal a severe defeat. But Cather makes the hiatus into a form of unspoken communication. She writes, just before the passage quoted above, 'They relapsed into the silence which was their usual form of intercourse' (91–2). Tolerant reticence might be a means to communicate (the title of one section – 'Stone Lips' – catches this paradoxical sense of mute communication). These silences or lacunae are a way for Cather to explore the gaps in understanding between two markedly different cultures. Writing about silence, Cather faced the problem of how one can write about the failure of communication. The pressure of language – as *Mornings in Mexico* demonstrated – is to *keep on*, to fill up the silence. Accepting the limitations of the realist text, Cather's solution is to write silences into her prose, dramatising these hiatuses and fissures in understanding.

Stadialism and savagism would not have countenanced the encounter between Latour and Jacinto; figures from different phases of societal evolution, they would have been kept apart within their demarcated stages. The new interest in the South-west and its primitive civilisations loosened this hierarchy, blurring boundaries to allow the meeting of previously polarised cultures. Ironically, though, Americans (as anthropologists, photographers and writers) began to appreciate the Indians just at the point when their culture was dying out, finally extinguished after a century of exterminations and forced removals. The new primitivism focuses on a way of life which is, or is about to be lost. The stadialist had felt a lingering fondness for the outmoded civilisation, but this nostalgia now gained a keener edge. Anthropology, photography and writing became the media to record America's loss of its indigenous peoples. A fundamental question then arose: as civilisations progress, is there an unavoidable loss of admirable qualities (of integrity, passion, community – the qualities often associated with the 'primitive')? If there is loss, is it balanced by the gains of entering a more advanced phase of civilisation?

Cather dramatises these questions: in the late 1920s she was drawn to the dilemma of societal progress. *The Professor's House* and *Death Comes for the Archbishop* are mapped to represent that dilemma, being divided between the 'primitive' and the civilised, the South-west and the East Coast or Europe, agrarian and technological communities. On one side, mesas and cliff-dweller settlements; on the other, the civilised centres of progressive power (bureaucracy, business, academe). It is to the issue of progress that I now want to return.

DEATH COMES FOR THE ARCHBISHOP AND PROGRESS

Death Comes for the Archbishop seems on first reading to endorse progress. Entitling one section 'The Old Regime' and including episodes which, with the precision of moral exempla, delineate the corruption of the Mexican clergy ('The Legend of Fray Baltazar'), Cather foregrounds the conflict of old and new authorities. Her alterations to the historical actuality serve to sharpen this conflict. The real Padre Martinez was not as bad as Cather makes him, and she probably overstates the inadequacies of the old regime.[21] Her exaggeration of his evil heightens the novel's morality-play structure – the schematic contrast between good and bad priests.

Other changes to her historical sources affect the politics of the novel; Cather gives us her own idiosyncratic reading of the progress of civilisation. Lamy, the prototype of Latour, had been strongly identified with the Americanisation of the South-west. An ultramontane (that is, an advocate of firm Papal power), his authority was harnessed to the extension of American influence throughout the new territories; he worked as an agent of centralised spiritual and temporal power. The US Government in turn supported Lamy's efforts.[22] Cather, however, plays down Latour's links with the Government; Americanisation is referred to but once, and then Latour claims that the Church is the best medium for this policy:

> The church can do more than the Fort to make these poor Mexicans 'good Americans'. And it is for the people's good; there is no other way in which they can better their condition. (36)

Latour is less fervent and more pragmatic than the historical Lamy. Cather's progressivism is apolitical; she takes the politics out of progress by suppressing or eliding the ideological implications of her sources. The novel's correlation of corrupt administration, private vice and reforming zeal reminds us that Cather had worked at *McClure's* just after the heyday of 'muckraking'. Like the muckraking journalists who exposed the political and business scandals of early twentieth-century America, Cather attacks maladministration and champions reform but refuses to enter into wider political debate. Latour's pragmatic and non-partisan reforms echo the missions of Cather's fellow-journalists, for example Lincoln Steffens. Exposing municipal corruption in *The Shame of the Cities* (1904), Steffens rejected 'a ready-made reform scheme', adding that for the muckrakers, 'The only editorial scheme we had was to study a few choice examples of bad city government'.[23] Although the tone is different, this is the spirit of *Death Comes for the Archbishop*: a circumscribed analysis in which the faults of a system are personalised or moralised rather than being interpreted in terms of underlying economic or political structures. Hence Cather's highly individualised images of evil: corruption becomes the manifestation of personal turpitude, a grotesque defect denoted by virulent physical appearance. Thus Buck Scales:

> He was tall, gaunt and ill-formed, with a snake-like neck, terminating in a small, bony head. Under his close-clipped hair this repellent head showed a number of thick ridges, as if the skull joinings were overgrown by layers of superfluous bone. With its small, rudimentary ears, this head had a positively malignant look. (67)

Cather's externalised, reified portrait of malice could come from a scheme of humours, and the allegorical name of this character (Buck Scales) emphasises his reptilian two-dimensionality. Instead of social process and interaction Cather projects a frozen, tableau-like image of personal corruption.

But elsewhere another form of progress emerges – Cather develops a more pointedly political sense of injustice and reform. Her treatment of Kit Carson is a case in point. She undermines Carson's heroic status. He had passed into American mythology as soon as his explorations of the West were reported in John Frémont's journals in the 1840s, and after he served in the Mexican War Carson became a national hero. In *Moby Dick*, published just after the War, Melville mock-heroically refers to Carson when Ishmael asks whether Hercules, described as 'that antique Crockett and Kit Carson', should be admitted into the pantheon of whalemen. As Carson became a prototypical American hero, his many biographers iconised a muscular Christian devoid of the usual cowboy vices.[24] Cather's Carson is demythologised. He is smaller and slighter than Latour expects; a Catholic (nineteenth-century biographers glossed over this fact); and his role in the capture of the Navajo in their ancestral lands is squarely acknowledged:

> Carson followed them down into the hidden world between those towering walls of red sandstone, spoiled their stores, destroyed their deep-sheltered corn-fields, cut down the terraced peach orchards so dear to them. When they saw all that was sacred to them laid waste, the Navajos lost heart. They did not surrender; they simply ceased to fight, and were taken. Carson was a soldier under orders, and he did a soldier's brutal work. (293–4)

Whereas there was a seamless correspondence between Buck Scales's appearance and his character, in this case there is disparity; Carson's 'far-seeing blue eyes' and mouth of 'singular refinement' (75) belie his 'brutal work'. Evil becomes a complex matter; appearance and reality do not match. Latour says at the end of his life that '"I have lived to see two great wrongs righted; I have seen the end of black slavery, and I have seen the Navajos restored to their own country"' (292). Carson's removal of the Navajos constituted one of the 'great wrongs', but to look at him you would never have guessed his involvement in wrongdoing. It is important that his actions are presented as the result of a larger process of political decision-making; Carson is an employee and not an autonomous free agent. He is 'a soldier under orders, and he did a soldier's brutal work'. The implication is that potential good is corrupted by institutional duty, by the political machine. Buck Scales's corruption seemed to arise from the very shape of his body; Carson's body is pure but his actions are warped into badness by political imperatives. As Latour thinks of the Indian wars, 'a political machine and immense capital were employed to keep it going' (292).

The problem with these comments is that they sit uneasily alongside the novel's earlier presentations of individualised corruption. The tone of the novel is disrupted. After accommodating his reforms to the contingencies of the situation, Latour's meditation on progress in the South-west now suggests a trenchant, idealistic, politicised overview. We can see that Cather's ironic undercutting of Carson (she replaces the myth with an historically culpable figure) has led her towards the kind of political questions which the rest of the text seemed to overlook. She has, in fact, raised just those questions provoked by the Mexican War which were to lead to the Civil War, questions about exploitation, expansion and slavery. Having apparently turned away from these topics, Cather then turns back to them, but too late in her text to grasp fully the implications of Latour's comments. Hence the contradictions besetting *Death Comes for the Archbishop*. Cather condemns the corruption of the old regime, making Lucero and Martinez unequivocally evil, but she also records the savagery of the new order, for instance in the hunting down of the Navajo. Looked at from a stadialist perspective this might seem readily explicable. Stadialism accepted the savagery of the old and the inevitable harshness of the new because it believed nevertheless that there was an underlying movement towards better civilisations. Cather therefore seems to be taking a classically stadialist line on the necessary evils of historical progress. But, as we saw earlier, for much of the novel Cather works against the stadialist model, notably in her sympathetic portraits of so-called 'primitive' peoples. Behind this contradiction lies a basic paradox: Cather simultaneously envisages the history of the South-west as a matter of personalities and ideologies. It is possible to read the novel in either way, and finally one has to recognise the astigmatism of this text: Cather cannot quite focus her conflicting interpretations of American history.

At the troubled core of the progressive ideology (where, as I wrote earlier, the relative worth of old and new civilisations is evaluated, and where the benefits or losses of progress are finally accounted for) Cather found herself unable to resolve this contradiction. She then moved away from the Common Sense, laconic style of the historical romance, finding that this medium could not account for the conflicting, paradoxical pressures of progressivism. Occasionally a compromise could be found within the boundaries of Common Sense. With the story of the Navajo, Cather illustrated the persistence of the old ways (the Navajos are accommodated in their government reservations) *and* a shift into a new phase of civilisation (the US administration is, after all, responsible for the South-west). But other Indian tribes presented less purchase for Cather's desire to find a middle-way between the old and the new. Thus Jacinto's dying pueblo:

> It seemed much more likely that the contagious diseases brought by white men were the real cause of the shrinkage of the tribe. Among the Indians, measles, scarlatina and whooping-cough were as deadly as typhus or cholera. Certainly, the tribe was decreasing every year. Jacinto's house was at one end of the living pueblo; behind it were long rock ridges of dead pueblo, – empty houses ruined by weather and now scarcely more than piles of earth and stone. The population of the living streets was less than one hundred adults. (123)

In this tale of decline-and-fall the white men's diseases are to blame. In the text, at the end of the last sentence ('one hundred adults') an asterisk takes the reader to a footnote: 'In actual fact, the dying pueblo of Pecos was abandoned some years before the American occupation of New Mexico.' That is, although the extinction of Pecos is clearly attributed to white civilisation, it is disengaged from American imperialism; Cather separates the US involvement in the South-west from Indian deaths caused by European diseases. All this is later explained in the main body of the text since Cather goes on to discuss Coronado's expedition to the area, thereby pinpointing the Spanish origin of the various contagions. Cather, then, chooses to refute emphatically the United States's role in this destruction, even to the extent of breaking up her prose with a footnoted insertion. The footnote authoritatively overrides the main body of the text, supplanting fictional history with the 'objective' history of footnotes, facts and authenticated chronology. In effect, this is a convoluted negotiation of the progressive dilemma: Cather acknowledges the white man's destruction of the Indian settlements but circuitously evades the question of American involvement. The fact that Cather uses a footnote to achieve this solution shows how much strain the progressive dilemma puts on her prose. The disruptions, contradictions and anomalies of 'progress' fissure the even surface of Cather's prose. Indeed, at this point the problem cannot be contained within the main body of the text.

A progressive contradiction is recognised and focused, but in order to 'solve' the problem Cather shifts into a different discourse – the overriding footnote. Elsewhere, especially when writing about superseded or outmoded civilisations, her writing becomes symbolic, mythic or parable-like. Her 'transparent', laconically factual style is then disrupted by an ambiguous, shifting, layered mode. Cather returned at several points in her career to a story which repeatedly produced this discourse. The myth of the Enchanted Mesa was the subject of an early story ('The Enchanted Bluff', 1909), a section of *The Professor's House*, and recurs in *Death Comes for the Archbishop*. The fable tells how an Indian tribe withdrew onto an isolated rock in fear and defiance of the outside world; they died from hunger after the only stairway from their fortress was destroyed:

> All this plain, the Bishop gathered, had once been the scene of a periodic man-hunt; these Indians, born in fear and dying by violence for generations, had at last taken this leap away from the earth, and on that rock had found the hope of all suffering and tormented creatures – safety. They came down to the plain to hunt and to grow their crops, but there was always a place to go back to. If a band of Navajos were on the Ácoma's trail, there was still one hope; if he could reach his rock–Sanctuary! On the winding stone stairway up the cliff, a handful of men could keep off a multitude. The rock of Ácoma had never been taken by a foe but once, – by Spaniards in armour. It was very different from a mountain fastness; more lonely, more stark and grim, more appealing to the imagination. The rock, when one came to think of it, was the utmost expression of human need; even mere feeling yearned for it; it was the highest comparison of loyalty in love and friendship. Christ Himself had used that comparison for the disciple to whom He gave the keys of His Church. And the Hebrews of the Old Testament, always being carried captive into foreign lands, – their rock was an idea of God, the only thing their conquerors could not take from them.

Already the Bishop had observed in Indian life a strange literalness, often shocking and disconcerting. The Ácomas, who must
share the universal human yearning for something permanent,
enduring, without shadow of change, – they had their idea in
substance. They actually lived upon their Rock; were born upon
it and died upon it. There was an element of exaggeration in
anything so simple! (97–8)

The rock embodies the Indians' faith, devotion and steadfastness;
to Latour the rock exemplifies the 'strange literalness' of Indian life.
Latour, or the narrator – the style becomes noticeably more indirect
as the passage proceeds, making it difficult to attribute the
thoughts to one or the other – speak a heightened, sacred language.
Using phrases such as 'when one came to think of it' the prose
mimes a kind of Biblical exegesis, an extended interpretation of the
rock's significance. That meaning is largely theological. In heightened religious language and with devotional intensity the passage
occludes the historical status of the rock, its place in a story of con-
quest and resistance. All that is left are fleeting references to the
pursuing Navajo and the 'Spaniards in armour' who finally took
the fortress.

It seems as if the importance of the mesa is as a theological
symbol; but the Enchanted Mesa originally suggested itself in *The
Professor's House* as a tale about the primitive peoples of America
and their defeat by white civilisation. The story of the mesa was a
vehicle for Cather to ask questions about this historical process.
Should the earlier communities be mourned? Why did they fail to
survive? Patricia Lee Yongue believes that Cather then used the
Enchanted Mesa story to answer these questions. The story of the
cliff-dwellers in *The Professor's House* is, in Lee Yongue's view, a
cautionary tale about societies which fail to progress. The cliff-
dwellers 'allowed their beautiful, naturally-endowed culture to de-
teriorate into a waste land by all avoidance of technological
change…by failure to make any effort to save themselves or ac-
tively to expand their customs to the rest of the New World'.[25]
Technological acumen and territorial acquisitiveness, qualities
absent from cliff-dweller life, were of course the foundation of
America's nineteenth-century progress. Cather, it is argued, transformed the mesa story into an exemplary parable about the value of
Yankee progress. The cliff-dwellers were not, in effect, sufficiently

similar to the civilisation which overtook them; if they had been, they might have survived.

It is surely more convincing to interpret the cliff-dwellers and the Enchanted Mesa as expressions of Cather's nostalgia for older and 'purer' civilisations. The lack of commercialism or covetousness, the dedication to craftsmanship, the pacific sense of community – all are qualities admired by Cather. We might even interpret the story as a kind of Utopian fiction. The cliff-dwellers are, after all, presented as an idealistic ur-Christian community. Their Utopian, godly settlement is another version of the American 'city on the hill' – the theocratic community at one with itself and with the landscape in which it is placed. Cather's heightened rhetoric signals her own fascination with (and yearning for?) this Utopia. But then there is the fall of the rock to the invading Spaniards. One does not have to agree completely with Lee Yongue to admit that Cather *is* interested in the fall of the ideal community; in the moment of envisaging her city on the hill she cannot hold off awareness of the city's inevitable demise.

The cliff-dweller settlement, like Ántonia's homestead on the prairies, demonstrates Cather's interest in what we might call a fragile or compromised Utopianism. In these cultured and harmonious communities she imagined her own version of the American ideal society; but in both cases the Utopia is circumscribed. Ántonia's home, beautifully poised between the Old and New Worlds and their languages, is an idealised projection of a liberal Americanisation that would accommodate European ways in the New World. Yet the simple fact that this Utopia extends to just one house and not the wider society shows that the dream was limited. The Enchanted Mesa likewise possessed a doubleness in Cather's imagination: the incarnation of a craft-based, theocratic Utopia; the disintegration of that ideal, whether through a combination of insularity and rapacious mobility, as here, or through the community's own cruelties, as in *The Professor's House*. Cather interlarded the two versions (Utopia and dystopia), producing the layered parables of the rock and the Enchanted Mesa. And the reason that the Enchanted Mesa can sustain a variety of interpretations (theological exemplum, progressive dystopia or nostalgic idyll) is that Cather is caught between conflicting discourses. She is simultaneously drawn towards idealism and disillusion, trying to imagine a progressive ideal even as she turns back on herself and undermines those ideals. The writer's imagination is attracted towards an ideal which it knows cannot be sustained.

Cather's narrative relaxation (her ability to accommodate or incorporate elements which seemed to be beyond the immediate scope of her ostensible themes) led to a liberal openness in her fiction; we have seen how this led her to define her text as a 'narrative' rather than as a novel. Now, however, we can also see that expansiveness might become a form of evasion. Unable to unravel the dilemma of progress, Cather accreted various answers rather than resolving the central issues. She described her novel as an exploration of narrative, deploying examples of archaic forms of story such as the legend or the frieze. The 'essence' of this method, she wrote, is 'not to hold the note...but to touch and pass on'. She wanted 'to do something in the style of legend, which is absolutely the reverse of dramatic treatment', 'something without accent, with none of the artificial elements of composition'.[26] Her formalist claims have been honoured by critics who read the novel either as a homage to older storytelling or as a modernist experiment. For Mary-Ann and David Stouck the novel utilises the medieval 'paratactic' structures identified by Eric Auerbach, 'a series of loosely related "pictures", each of which captures a gesture from a decisive moment in the subject's life'. And for Hermione Lee this structure is not an antiquarian idiosyncrasy but 'a sophisticated version of symbolism, a modernist refusal of naturalism'.[27]

Homage to medieval storytelling or modernist abjuration of traditional narrative: neither reading seems to me fully satisfactory. Is the formal experiment simply that – a structural idiosyncrasy – or does it have broader implications? Might it not affect the ways Cather represents American history? We have already seen that the swerve from naturalism into symbolism, noted by Lee, has much to do with the inability of straightforward realist prose to contain the conflicting pressures of Cather's America. The discussions of the novel's form quoted above posit a formalism hermetically sealed-off from the historical matrix in which Cather wrote. Yet the novel's form cannot, I believe, be isolated from the issues discussed in this chapter (race, primitivism, Catholicism, progress). In the novel's form we find the embodiment of Cather's thought, the grammar and syntax with which and through which she articulated her investigation into America's past.

The novel's discontinuous storyline, discrete tableaux and anecdotes, interpolated legends and historical asides, lack of dynamic plot or taut structure, give it an open paratactic form. Parataxis presents a story without the hierarchical structure to combine and rank its constituent elements; it is the opposite of a historiography which causally locks one event onto another in a chain of historical connexion. Even if at certain points the text is clear about its ideological stance (for example, Carson and the Navajo), the episodic construction isolates these moments because Cather has chosen 'not to hold the note...but to touch and pass on'. Faced with the jostling, contradictory evidence about the benefits of American progress, Cather favoured narrative structures which revealed ideological tensions but refused to work out solutions to these dilemmas. The narrative structure becomes the embodiment of her simultaneous opening up and occlusion of the progressive dilemma. As we have seen, the text incorporates the new primitivism, carrying with it a tolerant receptivity to Indian culture, racial heterogeneity and Catholicism – all of these aspects of American culture which narrow definitions of American progress would have excluded. Nonetheless, Cather cannot finally combine, incorporate or reconcile her own perspectives on progress, and her open text shades into an evasive text.[28]

Notes

1. Introduction

1. Willa Cather, *Not Under Forty* (London, 1936), p. v. The *Nation*, 117 (1923), 236–8.
2. Granville Hicks, 'The Case against Willa Cather' in *English Journal*, November 1933, reprinted in *Willa Cather and her Critics*, ed. James Schroeter (New York, 1967), pp. 139–47. Lionel Trilling, 'Willa Cather', *New Republic* 90 (1937), reprinted Schroeter, pp. 148–55. Harold Bloom, 'Introduction' to his collection, *Modern Critical Views: Willa Cather* (New York, 1985), pp. 1 and 3.
3. MS. letters to Kate Cleary (13 February 1905), to Carrie Sherwood (1 September 1922; 27 January 1934; 9 June 1943), Willa Cather Pioneer Memorial Collection, Nebraska State Historical Society, Red Cloud, Nebraska (hereafter abbreviated as WCPM). The other letter to Dorothy Canfield Fisher (15 March 1916) is in the Dorothy Canfield Fisher Collection, Bailey/Howe Library, University of Vermont, Burlington, VT (hereafter abbreviated as UVM). These letters are summarised in Mark J. Madigan's valuable work, 'Letters from Willa Cather to Dorothy Canfield Fisher 1899–1947' (unpublished MA dissertation, University of Vermont, 1987) – abstracts of letters from the Canfield Fisher papers.
4. Ernest Hemingway to Edmund Wilson, 25 November 1923, *Selected Letters 1917–1961*, ed. Carlos Baker (London, 1981), p. 105.
5. 'Willa Cather' in Schroeter, pp. 154–5.
6. Sacvan Bercovitch, 'The Problem of Ideology', *Critical Inquiry* 12 (1985–6), 631–53 (635–6). Allen Tate, 'Religion and the Old South', *Essays of Four Decades* (London, 1970), p. 568.
7. 'Problem of Ideology', 645.
8. Hicks, 'Case against', Schroeter, p. 147.
9. Other articles from this period which condemned Cather for evasion, nostalgia and the flight from modernity were as follows. Newton Arvin, 'Quebec, Nebraska, and Pittsburgh', *New Republic* 67 (12 August 1931), 345–6. Robert Cantwell, 'A Season's Run', *New Republic* 85 (11 December 1935), 149–53. Clifton Fadiman, 'Willa Cather: The Past Recaptured', *Nation* 135 (7 December 1932), 563–5. Even sympathetic readers understood Cather primarily as a nostalgist: 'It is not realism that colors these volumes, it is youth seen through the golden haze of later years, in far exile. She has given us the Nebraska of the eighties and nineties as it lies rich and warmly lighted in her memory' commented Fred Lewis Pattee in his critical overview of *The New American Literature 1890–1930* (1930. Reprinted New York, 1968), p. 264.
10. Willa Cather, *On Writing*, with a foreword by Stephen Tennant (New York, 1949. Reprinted 1968), pp. 23, 27.

11. On Populism see Norman Pollack, *The Populist Response to Industrial America: Midwestern Populist Thought* (Cambridge, Mass., 1962).

12. Pollack, p. 54 discusses *Wealth Makers*. Robert W. Cherny, 'Willa Cather and the Populists', *Great Plains Quarterly* 3 (1983), 206–18, argues that Cather's associations were with Nebraskans unsympathetic to Populism.

13. Willa Cather, *The World and the Parish: Willa Cather's Articles and Reviews, 1893–1902*, ed. William Curtin, 2 vols (Lincoln, 1970), pp. 308–13, 782–9.

14. *The World and the Parish*, p. 789.

15. When Cather came to revise *The Song of the Lark* she also turned away from political topicalities – in this case by cutting earlier references to Colorado politics. See Robin Heyeck and James Woodress, 'Willa Cather's Cuts and Revisions in *The Song of the Lark*', *Modern Fiction Studies* 25 (1979), 651–8.

16. Dorothy Canfield Fisher, 'Willa Cather: Daughter of the Frontier', *New York Herald–Tribune* (28 May 1933), sec. 2, pp. 7, 9.

17. Robert M. Crunden, *Ministers of Reform: The Progressives' Achievement in American Civilization 1889–1920* (New York, 1982), p. ix. Peter Filene, 'An Obituary for "The Progressive Movement"', *American Quarterly* 22 (1970), 20–34 (31).

18. Benjamin De Witt, *The Progressive Movement: A Non-partisan Comprehensive Discussion of Current Tendencies in American Politics* (New York, 1915), pp. 4–5.

19. David W. Noble, 'The Religion of Progress in America, 1890–1914', *Social Research* 22 (1955), 417–40 (439).

20. 'In general they shared moral values and agreed that America needed a spiritual reformation to fulfill God's plan for democracy in the New World' writes Crunden in *Ministers of Reform*, p. ix. On the Social Gospel see J. A. Thompson, *Progressivism*, BAAS pamphlet (Durham, 1979), pp. 18–34.

21. J. A. Thompson, *Progressivism*, p. 12. Crunden, *Ministers of Reform* covers the broad intellectual context of progressivism including work in music and the visual arts. Jean B. Quandt, *From the Small Town to the Great Community: The Social Thought of Progressive Intellectuals* (New Brunswick, 1970) examines the communitarian Utopias of progressive thinkers such as Josiah Royce and John Dewey.

22. Marilyn Butler, *Jane Austen and the War of Ideas* (Oxford, 1975).

23. For a valuable discussion of disillusion and idealism in the 1920s see Lawrence W. Levine, 'Progress and Nostalgia: The Self Image of the Nineteen Twenties', *The American Novel and the Nineteen Twenties*, ed. Malcolm Bradbury and David Palmer (London, 1971) pp. 36–56.

24. Filene, 'An Obituary', discusses differing views on the nativism of the progressives. Richard Hofstadter, *The Age of Reform: From Bryan to F.D.R.* (New York, 1955), pp. 179–81 describes the progressive reaction against immigration.

25. Cather, 'Nebraska', 237.

26. Gillian Beer, *Darwin's Plots: Evolutionary Narrative in Darwin, George Eliot and Nineteenth-Century Fiction* (London, 1985) provides a wealth

of information to demonstrate Darwin's rapid fertilisation of the British fictional imagination.

27. Robert Clark, *History, Ideology and Myth in American Fiction, 1823–52* (London, 1984), pp. 11–22.

28. Robert Weimann, 'Past Origins and Present Functions in American Literary History' in *Structure and Society in Literary History* (London, 1977), pp. 91, 115. Gerald Graff, *Professing Literature* (Chicago and London, 1987), p. 220. Warner Berthoff, 'Ambitious Scheme', *Commentary* 44, no. 4 (October, 1967), 111. Bruce Kuklick, 'Myth and Symbol in American Studies', *American Quarterly* 24 (1972), 435–50 exhaustively demolishes the theoretical assumptions of critics such as Leo Marx and Henry Nash Smith. I have used Clark's book as an example of historicised American studies but other works could have been cited. See especially Michael Paul Rogin, *Subversive Genealogy: The Politics and Art of Herman Melville* (New York, 1983) and David S. Reynolds, *Beneath the American Renaissance: The Subversive Imagination in the Age of Emerson and Melville* (Cambridge, Mass., 1989). A good recent account of American studies is Philip Fisher, 'American Literary and Cultural Studies since the Civil War' in *Redrawing the Boundaries: The Transformation of English and American Literary Studies*, ed. Stephen Greenblatt and Giles Gunn (New York, 1992), pp. 232–50.

29. Alvin Kernan, *The Death of Literature* (New Haven, 1990), p. 70. Laura Brown, *Alexander Pope* (Oxford, 1985), p. 3. Alan Sinfield, 'Four Ways with a Reactionary Text', *Literature Teaching Politics* 2 (n.d.), 81–95 (81). Kiernan Ryan, *Shakespeare* (Hemel Hempstead, 1989), p. 10.

30. 'The Marriage of Phaedra' in *The Troll Garden* (1905), reprinted in *Willa Cather's Collected Short Fiction 1892–1912*, ed. Virginia Faulkner, revised edition (Lincoln, 1970), pp. 219–34 (p. 229). Three other stories which illustrate Cather's prejudice are 'The Diamond Mine' and 'Scandal' (both in the 1920 collection, *Youth and the Bright Medusa*), and 'The Old Beauty', a 1936 story which appeared in the 1948 collection of the same name.

31. Sharon O' Brien, *Willa Cather: The Emerging Voice* (New York, 1987), pp. 239–40 deals with the marriage and the feelings it provoked in Cather.

32. James Schroeter, 'Willa Cather and *The Professor's House*', *Yale Review* 54 no. 4, reprinted in *Willa Cather and her Critics*, pp. 363–81 (p. 365). James Woodress, *Willa Cather: A Literary Life* (Lincoln, 1987), p. 284. O' Brien, *Willa Cather*, p. 240. The other biographical discussion of the topic is in Phyllis Robinson, *Willa: The Life of Willa Cather* (New York, 1983), pp. 48–9, 205–7.

33. Christopher Ricks, *T. S. Eliot and Prejudice* (London, 1988).

34. Heyeck and Woodress, 'Willa Cather's Cuts and Revisions'.

2. 'American Literature' and the Failure of American Culture

1. On the 'feminisation' of literary culture, the formation of the literary canon and the growth of American Studies in the universities, see:

Paul Lauter, 'Race and Gender in the Shaping of the American Literary Canon: A Case Study from the Twenties', *Feminist Studies* vol. 9 no. 3 (1983), 435–63; Kermit Vanderbilt, *American Literature and the Academy* (Philadelphia, 1986); Richard Ruland, *The Rediscovery of American Literature: Premises of Critical Taste, 1900–1940* (Cambridge, Mass., 1967); Russell J. Reising, *The Unusable Past: Theory and the Study of American Literature* (London, 1986). The two best accounts of Cather and the canon, from which I have learned a great deal, are: Deborah Carlin, 'Categorical Cather: Reading the Canon(s)', *Cather, Canon, and the Politics of Reading* (Amherst, 1992), pp. 3–26; and Sharon O' Brien, 'Becoming Noncanonical: The Case Against Willa Cather', *American Quarterly* 40 (1988), 110–26.

2. Henry C. Vedder, *American Writers of To-day* (New York, 1894), p. 3.

3. *American Writers*, p. 116.

4. Barrett Wendell, *A Literary History of America* (1900. London, 1901), p. 6.

5. Van Wyck Brooks, 'The Culture of Industrialism' (1917) and 'On Creating a Usable Past' (1918) in *Critics of Culture*, ed. Alan Trachtenberg (New York, 1976), pp. 89–98 and pp. 165–71. 'Toward a National Culture' (1917) in *Van Wyck Brooks: The Early Years* ed. Claire Sprague (New York, 1968), pp. 180–92. See also Ruland, *Rediscovery*, pp. 1–10.

6. Brooks, '"Highbrow"and "Lowbrow"' in *Critics of Culture*, p. 34.

7. *Van Wyck Brooks: The Early Years*, p. 187.

8. 'The importance of *The Ordeal of Mark Twain* is that it is so typical of the literary criticism of its era. Instead of being a scholarly attempt to discover and evaluate the evidence, it is propaganda: the marshalling of selected evidence to support a doctrinaire thesis. It was part of the contemporary war on Puritanism, business, and the alleged American hostility to the artist.' Ernest Earnest, *The Single Vision: The Alienation of American Intellectuals* (New York, 1970), p. 20.

9. Van Wyck Brooks, *The Ordeal of Mark Twain* (London, 1922), pp. 29–30, 59.

10. *Ordeal*, p. 144.

11. *Ordeal*, p. 144.

12. *Ordeal*, p. 41.

13. Wendell, *A Literary History*, p. 229.

14. Raymond Weaver, *Herman Melville – Mariner and Mystic* (New York, 1921). Lewis Mumford, *Herman Melville* (London, 1929), pp. 3–4, 15.

15. Earnest, *The Single Vision*, p. xi.

16. Van Wyck Brooks, 'The Literary Life' in *Civilization in the United States: An Enquiry by Thirty Americans*, ed. Harold E. Stearns (London, 1922), pp. 179–97 (p. 185).

17. *Civilization in the United States*, p. 193.

18. Warner Berthoff, *The Ferment of Realism: American Literature, 1884–1919* (1965. Cambridge, 1981), pp. 292–4.

19. Brooks, 'On Creating a Usable Past', *Critics of Culture*, pp. 165–71.

20. Vanderbilt, *American Literature*, pp. 257–69 discusses the universities in the 1920s.

21. Woodress, *Willa Cather: A Literary Life*, p. xvii.
22. H. L. Mencken, 'The National Letters' in *Prejudices: Second Series* (London, 1921), pp. 9–101.
23. On expatriation and foreign experience see Frederick J. Hoffman, *The Twenties: American Writing in the Postwar Decade*, revised edition (New York, 1965), pp. 43–55.
24. Harold E. Stearns, 'The Intellectual Life' in *Civilization*, pp. 135–50 (p. 135).
25. *Civilization*, p. 136.
26. *Civilization*, pp. 138–9.
27. Henry James, *The American Scene* (Bloomington, 1969), p. 66.
28. *Civilization*, p. 143.
29. Harold E. Stearns, *America and the Young Intellectual* (1921. Westport, Connecticut, 1973), pp. 9, 69.
30. *Civilization*, p. 145.
31. John Dos Passos, 'Against American Literature', *New Republic* 8 (14 October 1916), 269–71 (269–70).
32. For a view of the male critical reaction to Cather see Sharon O' Brien, 'Becoming Noncanonical: The Case Against Willa Cather', 110–26. O' Brien's psycho-sexual study of gendered displacement and succession suggests that the 'fathers' who paternally introduced Cather were followed by aggressive 'sons' keen to overthrow their forebears and establish a new critical order. The woman writer is trapped between competing generations of male critics.
33. Joseph Hergesheimer, 'The Feminine Nuisance in American Literature', *Yale Review* 10 (July 1921), 716–25 (718).
34. Hergesheimer, 722.
35. Hergesheimer, 723, 725.
36. Ernest Hemingway, 'Big Two-Hearted River' (originally in *In Our Time*, 1925), *The Nick Adams Stories* (New York, 1972), pp. 177–99 (p. 183).
37. 'Big Two-Hearted River', p. 189.

3. Imperial History: *O Pioneers!* and the Settlement of the Plains

1. Howard Erskine-Hill, *The Augustan Idea in English Literature* (London, 1983), pp. 350–9 deals with modern representations of empire.
2. Cather to Canfield Fisher, 8 November 1939, UVM.
3. Jules Michelet, *The History of France*, translated by G. H. Smith, 2 vols. (London, 1845–7), p. 109. This mid-Victorian text was almost certainly familiar to Cather, as it was the major translation of Michelet and published in both London and New York. The *New York World* interview is reprinted in *Willa Cather in Person: Interviews, Speeches, and Letters*, selected and ed. L. Brent Bohlke (Lincoln, 1986), p. 76.
4. Michelet, pp. 110, 142.
5. Donald Sutherland, 'Willa Cather: The Classic Voice' in *The Art of Willa Cather*, eds Bernice Slote and Virginia Faulkner (Lincoln, 1974), pp. 156–79.

6. Cather, 'Nebraska', 236–8.

7. Attractive as the novels are to film-makers, Cather's will forbids movie adaptations. She was disappointed by an early film of *A Lost Lady*.

8. The composition of *O Pioneers!* is discussed by Woodress, *Willa Cather*, p. 232.

9. Woodress writes that 'Cather had no interest in these matters', *Willa Cather*, p. 236.

10. Cather's letter to Elizabeth Sergeant, 22 April 1913 (Morgan Library, New York), paraphrased in Woodress, *Willa Cather*, p. 238.

11. Stephen Fender, *Plotting the Golden West – American Literature and the Rhetoric of the California Trail* (Cambridge, 1981), p. 8.

12. For Susan Rosowski *O Pioneers!* confronts 'centrally the problem of establishing spatial order': 'from chaos has come order, from a wasteland a great, rich farm'. Rosowski, 'Willa Cather and the Fatality of Place: *O Pioneers!*, *My Ántonia*, and *A Lost Lady*' in *Geography and Literature: A Meeting of the Disciplines* ed. William E. Mallory and Paul Simpson-Housley (Syracuse, 1987), pp. 86, 88.

13. Robert P. Swierenga, 'The Land Speculation Tradition' in *Pioneers and Profits: Land Speculation on the Iowa Frontier* (Ames, Iowa, 1968). Allan G. Bogue, 'Farm Tenants in the Nineteenth-Century Middle West' in *Farmers, Bureaucrats and Middlemen – Historical Perspectives on American Agriculture* (Washington, DC, 1980), pp. 103–19. Two important works on the development of the West which have generally informed my discussion are *The Frontier in American Development*, ed. David M. Ellis (Ithaca, 1969) and Ray Allen Billington, *Westward Expansion*, fourth edition (New York, 1974).

14. Paul W. Gates, *Landlords and Tenants on the Prairie Frontier* (Ithaca and London, 1973), pp. 48–71 and 238–302, writes on 'The Role of the Land Speculator in Western Development' and 'Frontier Landlords and Pioneer Tenants'. The latter supplies an account of William Scully and the anti-alien land agitation in the Midwest.

15. Ellen Moers, *Literary Women* (London, 1978), p. 231. Susie Thomas, *Willa Cather* (London, 1990), pp. 54–76.

16. Annette Kolodny, *The Lay of the Land: Metaphor as Experience and History in American Life and Letters* (Chapel Hill, 1975), pp. 4, 6. Kolodny's later work surveys the largely overlooked female response to the frontier: *The Land Before Her: Fantasy and Experience of the American Frontiers, 1630–1860* (Chapel Hill, 1984).

17. Moers, *Literary Women*, p. 258.

18. Cather to Dorothy Canfield Fisher, 7? April 1922, UVM.

19. Jefferson, letter to William Ludlow (6 September 1824), *The Writings of Thomas Jefferson*, ed. Andrew A. Lipscomb (Washington, DC, 1904), XVI, pp. 74–5.

20. George Dekker, *The American Historical Romance*, paperback edition (Cambridge, 1990), pp. 73–98. The classic study of nineteenth-century attitudes to the 'savage' is Roy Harvey Pearce, *Savagism and Civilization: A Study of the Indian and the American Mind*, revised paperback edition (Baltimore and London, 1967).

21. Dekker, pp. 73–4.
22. George W. Stocking, *Race, Culture, and Evolution* (New York, 1968), p. 229.
23. On changing attitudes to 'primitivism', see Pearce, *Savagism* and Lee Clark Mitchell, *Witnesses to a Vanishing America: The Nineteenth-Century Response* (Princeton, 1981). Mitchell argues that there was a shift towards cultural relativism as the century wore on, and that this was signalled in the growth of anthropology, pp. 215–51. For an account of the harsher views of social Darwinists, see Richard Hofstadter, *Social Darwinism in American Thought, 1860–1915* (Philadelphia, 1945), pp. 146–73, 'Racism and Imperialism'.
24. Theodore Roosevelt, *The Winning of the West* (New York, 1889), p. 1. Brooks Adams, *America's Economic Supremacy* (New York, 1900), pp. 24–5, 83.
25. Roosevelt, 'The World Movement' in *History as Literature and Other Essays* (London, 1914), pp. 109, 99, 125. This is a progressive thesis in both the broader and the narrower senses of the word: Roosevelt stood and lost as a Progressive candidate in the Presidential election of 1912.
26. Turner, 'Social Forces in American History' in *The Frontier in American History* (1920. New York, 1976), p. 323. R. A. Billington, *The Genesis of the Frontier Thesis: A Study in Historical Creativity* (San Marino, 1971), pp. 3–4 discusses the dominance of the Turner thesis among American historians. Howard R. Lamar reviews Turner's contribution to American historiography in *Pastmasters: Some Essays on American Historians*, eds Marcus Cunliffe and Robin W. Winks (New York, 1969), pp. 74–109.
27. Letters of July 16 1913 and March 7 1925 in *'Dear Lady': The Letters of Frederick Jackson Turner and Alice Forbes Perkins Hooper, 1910–1932*, ed. R. A. Billington (San Marino, 1970), pp. 149, 365.
28. Hermione Lee, *Willa Cather – A Life Saved Up* (London, 1989), p. 118.
29. F. Scott Fitzgerald, *The Great Gatsby* (1926. Harmondsworth, 1950), p. 171.
30. *Gatsby*, pp. 171–2.

4. *My Ántonia* and the Americanisation Debate

1. Werner Sollors, *Beyond Ethnicity: Consent and Descent in American Culture* (New York and Oxford, 1986), p. 6.
2. Royal Dixon, *Americanization* (New York, 1916), pp. 4, 31, 17.
3. Maldwyn A. Jones, *The Limits of Liberty: American History, 1607–1980* (Oxford, 1983), p. 648.
4. Peter Roberts, *The Problem of Americanization* (New York, 1920), p. 68.
5. George M. Stephenson, *A History of American Immigration, 1820–1924* (Boston and New York, 1926), p. 235.
6. Surveys of Americanisation include *Americanization* ed. Winthrop Talbot (New York, 1917), a handbook of articles and speeches, and

Robert A. Carlson, *The Americanization Syndrome: a Quest for Conformity* (London, 1987), especially pp. 92–100.

7. Dixon, p. 176.
8. Gino Speranza, 'Does Americanization Americanize?', *Atlantic Monthly*, 125 (1920), 263–9.
9. John Kulamer, 'Americanization: the other side of the case,' *Atlantic Monthly*, 125 (1920), 416–23.
10. William I. Thomas with Robert E. Park and Herbert A. Miller, *Old World Traits Transplanted* (1921. New Jersey, 1971), pp. 83, 259, 295.
11. Carol Aronovici, 'Americanization: Its Meaning and Function,' *American Journal of Sociology*, 25 (1919–20), 695–730.
12. James D. Hart, *The Popular Book: A History of America's Literary Taste* (New York, 1950), p. 242.
13. Edward Bok, *The Americanization of Edward Bok*, 29th edition (New York, 1924), p. 438.
14. Newspaper reports of Cather's speeches and the *NYTBR* interview in Bohlke, pp. 71–2, 146–7.
15. Willa Cather, 'Nebraska', 236–8.
16. Edward A. Ross, *Roads to Social Peace – the Weil Lectures, 1924, On American Citizenship* (Chapel Hill, 1924), p. 60.
17. Cited by Shirley Brice Heath, 'English in our Language Heritage', in Charles A. Ferguson and S. B. Heath, (eds), *Language in the USA* (Cambridge, 1981), p. 18. The adjudication reference was 262 US390 (1923). See Kenneth B. O'Brien Jr, 'Education, Americanization and the Supreme Court: the 1920s', *American Quarterly*, 13 (1961), 161–71.
18. Interview with John Chapin Mosher in The *Writer* (November, 1926), rept Bohlke, p. 94.
19. Lee. p. 136.
20. Edward G. Hartmann, *The Movement to Americanize the Immigrant* (New York, 1948), pp. 187, 200, 207.
21. Tony Tanner, *The Reign of Wonder* (Cambridge, 1977), pp. 1–15.
22. Immigrant names were often anglicised. See J. B. Dudek, 'The Americanization of Czech given names', *American Speech*, I (1926), 18–22. Cather's interest in the names of immigrants anticipates recent work on ethnicity and naming. 'From such a perspective, contrastive strategies – naming and name-calling among them – become the most important thing about ethnicity' writes Sollors, *Beyond Ethnicity*, p. 28.
23. On the Protestant hegemony see John Higham, *Strangers in the Land: Patterns of American Nativism 1860–1925*, revised edition (New York, 1971), pp. 234–99.
24. James E. Miller, '*My Ántonia* and the American Dream', *Prairie Schooner* 48 (1974), 112–23.
25. Bohlke, p. 10.
26. Letter to Carrie Sherwood, 27 January 1934, WCPM.
27. Interview with Flora Merrill for the *New York World*, 19 April 1925, in Bohlke, p. 77. This interview develops points Cather made in a letter, where she highlighted the lack of action in *My Ántonia* and suggested

that this novel omitted almost everything deemed necessary to a story. To Mrs. Seibel, 2 February 1919, WCPM.

28. Cather, 'The Novel Démeublé' (1922), in *On Writing*, pp. 40–2.
29. Louis Auchincloss, *Pioneers and Caretakers: A Study of Nine American Women Novelists* (Minneapolis, 1965), p. 103. James E. Miller, 'My *Ántonia*: A Frontier Drama of Time,' *American Quarterly*, 10 (1958), 476–84. For another attack on the structure of the novel, see David Daiches, *Willa Cather: A Critical Introduction* (Ithaca, 1951), pp. 43–61.
30. Paul Schach, 'Russian Wolves in Folktales and Literature of the Plains: A Question of Origins', *Great Plains Quarterly* 3 (1983), 67–78.
31. Cather detailed her working methods in a letter to Sinclair Lewis, 22 March 1944, WCPM. The basic process consisted of drafts in manuscript and typescript by Cather herself, followed by a professional typist's copy in a different colour of ink.
32. Letters to Carrie Sherwood, 9 June 1943, 27 January 1934, 28 June 1939, WCPM.
33. Woodress, *Willa Cather*, pp. 289–90. For a bleaker account of memory in the novel see Blanche H. Gelfant, 'The Forgotten Reaping-Hook: Sex in *My Ántonia*,' *American Literature*, 43 (1971), 60–82. On the male narrator see Susan J. Rosowski, *The Voyage Perilous: Willa Cather's Romanticism* (Lincoln, 1986), p. 88 and Deborah G. Lambert, 'The Defeat of a Hero: Autonomy and Sexuality in *My Ántonia*,' *American Literature*, 53 (1982), 676–90.
34. Randolph Bourne, review of *My Ántonia*, *The Dial*, 65 (1918), 557.
35. Bourne, 'Trans-National America,' *Atlantic Monthly*, 118 (1916), 86–97. A recent account of Bourne's work is Lesley J. Vaughan, 'Cosmopolitanism, Ethnicity and American Identity: Randolph Bourne's "Trans-National America"', *Journal of American Studies*, 25 (1991), 443–59.
36. Bourne, 87, 90.
37. Bourne, 91.
38. Bourne, 96.
39. Woodress, *Willa Cather*, pp. 84–8 and O'Brien, *Willa Cather*, pp. 129–31.
40. Herbert H. Vaughan, 'Italian and its Dialects,' *American Speech*, I (1926), 431–5. Louise Pound, 'An American Text' and 'Walt Whitman and the French language,' *American Speech*, I, 481–3 and 421–30. 'Oral Literature' in *A History of American Literature* ed. W. P. Trent, John Erskine *et al.*, 4 vols (Cambridge and New York, 1918–21), IV, 502–16.
41. Louise Pound, *Poetic Origins and the Ballad* (New York, 1921), p. 116.
42. *Poetic Origins*, p. 9.
43. *Poetic Origins*, p. 35.
44. *Poetic Origins*, pp. 218–19.

5. *One of Ours*: The Progressive *Bildungsroman* and the Death of Idealism

1. Malcolm Cowley, *Exile's Return: A Literary Odyssey of the 1920s* (New York, 1951), p. 39.

2. Schroeter, *Willa Cather and her Critics*, p. 151.

3. Alfred Kazin in *On Native Grounds* (1942), reprinted in Schroeter, pp. 161–70 (p. 166).

4. Cather commenting in New York, 1925, cited Mildred R. Bennett, *The World of Willa Cather*, new edition (Lincoln, 1961), p. 15.

5. Ferenc Morton Szasz, *The Divided Mind of Protestant America, 1880–1930* (Alabama, 1982).

6. Edmund Wilson, review of *One of Ours* (1922) in Schroeter, pp. 25–7 (p. 26).

7. H. L. Mencken in Schroeter, p. 12.

8. *New York Sun* Editorial (1914), cited Daniel M. Smith, *The Great Departure: The United States and World War I, 1914–1920* (New York, 1965), p. 2.

9. Smith, *The Great Departure*, pp. 24–5. See also pp. 83–109.

10. Arthur S. Link, *Woodrow Wilson and the Progressive Era, 1910–1917*, Harper Torchbook edition (New York, 1963), p. 265.

11. Link, pp. 223–282.

12. Woodrow Wilson, *Why We Are At War* (New York, 1917), p. 16.

13. Wilson, p. 58.

14. H. L. Mencken, review of *One of Ours* (*Smart Set*, October 1922), in Schroeter, p. 10. Hicks wrote in his 'Case Against Willa Cather' that 'the second part bears no relation to the issues raised in the account of Claude's unhappiness in Nebraska.' Schroeter, p. 143.

15. Robert J. Nelson, *Willa Cather and France* (Urbana, Illinois, 1988), p. 31.

16. Sinclair Lewis, review in the *New York Evening Post* (16 September 1922), in Shroeter, pp. 30–34 (p. 32). Mencken in Schroeter, p. 11.

17. Thomas, p. 44.

18. Vachel Lindsay, 'Bryan, Bryan, Bryan, Bryan' in *Collected Poems*, reprinted edition (New York, 1966), p. 98.

19. Edmund Wilson in Schroeter, p. 25.

6. *The Professor's House* and the Incorporation of America

1. Leo Marx, *The Machine In the Garden: Technology and the Pastoral Ideal in America* (New York, 1964).

2. In a letter to Mr. Phillipson, Cather said that stories were made from the grafting of an outside figure with part of the writer's own personality. 15 March 1943, WCPM.

3. Cather, 'The Carnegie Museum' in *Home Monthly* (March, 1897), 1–4. This article has unfortunately not been reprinted.

4. Alan Trachtenberg, *The Incorporation of America: Culture and Society in the Gilded Age* (New York, 1982), p. 5.

5. John Fiske, *Essays Historical and Literary*, 2 volumes (New York, 1902), II, pp. 29–30, 253.

6. William Jennings Bryan cited in Lawrence W. Levine, *Defender of the Faith – William Jennings Bryan: The Last Decade, 1915–1925* (New York, 1965), p. 339. Bryan's 'God and Evolution' appeared in the *New York Times* (26 February 1922). On the Scopes trial and its context see: Ray Ginger, *Six Days or Forever: Tennessee v. John Thomas Scopes*, paperback

edition (London, 1974); Paolo E. Coletta, *William Jennings Bryan* vol 3, *Political Puritan 1915–1925* (Lincoln, 1969), pp. 198–281; Norman F. Furniss, *The Fundamentalist Controversy, 1918–31* (New Haven, 1954), pp. 76–100, 'The Fundamentalist Attack Upon Evolution.' Cather on 'The Personal Side of William Jennings Bryan', reprinted in *The World and the Parish*, pp. 782–9. In the story 'Two Friends' Mr. Dillon hears Bryan's speech: *Obscure Destinies* (New York, 1932), p. 222.

7. John Dewey, 'The Influence of Darwinism on Philosophy' (lecture delivered at Columbia University, 1909) in *The Middle Works, 1899–1924*, ed. Jo Ann Boydston, 15 vols (Carbondale, Illinois, 1976–83), IV, p. 3.

8. Thorstein Veblen, *The Place of Science in Modern Civilisation* (1919. 3rd printing, New York, 1932), p. 26.

9. Fiske, *Essays Historical and Literary*, II, p. 31.

10. Elizabeth Sergeant, *Willa Cather: A Memoir* (Lincoln, 1963), p. 54. Cather's trip to the South-west in 1912 is often placed as the crucial turning-point in her growth as an artist. O'Brien, *Willa Cather*, pp. 403–27.

11. Leon Edel, *Literary Biography*, revised edition (Bloomington, 1973), p. 109.

12. J. R. Bash, 'Willa Cather: A Study in Primitivism' (Unpublished Ph.D. thesis, University of Illinois, 1954).

13. Thorstein Veblen, *The Theory of the Leisure Class* (1899. London, 1970), pp. 152, 110–11.

14. *The Place of Science*, pp. 16–17.

15. Thorstein Veblen, *The Instinct of Workmanship and the State of the Industrial Arts* (New York, 1914), pp. 1, 25, 28, 79.

16. Frank Kermode, 'Secrets and Narrative Sequence' in *Essays on Fiction 1971–1982*, paperback edition (London, 1983), p. 138.

17. Richard Slotkin, *The Fatal Environment: The Myth of the Frontier in the Age of Industrialization 1800–1890* (New York, 1985), p. 531.

18. *The Instinct of Workmanship*, p. 100.

19. *The Instinct of Workmanship*, p. 36.

20. Fechtig's raid on the mesa is, as this detail makes clear, facilitated by horses and mules. Writing about the isolated safety of Pueblo communities, Veblen had arrived at a similar conclusion about the danger posed by horses. He mentioned as a feature of Pueblo culture 'the absence of beasts of burden, such as have enabled the inhabitants of analogous regions of the old world effectually to cover long distances and make raiding a lucrative, or at least an attractive enterprise.' Cather's settlement is disrupted in exactly the way that Veblen had outlined in 1914. *Instinct of Workmanship*, p. 154.

21. *Instinct of Workmanship*, p. 154.

22. A recent powerful account of the novel enmeshes it in debates about assimilation, cultural identity and the 'vanishing American' (*The Professor's House* deals with both extinct Indian tribes and immigrant Jews). Walter Benn Michaels interprets the Pueblo as an example of an anti-assimilationist American community, and an American *polis* which can be idealised because it has now become extinct. 'The cliff dwellers provide for Cather a paradigm of the American but they

provide, more generally, a paradigm of cultural identity itself.' Walter Benn Michaels, 'The Vanishing American,' *American Literary History*, 2 (1990), 220–41 (237). Michaels fails, however, to take account of the figure of Mother Eve: Cather is drawn to idealised American communities based on the 'vanishing American', but she also records the violence and exclusion which underwrote such cultures. It is also significant that Cather should use sexual violence (a literal war between the sexes) to critique this idealised, mythic America. Ian F. A. Bell also writes on race, gender and ideas of 'origin' in American culture: 'Re-Writing America: Origin and Gender in Willa Cather's *The Professor's House*,' *Yearbook of English Studies*, 24, 'Ethnicity and Representation in American Literature,' (1994), pp. 12–43.

23. *Instinct of Workmanship*, p. 153.
24. Adrienne Rich, *Of Woman Born: Motherhood as Experience and Institution* (London, 1977), p. 96.
25. Sharon O'Brien, 'Mothers, daughters, and the "Art Necessity": Willa Cather and the Creative Process' in *American Novelists Revisited: Essays in Feminist Criticism*, ed. Fritz Fleischmann (Boston, 1982), pp. 265–98 (p. 291). Nina Baym, 'Melodramas of Beset Manhood – How Theories of American Fiction exclude women authors' in *The New Feminist Criticism*, ed. Elaine Showalter (London, 1986), pp. 63–80.
26. Fender, p. 60.
27. Peter Schwenger, *Phallic Critiques* (London, 1984), p. 98.
28. On the composition of 'The Blue Mesa' and *The Professor's House* see Woodress, *Willa Cather*, pp. 282, 353.
29. Edel, *Literary Biography*, p. 109. Woodress, *Willa Cather*, p. 367, reads St Peter's malaise as veiled autobiography, a fictionalisation of Cather's own psychological distress in the 1920s.
30. *On Writing*, pp. 30–2.
31. Leo Marx, *The Machine in the Garden*.

7. *Death Comes for the Archbishop*: The Ideology of Cather's Catholic Progressivism

1. Emerson, journal entry of 1846, *The Journals and Miscellaneous Notebooks of Ralph Waldo Emerson*, ed. Ralph H. Orth and Alfred R. Ferguson, 16 vols (Cambridge, Mass., 1960–82), IX, 430–1. Details of the Mexican War and its aftermath in James M. McPherson, *Battle Cry of Freedom: The American Civil War*, paperback edition (London, 1990), pp. 47–77. For an exposition of 'Manifest Destiny' (as territorial expansion, as democratic mission) see Frederick Merk, *Manifest Destiny and Mission in American History: A Reinterpretation* (New York, 1963).
2. Terence Martin, *The Instructed Vision: Scottish common sense philosophy and the origins of American fiction* (Bloomington, 1961), pp. 107–48.
3. Robert Clark, *History, Ideology and Myth in American Fiction*, pp. 26–38. Susan Manning, *The Puritan-Provincial Vision: Scottish and American Literature in the Nineteenth Century* (Cambridge, 1990), pp. 53–9.

4. Hawthorne, 'Preface' to *The House of the Seven Gables* (1851), *The Centenary Edition of the Works of Nathaniel Hawthorne*, William Charvat, Roy Harvey Pearce and Claude M. Simpson (eds), 13 vols (Columbus, Ohio, 1965), II, p. 1.

5. Dorothy Foster Gilman, 'Willa Cather writes a fictional biography,' *Boston Evening Transcript*, 10 September 1927, 2. Marilyn Arnold, *Willa Cather: A Reference Guide* (Boston, 1986), pp. 50–7 summarises the reactions of other reviewers to *Death Comes for the Archbishop*.

6. For sources and the historical material with which Cather worked, see the following. Edward A. and Lillian Bloom, 'The Genesis of *Death Comes for the Archbishop*', *American Literature* 26 (1955), 479–506. John C. Scott, 'Between Fiction and History: An Exploration into Willa Cather's *Death Comes for the Archbishop*', unpublished doctoral dissertation, University of New Mexico, 1980. Paul Horgan, *Lamy of Santa Fe, his life and times* (New York, 1975). Critics who then use this material alongside a reading of the novel's spiritual and 'romance' elements include David Stouck, *Willa Cather's Imagination* (Lincoln, 1975), pp. 129–49 and James Woodress, *Willa Cather*, pp. 391–411.

7. Lee, p. 288.

8. Cather, *On Writing*, p. 12.

9. Mitchell, *Witnesses to a Vanishing America*, pp. 140–50 discusses the new South-western primitivism.

10. Higham, *Strangers in the Land*, pp. 264–99.

11. *The World and the Parish*, pp. 709–11. James D. Hart, *The Popular Book*, p. 242.

12. Harold E. Stearns, 'The Country versus the Town' in *America and the Young Intellectual*, p. 141.

13. Letter to 'Dear Little Neddius' (Ellen Gere) (1896), WCPM. 'Eric Hermansson's Soul', *Willa Cather's Collected Short Fiction*, pp. 359–79. Georgine Milmine, *The Life of Mary Baker G. Eddy and the History of Christian Science* (New York, 1909).

14. *On Writing*, pp. 12–13.

15. Cather to Mr. Phillipson, 15 March 1943, WCPM.

16. Edward Said, *Orientalism*, paperback edition (Harmondsworth, 1985), pp. 21, 201–2, 204.

17. Cather wrote in a letter of 4 August 1932 to Carrie Sherwood that she knew Lawrence well and liked him. She said that he was undoubtedly the most gifted author of his generation but he let his prejudices get the better of him. WCPM.

18. D. H. Lawrence, *Mornings in Mexico and Etruscan Places* (Harmondsworth, 1960), p. 15.

19. Lawrence, p. 55.

20. Letters to Carrie Sherwood, 9 June, 1943 and 27 January, 1934, WCPM.

21. Scott, 'Between Fiction and History', 66–7.

22. Scott, 121–46.

23. Lincoln Steffens, *The Shame of Cities* (New York, 1904), p. 233. On 'muckraking' and the wider context of progressivism, see Louis Filler, *Progressivism and Muckraking* (New York, 1976); David W. Noble, *The Paradox of Progressive Thought* (Minneapolis, 1958); J. Leonard Bates,

The United States, 1898–1928: Progressivism and a Society in Transition (New York, 1976), pp. 51–2; Arthur A. Ekirch, *Progressivism in America* (New York, 1974), pp. 58–63; J. A. Thompson, *Progressivism*.

24. Herman Melville, *Moby Dick*, ed. Tony Tanner (Oxford, 1988), p. 373. On Carson and his secular canonisation see Henry Nash Smith, *Virgin Land: The American West as Symbol and Myth* (Cambridge, Mass., 1950), pp. 81–9 and *The Frontier Experience: A Reader's Guide to the Life and Literature of the American West*, ed. Jon Tuska and Vicki Piekarski (Jefferson, NC, 1984), pp. 91–2.

25. Patricia Lee Yongue, 'Search and Research: Willa Cather in Quest of History,' *Southwestern American Literature* 5 (1975), 27–39.

26. *On Writing*, p. 9.

27. Mary-Ann and David Stouck, 'Hagiographical Style in *Death Comes for the Archbishop*', *University of Toronto Quarterly* 41 (Summer 1972), 293–307. Lee, *Willa Cather*, p. 270. On Cather's modernist techniques see Phyllis Rose, 'Modernism: The Case of Willa Cather' in *Harvard English Studies* 11: *Modernism Reconsidered*, ed. Robert Kiely (Cambridge, Mass., 1983), pp. 123–45.

28. My discussion of the ideological configurations of fictional form is indebted to John Barrell's discussion of the georgic (a classical genre Cather alluded to and borrowed from). The georgic 'had also traditionally been ventilated by digressions, and was thus hospitable to a diversity of topics...to represent the diversity of modern experience'. *Poetry, Language and Politics* (Manchester, 1988), p. 90.

Bibliography

1. WILLA CATHER: PRIMARY TEXTS AND MANUSCRIPTS

Bibliographies

Arnold, Marilyn, *Willa Cather: A Reference Guide* (Boston, 1986).
Crane, Joan, *Willa Cather: A Bibliography* (Lincoln, 1982).

Letters and interviews

Letters in the Cather archive, Willa Cather Pioneer Memorial Collection, Nebraska State Historical Society, Red Cloud, Nebraska.
Letters in the Dorothy Canfield Fisher Collection, Bailey/Howe Library, University of Vermont, Burlington.
Madigan, Mark J., 'Letters from Willa Cather to Dorothy Canfield Fisher 1899–1947' (unpublished M.A. dissertation, University of Vermont, 1987).
Willa Cather in Person: Interviews, Speeches and Letters (Lincoln, 1986), ed. L. Brent Bohlke.

Fiction, poetry, criticism

Alexandra's Bridge (1912. Lincoln, 1977).
April Twilights (1903), edited and with an introduction by Bernice Slote (Lincoln, 1976).
'The Carnegie Museum', *Home Monthly* (March, 1897), 1–4.
Death Comes for the Archbishop (1927. London, 1981).
The Kingdom of Art: Willa Cather's First Principles and Critical Statements 1893–1896, ed. Bernice Slote (Lincoln, 1966).
A Lost Lady (1923. London, 1980).
Lucy Gayheart (1935. London, 1985).
My Ántonia (1918. London, 1980).
My Mortal Enemy (1926. London, 1982)
'Nebraska: The End of the First Cycle', *The Nation*, 117 (1923), 236–8.
Not Under Forty (London, 1936).
Obscure Destinies (New York, 1932).
On Writing, with a foreword by Stephen Tennant (1949. New York, 1968).
One of Ours (1922. London, 1987).
O Pioneers! (1913. London, 1983).
The Professor's House (1925. London, 1981).
The Song of the Lark, revised edition (1937. London, 1982).
The Song of the Lark, 1915 edition (Lincoln, 1978).

Uncle Valentine and Other Stories: Willa Cather's Uncollected Short Fiction, 1915–1929, ed. Bernice Slote (Lincoln, 1973).

Willa Cather's Collected Short Fiction 1892–1912, ed. Virginia Faulkner (Lincoln, 1970).

The World and the Parish: Willa Cather's Articles and Reviews, 1893–1902, ed. William Curtin, 2 vols (Lincoln, 1970).

Youth and the Bright Medusa (New York, 1920).

2. WORKS AND ARTICLES ABOUT WILLA CATHER

Arvin, Newton, 'Quebec, Nebraska, and Pittsburgh', *New Republic* 67 (12 August, 1931), 345–6.

Auchincloss, Louis, *Pioneers and Caretakers: A Study of Nine American Women Novelists* (Minneapolis, 1965).

Bell, Ian F. A., 'Re-Writing America: Origin and Gender in Willa Cather's *The Professor's House*, *Yearbook of English Studies*, 24 (1994), pp. 12–43.

Bennett, Mildred R., *The World of Willa Cather*, new edition (Lincoln, 1961).

Bloom, Edward A. and Lillian, 'The Genesis of *Death Comes for the Archbishop*', *American Literature* 26 (1955), 479–506.

Bloom, Harold, *Modern Critical Views: Willa Cather* (New York, 1985).

Canfield Fisher, Dorothy, 'Willa Cather: Daughter of the Frontier', *New York Herald Tribune*, (28 May 1933), section 2, pp. 7, 9.

Cantwell, Robert, 'A Season's Run', *New Republic* 85 (11 December 1935), 149–53.

Carlin, Deborah, *Cather, Canon, and the Politics of Reading* (Amherst, 1992).

Cherny, Robert W., 'Willa Cather and the Populists', *Great Plains Quarterly* 3 (1983), 206–18.

Daiches, David, *Willa Cather: A Critical Introduction* (Ithaca, 1951).

Edel, Leon, *Literary Biography*, revised edition (1957. Bloomington, 1973).

Fadiman, Clifton, 'Willa Cather: The Past Recaptured', *The Nation* 135 (7 December 1932), 563–5.

Gelfant, Blanche H., 'The Forgotten Reaping-Hook: Sex in *My Ántonia*', *American Literature* 43 (1971), 60–82.

Heyeck, Robin and James Woodress, 'Willa Cather's Cuts and Revisions in *The Song of the Lark*', *Modern Fiction Studies* 25, no. 4 (1979), 651–8.

Hively, Evelyn, *Sacred Fire: Willa Cather's Novel Cycle* (Lanham, Maryland and London, 1994).

Lambert, Deborah G., 'The Defeat of a Hero: Autonomy and Sexuality in *My Ántonia*', *American Literature*, 53 (1982), 676–90.

Lee, Hermione, *Willa Cather – A Life Saved Up* (London, 1989).

Lewis, Edith, *Willa Cather Living: A Personal Record* (Lincoln, 1953).

Michaels, Walter Benn, 'The Vanishing American', *American Literary History*, 2 (1990), 220–41.

Miller, James E., '*My Ántonia*: A Frontier Drama of Time', *American Quarterly* 10 (1958), 476–84.

——, 'My Ántonia and the American Dream', *Prairie Schooner*, 48 (1974), 112–23.

Nelson, Robert J., *Willa Cather and France* (Urbana, Illinois, 1988).

O'Brien, Sharon, *Willa Cather: The Emerging Voice* (New York, 1987).

——, 'Becoming Noncanonical: The Case against Willa Cather', *American Quarterly* 40 (1988), 110–26.

——, 'Mothers, daughters, and the "Art Necessity": Willa Cather and the Creative Process', in Fritz Fleischmann (ed.), *American Novelists Revisited: Essays in Feminist Criticism* (Boston, 1982), pp. 265–98.

Robinson, Phyllis, *Willa: The Life of Willa Cather* (New York, 1983).

Rose, Phyllis, 'Modernism: The Case of Willa Cather' in Robert Kiely (ed.), *Modernism Reconsidered* (Cambridge, Mass., 1983), pp. 123–45.

Rosowski, Susan J., *The Voyage Perilous: Willa Cather's Romanticism* (Lincoln, 1986).

—— 'Willa Cather and the Fatality of Place: *O Pioneers!, My Ántonia and A Lost Lady*', *Geography and Literature: A Meeting of the Disciplines* (Syracuse, 1987), eds, William E. Mallory and Paul Simpson-Housley, pp. 81–94.

Schroeter, James (ed.), *Willa Cather and her Critics* (New York, 1967).

Scott, John C., 'Between Fiction and History: An Exploration into Willa Cather's *Death Comes for the Archbishop*' (unpublished Ph.D. thesis, University of New Mexico, 1980).

Slote, Bernice and Virginia Faulkner, (eds), *The Art of Willa Cather* (Lincoln, 1974).

Stouck, David, *Willa Cather's Imagination* (Lincoln, 1975).

Stouck, Mary-Ann and David, 'Hagiographical Style in *Death Comes for the Archbishop*', *University of Toronto Quarterly* 41 (Summer 1972), 293–307.

Thomas, Susie, *Willa Cather* (London, 1990).

Woodress, James, *Willa Cather: Her Life and Art* (New York, 1970).

——, *Willa Cather: A Literary Life* (Lincoln, 1987).

Yongue, Patricia Lee, 'Search and Research: Willa Cather in Quest of History', *Southwestern American Literature* 5 (1975), 27–39.

3.   SECONDARY LITERARY CRITICAL SOURCES

Barrell, John, *Poetry, Language and Politics* (Manchester, 1988).

Baym, Nina, 'Melodramas of Beset Manhood – How Theories of American Fiction Exclude Women Authors' in Elaine Showalter (ed.), *The New Feminist Criticism* (London, 1986), pp. 63–80.

Beer, Gillian, *Darwin's Plots: Evolutionary Narrative in Darwin, George Eliot and Nineteenth-Century Fiction*, paperback edition (London, 1985).

Bercovitch, Sacvan, 'The Problem of Ideology', *Critical Inquiry* 12 (1985–6), 631–53.

Berthoff, Warner, 'Ambitious Scheme', *Commentary* 44, no. 4 (October, 1967), 111.

——, *The Ferment of Realism: American Literature, 1884–1919* (1965. Cambridge, 1981).

Bibliography

191

Bradbury, Malcolm, *The Modern American Novel* (Oxford, 1983).

Bradbury, Malcolm, and David Palmer (eds), *The American Novel and the Nineteen Twenties* (London, 1971).

Brown, Laura, *Alexander Pope* (Oxford, 1985).

Butler, Marilyn, *Jane Austen and the War of Ideas* (Oxford, 1975).

Clark, Robert, *History, Ideology and Myth in American Fiction, 1823–52* (London, 1984).

Dekker, George, *The American Historical Romance* (Cambridge, 1990).

Erskine-Hill, Howard, *The Augustan Idea in English Literature* (London, 1983).

Fender, Stephen, *Plotting the Golden West – American literature and the rhetoric of the California Trail* (Cambridge, 1981).

Fisher, Philip, 'American Literary and Cultural Studies since the Civil War,'in *Redrawing the Boundaries: The Transformation of English and American Literary Studies*, ed. Stephen Greenblatt and Giles Gunn (New York, 1992), pp. 232–50.

Graff, Gerald, *Professing Literature* (Chicago and London, 1987).

Hart, James D., *The Popular Book: A History of America's Literary Taste* (New York, 1950).

Hoffman, Frederick J., *The Twenties: American Writing in the Postwar Decade*, revised edition (New York, 1965).

Kernan, Alvin, *The Death of Literature* (New Haven, 1990).

Kolodny, Annette, *The Lay of the Land: Metaphor as Experience and History in American Life and Letters* (Chapel Hill, 1975).

——, *The Land Before Her: Fantasy and Experience of the American Frontiers, 1630–1860* (Chapel Hill, 1984).

Kuklick, Bruce, 'Myth and Symbol in American Studies', *American Quarterly* 24 (1972), 435–50.

Lauter, Paul, 'Race and Gender in the Shaping of the American Literary Canon: A Case Study from the Twenties', *Feminist Studies* vol. 9, no. 3 (1983), 435–63.

Manning, Susan, *The Puritan-Provincial Vision: Scottish and American Literature in the Nineteenth Century* (Cambridge, 1990).

Martin, Terence, *The Instructed Vision* (Bloomington, 1961).

Reising, Russell J., *The Unusable Past: Theory and the Study of American Literature* (London, 1986).

Reynolds, David S., *Beneath the American Renaissance: The Subversive Imagination in the Age of Emerson and Melville*, paperback edition (Cambridge, Mass., 1989).

Rogin, Michael Paul, *Subversive Genealogy: The Politics and Art of Herman Melville* (New York, 1983).

Ruland, Richard, *The Rediscovery of American Literature: Premises of Critical Taste, 1900–1940* (Cambridge, Mass., 1967).

Ryan, Kiernan, *Shakespeare* (Hemel Hempstead, 1989).

Schach, Paul, 'Russian Wolves in Folktales and Literature of the Plains: a Question of Origins', *Great Plains Quarterly* vol. 3 no. 2 (1983), 67–78.

Schwenger, Peter, *Phallic Critiques* (London, 1984).

Sinfield, Alan, 'Four Ways with a Reactionary Text', *Literature Teaching Politics* 2 (n.d), 81–95.

Tanner, Tony, *The Reign of Wonder* (1965. Cambridge, 1977).

Tate, Allen, 'Religion and the Old South', *Essays of Four Decades* (London, 1970).

Tuska, John and Vicki Piekarski, (eds), *The Frontier Experience: A Reader's Guide to the Life and Literature of the American West* (Jefferson, NC, 1984).

Vanderbilt, Kermit, *American Literature and the Academy* (Philadelphia, 1986).

Weimann, Robert, *Structure and Society in Literary History* (London, 1977).

4.   THE LITERARY AND HISTORICAL CONTEXT: PRIMARY SOURCES

Adams, Brooks, *America's Economic Supremacy* (New York, 1900).

Aronovici, Carol, 'Americanization: Its Meaning and Function', *American Journal of Sociology* 25 (1919–1920), 695–730.

Bok, Edward, *The Americanization of Edward Bok* (1920. New York, 1924).

Bourne, Randolph, 'Trans-National America', *The Atlantic Monthly* 118 (1916), 86–97.

Brooks, Van Wyck, *The Ordeal of Mark Twain* (London, 1922).

Van Wyck Brooks: The Early Years, ed. Claire Sprague (New York, 1968).

De Witt, Benjamin, *The Progressive Movement: A Non-partisan Comprehensive Discussion of Current Tendencies in American Politics* (New York, 1915).

Dixon, Royal, *Americanization* (New York, 1916).

Dos Passos, John, 'Against American Literature', *The New Republic* 8 (14 October 1916), 269–71.

Dudek, J. B., 'The Americanization of Czech given names', *American Speech* 1 (1926), 18–22.

Fitzgerald, F. Scott, *The Great Gatsby* (1926. Harmondsworth, 1950).

Hawthorne, Nathaniel, *The House of the Seven Gables* (1851) in *The Centenary Edition of the Works of Nathaniel Hawthorne*, eds, William Charvat, Roy Harvey Pearce and Claude M. Simpson, 13 vols (Columbus, Ohio, 1962–77), II.

Hemingway, Ernest, *Selected Letters 1917–1961*, ed. Carlos Baker (London, 1981).

——, *The Nick Adams Stories* (New York, 1972).

Hergesheimer, Joseph, 'The Feminine Nuisance in American Literature', *Yale Review* 10 (July 1921), 716–25.

James, Henry, *The American Scene* (1907. Bloomington, 1969).

Jefferson, Thomas, *The Writings of Thomas Jefferson*, ed. Andrew A. Lipscomb (Washington, DC, 1904).

Kulamer, John, 'Americanization: the other side of the case', *The Atlantic Monthly* 125 (1920), 416–23.

Lawrence, D. H., *Mornings in Mexico and Etruscan Places* (1927. Harmondsworth, 1960).

Melville, Herman, *Moby Dick*, ed. Tony Tanner (1851. Oxford, 1988).

Mencken, H. L., *Prejudices: Second Series* (London, 1921).

Michelet, Jules, *The History of France*, translated G. H. Smith, 2 vols (London, 1845–7).

Milmine, Georgine, *The Life of Mary Baker G. Eddy and the History of Christian Science* (New York, 1909).

Mumford, Lewis, *Herman Melville* (London, 1929).

Pattee, Fred Lewis, *The New American Literature 1890–1930* (1930. New York, 1968).

Pound, Louise, *Poetic Origins and the Ballad* (New York, 1921).

——, 'Oral Literature' in W. P. Trent, John Erskine *et al.*, *A History of American Literature*, vol. 4 (Cambridge and New York, 1921), pp. 502–16.

——, 'An American Text of "Sir James the Rose"', *American Speech* 1 (1926), 481–3.

——, 'Walt Whitman and the French Language', *American Speech* 1 (1926), 421–30.

Roberts, Peter, *The Problem of Americanization* (New York, 1920).

Ross, Edward A., *Roads to Social Peace – the Weil Lectures, 1924, On American Citizenship* (Chapel Hill, 1924).

Roosevelt, Theodore, *The Winning of the West* (New York, 1889).

——, *History as Literature and Other Essays* (London, 1914).

Speranza, Gino, 'Does Americanization Americanize?', *The Atlantic Monthly* 125 (1920), 263–9.

Stearns, Harold E., *America and the Young Intellectual* (1921. Westport, Conn., 1973).

—— (ed.), *Civilization in the United States: An Enquiry by Thirty Americans* (London, 1922).

Steffens, Lincoln, *The Shame of the Cities* (New York, 1904).

Stephenson, George, *A History of American Immigration, 1820–1924* (Boston, 1926).

Thomas, William I., with Robert E. Park and Herbert A. Miller, *Old World Traits Transplanted* (1921. Montclair, N J, 1971).

Talbot, Winthrop (ed.), *Americanization* (New York, 1917).

Trachtenberg, Alan (ed.), *Critics of Culture* (New York, 1976).

Turner, Frederick Jackson, *The Frontier in American History* (1920. New York, 1976).

——, 'Dear Lady': *The Letters of Frederick Jackson Turner and Alice Forbes Perkins Hooper, 1910–1932*, ed. R. A. Billington (San Marino, 1970).

Vaughan, Herbert H., 'Italian and its Dialects as Spoken in the United States', *American Speech* 1 (1926), 431–5.

Veblen, Thorstein, *The Theory of the Leisure Class* (1899. London, 1970).

——, *The Instinct of Workmanship and the State of the Industrial Arts* (New York, 1914).

——, *The Place of Science in Modern Civilisation* (1919. New York, 1932).

Vedder, Henry C., *American Writers of To-day* (New York, 1894).

Weaver, Raymond, *Herman Melville – Mariner and Mystic* (New York, 1921).

Wendell, Barrett, *A Literary History of America* (1900. London, 1901).

Wilson, Woodrow, *Why We Are At War* (New York, 1917).

5. THE HISTORICAL AND CULTURAL CONTEXT: SECONDARY SOURCES

Bates, J. Leonard, *The United States 1898–1928: Progressivism and a Society in Transition* (New York, 1976).

Billington, R. A., *The Genesis of the Frontier Thesis: A Study in Historical Creativity* (San Marino, 1971).

Bogue, Allan G., *Farmers, Bureaucrats, and Middlemen – Historical Perspectives on American Agriculture* (Washington, DC, 1980).

Carlson, Robert A., *The Americanization Syndrome: A Quest for Conformity* (London, 1987).

Cochrane, Willard W., *The Development of American Agriculture: A Historical Analysis* (Minneapolis, 1979).

Coletta, Paolo E., *William Jennings Bryan* vol. 3, *Political Puritan 1915–1925* (Lincoln, 1969).

Crunden, Robert, *Ministers of Reform: The Progressives' Achievement in American Civilization 1889–1920* (New York, 1982).

Cunliffe, Marcus, and Robin W. Winks, (eds), *Pastmasters: Some Essays on American Historians* (New York, 1969).

Earnest, Ernest, *The Single Vision: The Alienation of American Intellectuals* (New York, 1970).

Ekirch, Arthur A., *Progressivism in America* (New York, 1974).

Ellis, David M. (ed.), *The Frontier in American Development* (Ithaca, 1969).

Filene, Peter, 'An Obituary for "The Progressive Movement"', *American Quarterly* 22 (1970), 20–34.

Filler, Louis, *Progressivism and Muckraking* (New York, 1976).

Furniss, Norman F., *The Fundamentalist Controversy, 1918–31* (New Haven, 1954).

Gates, Paul W., *Landlords and Tenants on the Prairie Frontier* (Ithaca and London, 1973).

Ginger, Ray, *Six Days or Forever: Tennessee v. John Thomas Scopes*, paperback edition (London, 1974).

Hartmann, Edward G., *The Movement to Americanize the Immigrant* (New York, 1948).

Heath, Shirley Brice, and Charles A. Ferguson, (eds), *Language in the USA* (Cambridge, 1981).

Higham, John, *Strangers in the Land: Patterns of American Nativism 1860–1925*, second edition (New York, 1971).

Hofstadter, Richard, *Social Darwinism in American Thought, 1860–1915* (Philadelphia, 1945).

——, *The Age of Reform: From Bryan to F.D.R.* (New York, 1955).

Horgan, Paul, *Lamy of Santa Fe* (New York, 1975).

Jones, Maldwyn A., *The Limits of Liberty: American History 1607–1980* (Oxford, 1983).

Levine, Lawrence W., *Defender of the Faith – William Jennings Bryan: The Last Decade, 1915–25* (New York, 1965).

Link, Arthur S., *Woodrow Wilson and the Progressive Era, 1910–1917*, Harper Torchbook edition (New York, 1963).

McPherson, James M., *Battle Cry of Freedom: The American Civil War* (London, 1990).

Marx, Leo, *The Machine in the Garden: Technology and the Pastoral Ideal in America* (New York, 1964).

Mitchell, Lee Clark, *Witnesses to a Vanishing America: The Nineteenth-Century Response* (Princeton, 1981).

Noble, David W., *The Paradox of Progressive Thought* (Minneapolis, 1958).

——, 'The Religion of Progress in America, 1890–1914', *Social Research* 22 (1955), 417–40.

O'Brien Jr., Kenneth B., 'Education, Americanization and the Supreme Court: the 1920s', *American Quarterly* 13 (1961), 161–71.

Pearce, Roy Harvey, *Savagism and Civilization: A Study of the Indian and the American Mind* (1953. Baltimore and London, 1967).

Pollack, Norman, *The Populist Response to Industrial America: Midwestern Populist Thought* (Cambridge, Mass., 1962).

Quandt, Jean B., *From the Small Town to the Great Community: The Social Thought of Progressive Intellectuals* (New Brunswick, 1970).

Rich, Adrienne, *Of Woman Born: Motherhood as Experience and Institution* (London, 1977).

Said, Edward, *Orientalism* (1978. Harmondsworth, 1985).

Slotkin, Richard, *The Fatal Environment: The Myth of the Frontier in the Age of Industrialization 1800–1890* (New York, 1985).

Smith, Daniel M., *The Great Departure: The United States and World War I, 1914–1920* (New York, 1965).

Smith, Henry Nash, *Virgin Land* (Cambridge, Mass., 1950).

Sollors, Werner, *Beyond Ethnicity: Consent and Descent in American Culture* (New York and Oxford, 1986)

Stocking, George W., *Race, Culture, and Evolution* (New York, 1968).

Swierenga, Robert P., *Pioneers and Profits: Land Speculation on the Iowa Frontier* (Ames, Iowa, 1968).

Szasz, Ferenc Morton, *The Divided Mind of Protestant America, 1880–1930* (Alabama, 1982).

Thompson, J. A., *Progressivism*, BAAS pamphlet (Durham, 1979).

Trachtenberg, Alan, *The Incorporation of America: Culture and Society in the Gilded Age* (New York, 1982).

Vaughan, Lesley J., 'Cosmopolitanism, Ethnicity and American Identity: Randolph Bourne's "Trans-National America"', *Journal of American Studies*, 25 (1991), 443–59.

Index

Whenever possible, major discussion of a topic, work or individual is indicated in **bold** type.